# WHAT WAS FOOTBALL LIKE IN THE 1980s?

# WHAT WAS FOOTBALL LIKE IN THE 1980s?

RICHARD CROOKS

First published by Pitch Publishing, 2020

Pitch Publishing
A2 Yeoman Gate
Yeoman Way
Worthing
Sussex
BN13 3QZ
www.pitchpublishing.co.uk
info@pitchpublishing.co.uk

ISBN 978 1 78531 553 4

Typesetting and origination by Pitch Publishing
Printed and bound in India by Replika Press Pvt. Ltd.

# Contents

*For my grandsons*
*Charlie, Edward,*
*Cameron and William*

# Acknowledgements

MY GRATEFUL appreciation to Jennifer Ann Wiles for her support and encouragement in the writing of this book – her thoughts, comments and suggestions have been unerringly helpful.

I would like to thank Michael Griffiths and Ian Carter for their comments and observations, which have undoubtedly improved the narrative. Additionally, Mike Firth provided very useful input and my thanks to him.

Thank you to Duncan Olner for the design of the cover, and to Richard Fletcher for editing the book. And thank you particularly to Jane Camillin at Pitch Publishing for her continued support and advice in producing this book.

Quotations used in this book are referenced by their source – the book, author and publisher. Permission for quotations used in this book has been sought from the publisher.

From *Motty* by John Motson published by Ebury. Reproduced by permission of The Random House Group Ltd copyright 2008.

# Preface

WHY WRITE a book about football in the 1980s?

I've written books about football in the previous two decades – *Grandad – What was Football like in the 1960s?* and *Grandad What was Football like in the 1970s?* And having taken time to write a third book, *Wednesday v United: The Sheffield Derby*, it feels right to continue a narrative about football, this time in the 1980s.

Unlike the previous book titles, you'll see there's no reference to 'Grandad' in this one. That's not because of my grandsons' lack of interest in the historical perspective of football, quite the reverse as far as Charlie is concerned. He will ask 'what was football like in the old days, Grandad?' And whilst for him, at the age of 12, the 1980s are quite definitely 'the old days', for me they are certainly not – they are the third decade of my continuing passion for football, keen interest in the game and all that surrounds it.

The omission of 'Grandad' from the title is simply because there are many people who will recall football in the decade – through fond memories or otherwise – who are of a younger generation and reference to 'Grandad' in the title could potentially narrow interest in the book.

I have assured my ten-year-old grandson Edward that he should not be concerned about this omission from the book's title – his name is in the book!

# WHAT WAS FOOTBALL LIKE IN THE 1980s?

Aside from the title, the narrative follows a similar structure to the first two books – using personal experiences to supplement the perspective of football and the wider context of the 1980s.

# Foreword

THE 1980s are at least 30 years ago, 40 from the beginning of that decade.

For some, memories start to fade with time. For others, memories of events years ago remain as vivid today as if they took place yesterday.

For football the 1980s were a momentous time – on and off the pitch. For me, it was unquestionably the darkest decade for the game. Whilst there were many highs on the pitch, and great achievements by clubs, they were overshadowed by events off it – hooliganism, the Bradford fire, Heysel, Hillsborough … at times, the football seemed incidental at best.

The decades since have seen major changes – some for the better, some maybe not so.

Aside from the first chapter, which presents a perspective on current football, the book is focused on how things were in the 1980s.

# Chapter 1

# Four Decades Later – The Wasps, The Jags, The Gers...

IT SEEMED a good idea at the time. And POMO – Position of Maximum Opportunity – came to mind. I'd first heard the term used as the football mantra of Charles Hughes, the FA's director of coaching, in the 1960s. His approach on the football field was to get the ball into the opposition's six-yard box as quickly as possible – statistically the area where most goals are scored. In the 1980s, there were managers of clubs who applied this mantra.

My POMO was a little different. My partner, Jennifer, was away for six weeks visiting her daughter and granddaughter in New Zealand, giving me every opportunity to indulge my passion and interest in going to watch live football. Scottish football appealed. I'd been to a few grounds in Scotland but here was the chance to go to town and spend a weekend there.

Fixtures researched on the internet, the best weekend promised to be Friday, 4 October, Saturday, 5 October and Sunday, 6 October (2019) – respectively Alloa Athletic v Dundee United, 7.05pm kick-off, Partick Thistle v Queen of the South, 3pm kick-off, Glasgow Rangers v Hamilton Academical, 3pm kick-off.

I toyed with the idea of a 'double-header' on the Sunday – Livingston v Glasgow Celtic at 12 noon before the game at Ibrox. Logistics in the way – it was almost impossible to see a way of watching the Hoops play the full game at Livingston and travel to the Gers for a 3pm kick-off using public transport. Foolhardy to attempt the task.

The Scottish weekend would mean missing (Sheffield) Wednesday's game at home to Wigan Athletic on the Saturday afternoon, but sacrifices had to be made.

Internet again – check the train times, connections and costs, and then the hotels. The thought of travelling from home in Hertfordshire to Scotland and back by car was a non-starter. Travel by rail looked remarkably straightforward – Home to Alloa – train at 08.28 on Friday into London St Pancras International, London Kings Cross to Edinburgh, change for the train to Croy (where?), change at Croy for Alloa, arrive Alloa at 15.34.

Game kicks off at 7.05pm – televised live on BBC Scotland.

Cost of travel by train with railcard discount, £55.10 – plus £1.30 admin fee. Seemed good value. Booked two weeks in advance.

Tickets for the games – register online with Glasgow Rangers and Partick Thistle and tickets then purchased. Website only for Alloa Athletic, no tickets for purchase online.

Single tickets only available at Ibrox – purchased one in the Sandy Jardine Stand Lower for the game – £29 plus the admin charge; many tickets available at Partick Thistle's Firhill – purchased one in the Jackie Husband Stand, £20 plus the admin charge.

For Alloa, the website stated a ticket price of £18 – no further information. The capacity at the oddly named Indodrill Stadium was 3,100 – that looked low. This could be a problem

– the club website had an e-mail address for supporters to contact if they had any questions. 'Can I purchase in advance or is it pay at the turnstile on the night?' and 'How long to walk from the hotel to the ground?' The response was quick and very helpful – pay on the turnstile, the presumption must be they're not expecting a capacity crowd, I'd get there early in any event to beat any rush and guarantee a place in the ground.

All booked and done, the first leg of three at Alloa. But I had no idea of the location of Alloa. I'd booked everything without knowing that basic fact. I hadn't needed to. Indeed, for a while I felt a little ashamed that my education had not provided me with an understanding of the geography of Scotland. I checked. Alloa is in Clackmannanshire, five miles from the more well-known Stirling.

And the football club? I knew next to nothing about Alloa Athletic. They played in the Scottish Championship, wore yellow and black and were nicknamed 'The Wasps'. Beyond that, nothing. Disappointed with my ignorance, I set out to learn more. The club website was my primary source – the Wasps formed in 1883, were champions of Scottish League Division Two in 1921/22. And that was it – no other football honours. The capacity of their home ground, the Recreation Ground, was recorded in 1980 as 9,000.

Most individual league goals in a season – 49 – scored by Wee Crilley in 1931/32, and their most capped player, Jock Hepburn, made one international appearance for Scotland in 1890/91.

The Indodrill Stadium (sponsor's name) was referred to by many locals as the 'Rec' – they had been the second-to-last Scottish League club to install floodlights at their ground in 1979, Stranraer's Stair Park the only ground floodlightless for longer.

Having arrived in good time in Alloa, I made for the ground … and there it was, oddly shaped floodlights leaning over, almost apologetically, from the Clackmannan Road side of the ground. A quick walk around the three sides of the ground that were accessible – Alloa Athletic's home a 'stadium'? Not in my book.

Forty-five minutes before kick-off, there were many away supporters outside the ground sporting their tangerine and black favours.

The primary entrance to the ground was the best bet – on the same side that players and officials entered. Once inside, a look around – I'd call this a ground at best, and one that has most probably seen better days. An elevated section of ten rows of seating stretches half the length of one side from where the players' tunnel emerges, and opposite a smaller stand with seats similarly stretching halfway down one side. Standing at pitch level was possible at either end of the two stands.

The two ends – a covered end with shallow terracing, and an open end with similarly shallow terracing.

Refreshment bar, I joined a small queue – the guy in front of me asked for a 'stovie'. Looking at the refreshments available, no mention of a stovie. Intrigued, I asked the stovie purchaser,

'Excuse me, what's a stovie?'

'You dinnae know what a stovie is?' he responded with a marked tone of incredulity. Others turned and looked.

I resisted the temptation to respond, 'Why do you think I'm asking you if I knew what it was?' Diplomacy better here. 'No, I don't, I'm a Sassenach and live south of the border.'

This seemed to appeal to stovie man, chest puffed out a little. 'A stovie is basically pieces of meat with vegetables,' he paused momentarily, 'though the stovie here will not be as good as the ones I make myself.'

His timing in reflecting his prowess at stovie-making was ill judged – the stovie-serving lady had turned to him at that instant. The purchaser looked down, ensuring no eye contact, handed over his money (£1) and was on his way, stovie in hand.

For the record, the stovie was served in a polystyrene cup – the type that might contain soup. The content looked just like the purchaser had described – to the hitherto uneducated Englishman, it looked like the ingredients for a stew without gravy. And it was hot – a distinct benefit to warm the hands.

Time to find a place to sit in the ground – the stand opposite the players' tunnel looked the best spot, closest to the action. Walking round, it was clear it had been sectioned off, crates and pieces of tape across the terracing indicating it was out of bounds. Oh well, back to the main stand – up the stairs and to the steward. 'Am I OK to sit here?'

'Are you a season ticket holder?'

'No.'

'This is for season ticket holders only.'

'Where can I sit, then?'

'The stand over there.'

'But that's sectioned off just there,' I pointed out.

'Is it? Go around the other corner then and get in that way.'

No point engaging further. His knowledge of the apparent crowd-control measures in place was distinctly lacking. To the other corner – here a piece of tape stretched between two bins at the top and bottom of the terracing, presumably to denote this was sectioned off too. No matter – three girls lifted the tape and walked underneath towards the main stand. I lifted the tape and walked away from the main stand. Stewards watched and ignored.

I took a place amongst the Dundee United supporters in the stand. It became clear this stand and the open terracing

I'd walked across was for away fans. The main stand and covered stand for home fans. Away fans here in numbers and in confident mood ahead of the game – they were top of the Championship and Alloa Athletic were bottom.

The league placings were reflected on the Ladbrokes coupon offering odds on the game – 3/1 a home win, 4/6 a win for their opponents.

With the game televised live on BBC Scotland, there were two bright lights at pitch level illuminating the area for pre-match interviews and they were far brighter than the ground's floodlights.

The game under way, the home side gave as good as they got and more besides. Within 14 minutes they had cut open what purported to be a defence, quick, incisive one-touch passing, and the ball swept in. Disgruntlement amongst the away support. That disgruntlement was to increase as the game progressed – the Wasps, the part-timers, were certainly the better team on the night. It was a good, competitive, open game; the home team made more chances than their fully professional opponents.

Much had been made of the Tangerines' striker, Lawrence Shankland, a prolific goalscorer who had been called up to the Scotland national squad for the first time a couple of days earlier. He barely had the proverbial look-in.

And to rub salt into the travelling supporters' wounds, the Alloa fans' chant of 'When the Wasps go marching in' was heard again and again as the game drew to its conclusion. Quite where and when the Wasps had last marched in, I don't know; that had no relevance for the home support as they took the game, 1-0.

In the following morning's *Daily Record*, Alloa boss Peter Grant was quoted, 'I was chuffed with that.' His opposite number, Robbie Neilson, commented, 'If you're at Dundee United you have to win 50-50s, headers and second balls. You have to be aggressive with the press. We were letting people pass the ball around us. The quality wasn't there tonight.'

The crowd was 1,717, the majority supporting the away team. The programme for the game did not highlight previous attendances but it seemed reasonable to conclude that tonight's was likely to be the season's highest.

And the programme – £2, it had the usual information you'd expect to see – Manager's Notes, away team information and an 'On this Day' (4 October) feature ... which included club photographer David Glencross, born on this day in 1960.

A first for me at the game – the first time I'd seen a football team play in black and yellow hooped shirts – the Wasps.

Different colours at the next game – red and yellow striped shirts for Partick Thistle.

On the Thursday before the Scottish Football fest weekend, the postman had been and gone without delivering a ticket from Partick Thistle. He may come on the Friday morning, but my plan was to be travelling north on the Alloa Express by that time. The ticket would languish on the doormat.

Call to Partick Thistle – the usual automated voice came on identifying the caller's options, depending on who the call was intended for. Fortunately, option 1 for the ticket office – automated voice-man cut off in mid-flow as the number 1 was pressed. A lady's voice on the other end, engaging and friendly – problem explained, she said, 'Two seconds honey while I put you on hold briefly.' Not expecting to be called honey, very friendly. Time goes slower north of the border; her estimated time to come back was out by more than a 1,000 per cent, but no matter, the friendly and engaging voice was back:

'I've found you. I've got the ticket. I'll arrange for it to be at the Jackie Husband Stand reception on Saturday afternoon. You can collect it from there.'

'Thank you.'

'No problem, darling. I hope you enjoy the game.'

Call done and completed within two minutes and in that time I'd been referred to as 'honey' and 'darling'. You don't get that at the Hillsborough ticket office.

I needed to do a bit of research on Partick Thistle before my visit. I'd known only one 'Jags' supporter – Neil Roden, then HR Director for the Royal Bank of Scotland – when I worked there. I met Neil a couple of times and his passion for the club shone through. I recollect asking him about what I'd heard about Partick Thistle supporters, and whether it was true that in Glasgow the Protestants supported Rangers, the Catholics supported Celtic, and agnostics supported Thistle. Neil looked at me more than a little quizzically and said, 'No.'

And Thistle? – amongst other players, Alan Hansen started his career there before joining Liverpool and having great success in the 1970s and 1980s.

Now the football – train from Alloa to Glasgow on Saturday morning – £6. Book into the hotel, then a walk to Firhill, the home of Partick Thistle. Google Maps – journey 2.7 miles. Made it with the odd unintended detour as either the software, the iPhone or the operator failed to pick up a change of direction at the right point. No matter. Approaching Firhill there was one pub, the Star and Garter, clearly Thistle, red and yellow chequered flags hanging outside.

Closer to the ground on Firhill Road, the constituency office of Patrick Grady, the Scottish Nationalist Party MP who represented Glasgow North. A picture of a smiling

Mr Grady was included in the match day programme (£3), highlighting his availability for constituents.

I purchased a Thistle yellow, black and red bar scarf (£9) from the Thistle store – it was cold for early October and the scarf would serve a useful purpose. Noticing the label on it – 'Made in England' – I wondered what Mr Grady would make of it. Certainly, the whole issue of Brexit was to the fore at the time and the SNP were making clear they were looking for another independence referendum. Could the days of the Thistle scarf being produced south of the border be numbered?

I circumnavigated the ground – a steep hill from Firhill Road to walk behind both ends. Ticket collected from a man with a box of tickets in the Jackie Husband Stand (Google research showed Husband had played for Thistle from 1938–50, had made 371 appearances and been capped twice for Scotland, and that was not the half of it – he spent a total of 52 years at Firhill as player, captain, trainer, coach, physio and kitman).

One thing was noticeable about the frontage of the ground on Firhill Road – it looked dated and a little tired. There were turnstiles at one end of the road with faded lettering on signs above the turnstile doors, 'Parent and Child £5.00, OAPs and Boys £2.00.' It looked as if the turnstiles had not been used for some time.

Once inside the ground it became clear why – the all-seated Jackie Husband Stand runs the length of the pitch down one side, opposite the old main stand. To the left and behind the goal was open grass banking with a scaffold in place for a television camera. The old turnstiles would have provided access to this area, but no longer. It was not in use for spectators.

The other end had yellow and red banners and flags on display at the rear of this covered stand – it looked like the popular end for Thistle supporters. As kick-off approached, it became clear that the two areas of the ground used for spectators was the covered stand at one end of the ground and the Jackie Husband Stand. Except not quite – the main stand had no spectators apart from one area, the Directors' Box, which had a full complement in its seated area. It looked surreal – a large old stand with no spectators save for this isolated area in the middle.

Fans' singing took place before the game – I recognised none of the songs. This may have been in part because my ear was not attuned to the melodious tunes being sung with a marked Glaswegian accent. That said, I picked up one line, 'Oh Maryhill is wonderful.' Maryhill is the district of Glasgow where Firhill is situated. Wonderful? – its beauty would be in the eye of the beholder, with its many high-rise blocks.

Thistle were managed by Ian McCall – this his second game in charge in his second spell at the club. There was confidence in the air – the previous week Thistle had won 3-1 at Inverness. On the betting coupon Ladbrokes quoted 5/6 the win for Thistle, 5/2 a win for their opponents.

The confidence was misplaced – the only goal of the game a header in the second half by Queen of the South's Darren Brownlie, direct from a corner. The Thistle faithful were increasingly restless from that point – whether manager McCall's post-match assessment brought them any comfort is open to doubt. 'We did not deserve to lose the game – that's a given – although I don't think we deserved to win it.' *(Sunday Post)*. Seems a roundabout way of saying he thought it should have been a draw – for my part I thought Queen of the South were good value for the win.

The crowd totalled 2,910, of which the stadium announcer stated 259 were Doonhammers (Queen of the South's nickname). No attendances for previous games were shown in the match programme.

During the game, I kept up to date with other scores across the country – Wednesday won 1-0. That's a positive.

After the game, I found a different and more direct way to walk back into central Glasgow – follow the Forth and Clyde Canal situated directly outside the ground. Interesting information on boards by the canal highlighted the many sawmills that had been situated around this part of the canal in the 19th and early 20th centuries.

And now thoughts turned to Glasgow Rangers. From being a lad growing up in Sheffield, the Gers had been my second Scottish club (after Montrose). They played in blue and their name began with 'R', and they were one of the two clubs in 'The Old Firm'.

For the game at Ibrox, I decided on a taxi from the hotel, leaving at 1.30pm for a 3pm kick-off. The taxi driver was not overly impressed with his fare – he was a keen Celtic supporter and from a professional perspective he thought there would be major traffic problems getting to the ground.

His concerns misplaced. It took 20 minutes. Circumnavigate the ground – this is an impressive stadium. There was a Fan Zone behind the stand at one end of the ground – it was busy. Two guys with a microphone talking to the crowd and the European Cup Winners' Cup won by Rangers in 1972 on display in front of them. One was Derek Johnstone, a famous Rangers player of the 1970s. He was responding to questions – 'Who was the funniest guy in the Rangers' dressing room when you played?'

Johnstone considered the question.

'Jim Denny, some of our older supporters will remember him. And you know at this club as well as other clubs, supporters tend to make a judgement about a player quickly. And they did that with Jim – not a favourite.

'There was an Old Firm game here at Ibrox, Jim on the bench when manager Jock Wallace said to him, "Go and have a warm-up, it looks like you'll be coming on for Sandy [Jardine], who's injured."

'Jim went to have his warm-up at the end where the Celtic supporters were gathered. On returning to the bench, Jock asked him why he'd gone down to that end for his warm-up – "Simple boss, I get less stick down there than warming-up in front of our own supporters!"' Laughter from the gathered throng.

I purchased a programme, £3.50, and asked its seller who would win today. 'Rangers, easy, 3-0.' He told me my poster was inside the programme – it was a full team line-up of Rangers. Splendid. It would be staying in the programme.

Outside, at a corner of the stadium, a statue. At its base small plaques with names – 66 of them. Fresh flowers lay in front of the statue. People stopped and looked, and thought, saying little. The statue was of John Greig, Rangers' legendary full-back and captain in the 1970s. The names on the plaques were those of the 66 people who had died in the Ibrox tragedy on 2 January 1971 on Stairway 11, coming out of the ground as the end of the Old Firm game approached. People falling down, taking others with them, tumbling, a crush of bodies. At that time the worst football tragedy in the United Kingdom. Almost 50 years on it resonated.

Once inside, it was readily apparent this was a stadium, a place with atmosphere, a place with great support and passion, a place to play and watch football – I sat in the three-tiered Sandy Jardine Stand and the place looked magnificent. Atmosphere building as kick-off approached. Not a seat left to watch the game, except in the Hamilton Academical corner, where there looked to be no more than 50 hardy souls in their red and white favours, isolated by the hundreds of blue seats around them. They must have felt like strangers in a very foreign land.

Full house for the Rangers support – 48,838 in attendance. And if the Gers fans needed any geeing up for the game, it came in the form of a result from Livingston an hour before kick-off – the home team had defeated the Gers' arch-rivals Celtic for the first time ever, 2-0. Ibrox buoyant. A win this afternoon and they would leapfrog the Bhoys to go top of the Premiership table.

Interestingly, the Ladbrokes coupon had no reference to the Rangers game – perhaps like the programme seller they thought it was a foregone conclusion. For the game at Livingston they had 7/1 the home team, 2/9 Celtic. Coupon-buster.

And the game against the Accies – very one-sided. In the *Scottish Daily Mail*, John McGarry reported, 'It was plain in the opening seconds that Rangers were at it and Hamilton were all at sea. The only wonder was that it took seven minutes for the opener to arrive.' 5-0 the result – it could and should have been more. Jermaine Defoe, 37 the following day, scored a hat-trick.

From the second goal, the noise, the singing, the *joie de vivre* that was Ibrox, climbed the scales. 'We shall not be moved …', sung with feeling and with strength, reverberated and reverberated again around the stadium – the home support in full cry.

Half-time provided a brief interlude. Half-time draw for the winning lucky number to be drawn on the pitch. The ex-player making the draw is – small pause by the stadium announcer – 'Gazza ... Paul Gascoigne.' I barely heard the surname – the stadium erupted, the ovation for Gascoigne was incredible, like no other. He could not help but be moved and you could hear it in the cracking of his voice as he addressed the crowd. The legend returned 25 years and more after he'd left the club.

And now to the draw – 'Gazza, over to you', pause and then Gazza, 'The winning number is ... 9 ... 9 ... 9.'

The stadium announcer knew something was up. He took the ticket and read the number out – it was a six-digit number, the details of which I don't recollect. The crowd laughed heartily well before the announcer had time to put things right.

Gazza was thanked and gave a wave of acknowledgement to each side of the ground. Cue further loud applause.

Final whistle at the end of the second half – joy unconfined for the Gers supporters, a 5-0 demolition of the Accies and now top of the league. For the players on duty for their respective countries over the next two weeks, they would meet up with their international team-mates. For the clubs, it was the international break – no games the following weekend for those clubs with players away with national squads.

A look at the programme – well produced, glossy, lots of information both current and historical for the Rangers fan. And then one thing struck me – aside from the team line-up on the back page, there was no information about the visitors' team. If you wanted to know anything about Hamilton Academical and their players, the match programme was not the place to look! I think it's the only time I've seen a programme bereft of such information.

After the game, a walk back to the hotel in the city centre – a long walk, more than two miles, I was far from alone. A snake of people to the front and back made their way – many of them to Glasgow Central Station.

An interesting weekend. Three games in three days. Different experiences at the three venues. And how does it compare to the 1980s? In that decade:

- Two divisions in the Scottish League, not the current four
- No international break. Internationals were played midweek; club games continued
- No live second tier games on television
- No keeping up to date with scores at other games by smartphone – a portable radio was best for that purpose in the 1980s
- And the grounds – not all-seater, terracing covered the greater part of the ground with fencing
- No coupons for betting in the ground
- With no internet, there was no chance of easily understanding the rail journeys required, and booking those journeys was much more time-consuming and problematic.

A comparison of the three home clubs and how they fared 40 years ago is interesting.

In 1979/80, Alloa Athletic finished bottom (14th in Division Two) of the Scottish League (34 clubs). Their highest attendance that season was 1,600, the lowest 300, with an average of 691.

Partick Thistle finished seventh in the top flight, the Premier Division. Their highest attendance that season was 23,000, with a crowd lower than 3,000 recorded once (2,000) and an average attendance of 8,445.

Rangers finished fifth in the Premier Division. Their highest attendance was 36,000 for an Old Firm game against

Celtic, their lowest 8,000 against Kilmarnock and an average attendance of 21,154.

Aberdeen, managed by Alex Ferguson, were the Premier League champions in 1979/80.

And I thought about how things are nowadays following my club, Sheffield Wednesday. A season ticket at Hillsborough in the North Stand, £555 – for 23 home league games in the Championship. All turnstiles had stewards, who checked anyone carrying baggage into the home spectator areas.

Away games? Tickets available to supporters based on the 'points' achieved from attending home and away games. It was a meritocratic approach and ensured those who attended most games had the first opportunity to purchase tickets for away games.

All away games had stewards and police present – it usually entailed an outer body search, as well as baggage searched before entry into the ground. And a new one the previous season at local rivals Rotherham United – police and dogs present, and supporters checked for any so-called recreational drugs in their possession! It wasn't like that in the 1980s.

# Chapter 2

# On the Rise ... and Then

FOR SUPPORTERS of Sheffield Wednesday, the new decade offered distinct optimism, albeit in the Third Division. The penultimate game of the 1970s had seen Wednesday beat local rivals United 4-0 in the Sheffield derby on Boxing Day, a game that passed into local folklore as the 'Boxing Day Massacre'. That game was played in front of a Third Division record crowd of 49,309.

Aside from the result, the game proved to be a major turning point in the fortunes of the city's clubs for years to come – Wednesday were on the rise, promoted at the end of the 1979/80 season. Manager Jack Charlton observed before the start of the following season, 'I've been looking forward to this season, because I've always said that Sheffield Wednesday was like a big snowball. It was heavy and difficult to get moving, but now will be very difficult to stop. There is tremendous potential at the ground here and in the city. It will only be a matter of time before they get back to the First Division.'

It took four years for Wednesday to gain promotion, and by then under new manager Howard Wilkinson, putting them back amongst the elite of the game after 14 long seasons outside the top flight. Those 14 seasons were the longest absence from

First Division football Wednesday and their supporters had endured in their history.

That 1983/84 season promised much – and for once delivered. Howard Wilkinson had replaced Jack Charlton as manager before the campaign's start. A new, effective style of play – unbeaten in 15 games in the league. I saw that first defeat of the season at Crystal Palace. Wilkinson noted the reaction of the home team. 'Crystal Palace celebrated their victory over us with a glass of champagne,' he said. No matter – the team looked right and oozed confidence and belief. Spirit was high in the team and among supporters.

It looked good and was. They were promoted back to the First Division at season's end.

For the final game of the season at home to Manchester City, I decided to revisit my boyhood, taking the bus from close to my parents' home into town and then from the town centre to the ground – reliving countless such journeys of yore. But the journey had changed – or rather the buses had. One man operated them, no bus conductors. In the 1960s running to jump on the rear open platform of the 'Football Special' bus as it accelerated on its way to the ground, the bus conductor weaving in and out of the standing passengers on the lower deck in a frantic effort to get their fares. All seemed slow and synthetic. Pay the driver for the ticket. Leave when all passengers had paid and were on board the bus. The energy and pace of the 1960s and 1970s had gone.

The first game back in the top flight was against Brian Clough's Nottingham Forest at Hillsborough. That first game back is always a test – are we good enough to survive in this league? The test was passed with flying colours – a well-deserved 3-1 win, Imre Varadi scoring one of the finest individual goals I've seen by a Wednesday player. He took the ball from the edge of his own penalty area to the edge of the Forest area, following a mazy run, before delivering an unstoppable shot past the keeper. Clough remarked after the game, 'Wednesday murdered us, but it is good for football that this club and its supporters should be back in the First Division.'

But it's not the football, or the result, or the Varadi goal that really sticks in the memory. It's the crowd and the context of the times.

August 1984 was five months into what would turn out to be the year-long national miners' strike. A national strike called for one purpose – to prevent forced colliery closures and unemployment in mining communities. The Yorkshire coalfield – a total shutdown. Real hardship for the miners and their families. But not all areas were as one – notably Nottinghamshire. The Nottinghamshire area miners seceded from the National Union of Mineworkers in July 1984 and formed the Union of Democratic Mineworkers. They wanted to work and be paid. They returned to work and the strike was broken.

The atmosphere inside the Hillsborough ground was venomous towards the Forest supporters on the Leppings Lane terrace behind the goal – the loud, thunderous, passionate and heartfelt chant of 'scabs, scabs, scabs' rained down on them from three sides of the ground. The reaction and chorus of 'we're getting paid' fuelled the anger and resentment further. The atmosphere was approaching a powder keg: strike, unity, jobs, short-term pain – work, self, short-term gain, all played out at a football ground. Yorkshire v Nottinghamshire – much more than Wednesday v Forest. Wednesday's win helped lower the tension a degree.

Towards the end of the game, Wednesday hordes from the Spion Kop left the ground and made for the Leppings

Lane end. Their visit was not to exchange pleasantries with the away supporters – there were no pleasantries to exchange, and it was not to take on the opposition's football supporters. This was different. It was simply focused on demonstrating and underpinning a way of life, the solidity of the collective, the values of a community, and all that those values meant. I don't know the outcome of the visitation. As an away supporter it would not have been pleasant.

It's interesting to reflect and question what the Yorkshireman and socialist, Brian Clough, felt about his adopted county breaking the miner's strike. It would not have sat easy with him.

Over the next five seasons, Wednesday consolidated their position in the top flight without setting the division on fire.

In October 1988, Howard Wilkinson left and took his managerial skills up the M1 to Leeds United, in time proving to be a great success at Elland Road.

Wednesday appointed ex-player Peter Eustace to the helm. Not a success. After three months in charge, he was gone – and that period included the most defensively organised team set-up I've ever seen Wednesday adopt, at Millwall. A 1-0 win for the home side with a goal in the last minute.

The Millwall manager, John Docherty, summed up Wednesday's approach, 'Their only ambition was in winning a corner. They got two so it was a good day for them.' Fair comment.

Next came the appointment of the charismatic and outgoing Ron Atkinson, who joined Wednesday from Atletico Madrid … he'd apparently fallen out with their chairman, Jesus Gil. Things were never boring with big Ron in charge.

But it was not boring for all the wrong reasons the following season – Wednesday seemed safe from relegation in 14th place with six games to play, seven points clear of the drop zone. And then all change – four defeats in five games meant the last game of the season would decide relegation.

Atkinson's programme notes for that last game made the point. 'A few weeks ago we could not have envisaged being in our present situation. We face an exciting finale.' Indeed.

That afternoon, I'd committed to managing the Onslow Boys' under-9s team at the Guildford Saints 5-a-side tournament. The boys knocked out at the group stage ... news from around the grounds on BBC Radio was not promising. Wednesday were in the relegation zone if results stayed the way they were. That lack of promise became reality. 3-0 loss at home to Nottingham Forest, Wednesday relegated.

There was a sinking, empty feeling. Too many people came up and said, 'You know Wednesday have been relegated, don't you?' I don't recollect exactly how many, but it was a dozen at least. But if they thought I knew, then why come up and tell me? It didn't help.

Meanwhile, much to the chagrin of Wednesdayites and to the great delight of supporters of the red and whites in Sheffield, United had confirmed their promotion to the top flight on the same day as Wednesday's relegation with a win at Leicester City.

The United captain, Bob Booker, recollected that day at Filbert Street. 'With Sheffield Wednesday suffering relegation from the First Division that day, the Blades were singing, "United up, Wednesday down". It was fantastic.' (*Sheffield United: Match of My Life*, Nick Johnson, Pitch Publishing, 2012).

United had finished the decade on a real high, having achieved promotion to the Second Division the previous season – the Blades' centenary season. For the bulk of the 1980s they had been in the relative doldrums and played second fiddle to Wednesday in the city. Relegated to the Fourth Division for the first time in their history in 1981, they had a journey to make through the divisions.

Their fall to the basement prompted this observation, 'Bramall Lane was now the archetypal haunted house of English football, dilapidated and infested with a restless, resentful hooliganism.' (*The Rough Guide to English Football*, Dan Goldstein, Rough Guides, 2000).

For United, 1980/81 was to prove disastrous – with a last-game decider to determine the fate of their Third Division season.

They needed to draw at home to Walsall to stay up, while their visitors needed to win. The game was a real 'nail-biter'. Almost the inevitable happened. The game was goalless with five minutes to go, penalty to Walsall. And converted by Donald Penn!

Two minutes later, a penalty for the home side. The regular penalty-taker, John Matthews, once of Arsenal, did not step up for the kick but Don Givens – bought from Birmingham City earlier in the season – took the responsibility. He struck the ball and Ron Green saved it. Pandemonium. Minutes later, United relegated to the Fourth Division for the first time in their history.

Given the rivalry in the city, it may come as no surprise that Don Givens has a special place in the hearts of many Wednesdayites.

By the end of the decade, the clubs' positions were changing, and the start of the new decade had Wednesday playing second fiddle to their city rivals.

Promotion to the top division on the same day your rivals are relegated from it is the best/worst of times depending on which club you support. One man who didn't see it like that was the United manager, Dave Bassett. 'Sheffield Wednesday's unsuccessful bid to escape relegation to the Second Division saddened me. There had been no Sheffield derby in the First Division since 1967/68 – 24 years previously – and it would have been really good to have both teams in the top flight for the following season. Good for football, good for Sheffield and, perhaps more pertinently, good for both Bramall Lane and Hillsborough.' (*Settling the Score*, Dave Bassett, John Blake, 2002).

# Chapter 3

# Shrimpers and Shots ...

LOCAL CLUBS for me in the 1980s – the Shrimpers, Southend United at Roots Hall, and the Shots, Aldershot at the Recreation Ground.

Working for Ford Motor Company in the first half of the decade, home at Leigh-on-Sea in Essex, convenient for each of the locations I worked at – Dagenham, Brentwood, Basildon – and Southend United.

I'd first gone to the home of the Shrimpers for a game in April 1978 – Southend United were the club of my soon-to-be wife, Pauline, and all her family. They could go almost as far back supporting their club as I could with mine supporting Wednesday.

And in some ways, their support was all the more creditable given the Shrimpers' entire Football League history (joined the Football League in 1920) had been spent in divisions three and four, and their FA Cup exploits had seen them go no further than the fifth round. Progress in the League Cup was even less noteworthy, never beyond the third round.

For most of the 1980s Southend United could boast having the most recently built ground in the Football League, Roots Hall, opened in 1955. In his definitive book, *The Football Grounds of England and Wales* (Collins Willow, 1983), author

Simon Inglis observes, 'If there is a monument to the British football supporter, it is Roots Hall, for here is a ground built almost entirely through the efforts of a small, but dedicated group of people.' The Supporters' Club provided the finance to purchase the land for the new ground in 1950 and funded the setting up of a trust fund to build it.

By the time I became familiar with the ground, it was starting to show its age – one main wooden seated stand down one side, covered terrace opposite, large open terracing behind one goal and covered shallow terracing behind the other goal.

A comment from journalist Howard Southwood in the local *Evening Echo* in March 1986 caught the eye. 'News that Southend United have resurrected plans to build a super stadium in the town has got my pulses racing. Chairman Vic Jobson is confident that the plans presented this time will iron out any possible objections and that the whole package will go through and see Blues kicking off at the new venue in 1987/88.' It didn't.

By September 1986, things had taken a decided turn for the worse for the club's ambitions – the club's programme recorded, 'September 29th 1986 will go down in the minds of the board of directors as a black day in the democratic process of local government as it affects our own council.' The club's concern was simple – regarding planning permission for a new stadium, in block capitals in the programme, 'THE COUNCILLORS WERE DENIED A RIGHT TO VOTE', apparently because the 'applicant had withdrawn the application'. This was news to the club. No progress on a new stadium in the 1980s.

Southend United's keenness for home games to be played on Friday nights helped me see more games – with a young family, taking many Saturday afternoons off for football was not practical. The club's use of their car park for the Roots Hall Market on Saturdays (as well as Thursdays) suited me down to the ground.

During the first half of the 1980s, the Shrimpers oscillated between the third and fourth divisions – two relegations, one promotion. A handful of decent players – 'crowd pleasers' as they were often referred to in those times – including Derek Spence, the blond-haired forward who played for Northern Ireland, and midfielders Ron Pountney and Anton Otulakowski. Some good games there, too, particularly during their Fourth Division Championship-winning season of 1980/81, during which they set many club records.

At games, supporters were direct and honest in their assessment of the players – encouraged them, yes, no time for shirkers or 'fancy dans'.

Wednesday were not in the same division as the Shrimpers but were drawn against them in the FA Cup third round in 1982/83. A tough, uncompromising affair at Roots Hall ended 0-0 … the stand-out memory Wednesday captain Mick Lyons walking off the pitch at half-time with blood pouring down his face. The blood oozing from a wound for several minutes, he was not leaving the game. Lyons was a leader, hard as nails, and would run through a brick wall for the cause.

The tie went to a first and then second replay, both games at Hillsborough. Wednesday won the choice of venue for the third game on the toss of a coin, winning the tie 2-1. The outcome caused a little consternation with my in-laws, but they were very fair-minded and wished Wednesday well for the cup campaign.

My brother-in-law, Ray, became a director of the club during season 1988/89, and gained a clear insight into the issues facing a lower-division club. His discretion and the need to maintain confidentiality meant I learned little about the club from the inside.

Southend United's progress seemed to be mirroring my career progress to a degree – promotion, stalling and prospects not looking that bright. At Ford, having joined their graduate trainee scheme in 1977, that decade offered opportunity for advancement.

Not so much the next decade; 1981 seemed a watershed year for Ford – and the term 'AJ' came to mean a lot. It was 'After Japan'. The motor industry becoming ever more competitive worldwide – the Japanese increasingly demonstrating their capabilities. Senior Ford executives travelled to Japan to understand 'how they did it'.

The upshot back in the UK became clear – reduced time required for vehicle design, greater standardisation of parts across Europe, reduction in organisational structure, in management and in the number of employees required. Efficiency, rationalisation, quicker to market.

In the global motor industry this was all well and good – and necessary for Ford to compete. But for me and others, it meant career opportunities were substantially reduced. Time to look elsewhere.

And where better than the so-called 'sunrise industry' – the IT industry. A manager at Ford had moved to ICL (International Computers Limited) and recommended I might be interested in joining.

Fast forward. I joined ICL in April 1985, based at Putney in London. In that first role in employee relations I worked for Gareth Trevor, whose own background is interesting. Earlier in his career, he had worked alongside Peter Ridsdale in personnel. Ridsdale later went on to senior roles at a number of football clubs, most notably Leeds United. Gareth observed that Mr Ridsdale's skills were probably not best suited to personnel work.

Change of work location meant a change of home location – three months of commuting by car to Putney from Leigh-on-Sea underlined that living in Essex was not compatible with working in London. A move required – given ICL's locations in the South East, Guildford chosen for our home. And Aldershot was the nearest football club – a 15-minute drive.

The Recreation Ground was 'something else'. It's situated in a public park. The turnstiles front the main road – once in the ground, flowerbeds immediately in front, attractive flowerbeds in the spring and summer. A short walk up to pitch level. No terracing or stands behind this goal – the Flowerbed End. And not once in more than 50 visits to that ground were the flowerbeds disturbed by supporters – all very civilised.

The other three sides of the ground had a similar layout to other lower-division grounds I'd seen. Nonetheless, the Recreation Ground for me was bottom of the pile in terms of seating and basic facilities. Its location gave rise to Simon Inglis observing, 'The Recreation Ground is like part of an arboretum, with the nicely mildewed air of its surrounds.' (*The Football Grounds of England and Wales*, Collins Willow, 1983). His view of the ground was more flattering than mine.

But the three-sided ground didn't affect the football – except when the ball went out of play at the Flowerbed End. Ball boys were in short supply and it often took that bit longer to return the ball into play.

On Saturday afternoons Aldershot players not on duty with the first team walked up to the office building and into the stand – Steve Claridge being one I saw walking and talking with supporters. In truth he and they had no choice – it was the only way to access the ground from the main road.

The club shop was in a small supporters' club hut – a Portakabin. The shop was manned by real enthusiasts – products on offer were limited: scarf, bobble hat and biro about the extent of the range. In that hut, I first heard the expression 'Barcelona like Aldershot' – not a phrase you hear every day of the week. That comparison based on the blue and red striped shirts of the two clubs – and there the comparison ended.

My best description of Aldershot is 'a good local club' – patrons primarily from around the immediate area with some soldiers present from the nearby barracks. Expectations at the club – and most obviously from the supporters – were low. For most of their history, the club had been in the basement division and few expected anything higher.

Nonetheless, come the late 1980s the club had assembled a good, tight squad of players – unheard of optimism started to emerge ... the Shots made the play-offs for promotion to Division Three in 1987/88 ... made the final, and over two legs against the mighty Wolverhampton Wanderers won on aggregate and were promoted.

Heady days that lasted a couple of seasons before they made their way back from where they came.

But things were not going well financially for the club and an SOS – Save Our Shots – campaign was launched. To underline the problems, in the programme for the last home game in May 1989, it stated, 'As you are no doubt aware, a lot has happened off the field and at the time of writing, Colin Hancock (Chairman) is doing his utmost to save the club from being wound up.' Short term he was successful in his aim, albeit cash flow and revenue remained a problem. At the beginning of the following season, the club offered a 'Ticket for Life' – £600 for a seat.

Given the Shots were my closest league club, I went to games and took an interest in their results; Wednesday were separated from them by two divisions.

But they were drawn together in a two-legged first-round tie of the League Cup in August 1989 – shortly after the Shots' relegation to Division Four.

First leg at Hillsborough – a surprising 0-0 draw given Wednesday were in the First Division, and a season's lowest crowd of 9,237. The draw was all the encouragement Aldershot manager Len Walker needed – the local press full of how well the Shots had done, and more importantly it highlighted the manager's confidence that his boys could cause a surprise in the return leg.

The programme for the return game, the home club's chairman enthused about the pitch at Hillsborough. 'When I entered the stand at Hillsborough and looked at the pitch, it took my breath away. So perfect was the surface that it seemed sacrilege for anyone to step on to the grass.'

At the Recreation Ground the game drew a much larger crowd than normal, a season's best of 4,011. We had seats amongst a small number of Wednesdayites positioned in the main stand. Pre-match singing and chanting by the home support indicated Len Walker's confidence was shared on the terraces.

The game played out fairly evenly – for the first 20 minutes – and then Wednesday scored, and scored again, and again, and again. Wednesday ran out convincing 8-0 winners – a record away win for the League Cup.

Wednesday manager Ron Atkinson did not make much of the result, Aldershot's Len Walker even less. Given his pre-match confidence and prediction, this was close to a 24-carat embarrassment for him. Walker acknowledged, 'It was embarrassing at the end – they were taking the mickey out of us.'

In the programme, a 'One to Watch' was identified – Wednesday's Dalian Atkinson. On the button – Atkinson scored three.

# Chapter 4

# Mascots

THE APPEARANCE of matchday mascots had become increasingly popular with clubs as the decade progressed – for many it would have been an opportunity to provide football-mad youngsters with the chance to lead their team out on to the pitch, as well as provide a commercial opportunity for the club.

Sheffield Wednesday had matchday mascots for each of their home games at Hillsborough. A telephone call to the club early in season 1986/87 confirmed all Wednesday's home league games had been taken for a matchday mascot. Ben, my seven-year-old son, was first on the list for a home FA Cup game.

Come the third-round draw, Wednesday were paired with Derby County at Hillsborough. Living in Guildford meant an early start for the game – we had to be there for 1pm, with a reserved parking spot outside the stadium. The cost of the experience was £90 – each game had one matchday mascot.

The day arrived – Saturday, 10 January – but the weather had not been kind. The pitch at Hillsborough was unplayable and the match was postponed. The game was rearranged for a midweek evening kick-off. Problem. There was no way Ben could take time off school to be taken up for an evening kick-off in Sheffield. Call the club – problem explained, the club fully understood and said Ben could be the mascot for the next home FA Cup game played on a Saturday (at no additional cost).

Better than nothing but conditional on Wednesday progressing in the competition and being drawn at home. At the age of seven, Ben seemed much less concerned about this turn of events than his dad.

Wednesday progressed in the rearranged midweek game against Derby, a 1-0 win. Interestingly, the programme for the game had Ben's details as mascot and a small photo.

Now the cup draw – Chester away. No mascot duties available for the FA Cup fourth round – game drawn at Sealand Road, midweek replay won at Hillsborough. To the fifth round – Wednesday drawn at home to West Ham United on Saturday, 21 February. Now the matchday mascot could travel from Guildford.

The mascot experience provided the chance to look behind the scenes at Hillsborough before the game, meet the players in the dressing room prior to kick-off, lead the team out on to the pitch, have a kick-around with the players and a photograph with his favourite player. Additionally, there were two tickets for his parents in the South Stand.

Replica kit purchased it was up to Hillsborough early that Saturday morning. Bob Gorrill, the Wednesday commercial manager, our contact point – smartly dressed in a fashionable grey suit and tie, with a noticeable smell of after-shave, were the first impressions. Friendly, helpful and efficient, he pointed us in the right direction – Ben changed into his kit outside the trophy room.

A visit to the Wednesday dressing room at about 2.15pm. Gorrill knocked on the door to ensure the visit and more particularly its timing was right for the players. The inner sanctum – the dressing room almost square shaped, clothes pegs on each wall and a wooden bench running unbroken around each wall at knee height. The players had their own individual pegs, although none had changed at that point.

Time for Dad and mascot to meet them. Some banter between the players and much more between the players and Bob Gorrill. It was clear the commercial manager had a good relationship with them. All the players were friendly, some quieter than others – 'Shelly', Gary Shelton, one of the friendliest, Brian Marwood more reserved, quieter. In fairness, the game was less than an hour from starting. Autographs obtained on the matchday programme, we left the players, giving them encouragement and wishing them good luck – that came more from the mascot's dad than the mascot!

Now time to check that Ben was feeling okay and ready to lead the team out on to the pitch. Positive response. The tunnel is narrow at Hillsborough and the teams ran out on to the pitch separately.

Ben had been taken by Bob Gorrill to wait outside the dressing room and meet up with captain Martin Hodge at the front of the phalanx of players. Dad standing pitch-side by the tunnel entrance. The atmosphere was building – and there appeared to be trouble on the Spion Kop in the top right-hand corner, the crowd moving quickly in different directions and police visible there.

The away team first down the tunnel, Billy Bonds at the front, stopped briefly at the end of the tunnel – looked in my direction, his steely blue eyes focused and determined. He ran towards the Leppings Lane end with his team – their supporters in their claret and blue colours rapturous at their team's arrival.

Now Wednesday. Ben came down the tunnel with Hodgy, the captain picked up pace as the natural light appeared and he emerged from the tunnel – all the Wednesday players running on to the pitch. Ben was doing his best to keep up with the captain.

The noise was incredible – all focused on that tunnel area and I could feel it coming down on the players. It felt like wave after wave of noise from all four sides of the ground arrowing in on one small area and enveloping it. No doubt the players were used to it. I wasn't. And the seven-year-old mascot certainly wasn't.

At the Spion Kop goal Ben kicked the ball back and forth to Hodgy, looking a little nervously over his shoulder, I suspect to check where Dad was. The kickabout with the goalkeeper interrupted for a photograph with 'Shutty' (Carl Shutt), his favourite player. Shutty was substitute that day.

Referee's whistle blown for the captains to join him, toss of the coin for choice of ends. Hodgy encouraging Ben to move to the centre circle by pointing in that direction and ruffling his hair in a friendly way. Proceedings completed with the referee, Ben came away with the tossed 50p coin in his hand as the stadium announcer confirmed the name of the mascot leaving the field, the mascot waving to the crowd as he ran off the pitch.

Reunited with Dad, Ben said he was fine and wanted to know what happened next – now time to quickly change into his normal clothes and reunite with Mum (and Dad) to watch the game. By now sitting in the South Stand, it was clear events had taken a toll on the young mascot and he said he was not feeling well – at half-time, he left the ground with Mum to return to his grandparents' house in Sheffield. By the time Dad returned – after a feisty game had ended in a 1-1 draw – Ben was feeling much better.

A nice touch from Wednesday in the matchday programme – the same picture and brief details of the mascot were provided, with the notation that 'this is Ben's second cup game of the season; he safely saw us through the Derby tie'.

Video of the game obtained the following week cost £11.65 – VHS format, Beta also available. Ben featured prominently in the first minute – that increased video sales to his family!

The matchday experience at Hillsborough was something special for the mascot – and at least as special for his dad.

As a comparison, Third Division Southend United and Aldershot were keen to have mascots – they advertised in their home programmes. A replica strip, autographed football and tickets for the game were the attraction in 1986/87. Cost £40 at both clubs.

No advert for mascots at Hillsborough – perhaps not surprising given the profile of the club and its support.

# Chapter 5

# Grounds

FOOTBALL GROUNDS development in the 1980s was primarily focused on meeting the safety requirements of the Safety of Sports Grounds Act 1975 in the wake of the fire at Bradford City's Valley Parade ground in 1985.

The only ground to increase its capacity in the 1980s was Hillsborough, a result of the long-awaited roofing of the open Spion Kop, the large irregular-shaped hill – that 'alp of humanity' – providing shelter for Wednesday supporters on the popular home end for the first time. With £1 million spent on the project, the club added more terracing in both rear corners, increasing Hillsborough's capacity to over 54,000, of which 17,767 for standing on the Spion Kop terraces. It was the largest covered terracing of any ground in Europe.

Such was the pride in this achievement that the Queen was invited to formally open the covered Spion Kop in December 1986. Tickets and a commemorative programme for the occasion produced. The club's consulting engineer, Bill Eastwood, had told a council committee in August 1986 that, 'Hillsborough is probably the safest ground in the country'.

Other grounds had different issues. In a November 1982 matchday programme, Fulham chairman Ernest Clay commented, 'Bankruptcy is now a threat facing more league clubs than is generally appreciated. By the time you read this, one club may well have gone to the wall, and this could cause a "domino effect". Once one club goes, a lot of others will follow. No bank or creditor wants the opprobrium of being the first to pull the plug on a Football League team, but they will not mind being the third, fourth or fifth.' In the event, Clay's prediction was wide of the mark.

Clay's words were a preface to remarks about a new stand planned for Craven Cottage, an all-seater at the Putney end built by developers with their own money, with flats built behind the stand that look out on to Bishops Park. Clay went on, 'The only disadvantage I can see is that the Cottage must come down. It is a shame, but anyone who has worked inside will know it is not a very functional building. We must accept it has outgrown its usefulness. Remember, even Johnny Haynes got too old, and had to retire.' No doubt much to Mr Clay's chagrin, the plan was not implemented, the Cottage remains.

Other grounds were the subject of potential closure and property development. Chelsea's Stamford Bridge was owned by Marler Estates and for the first part of the 1980s there was real concern that the ground would be sold for development. Regular updates on the fate of the ground and 'Save the Bridge' articles featured in club programmes.

At Charlton Athletic's home game against Crystal Palace in September 1985, supporters were handed a leaflet outside the ground headed 'Message to Our Supporters'. It started, 'It is with regret that we must announce that we will be obliged to leave The Valley, the home of Charlton Athletic Football Club for 66 years.' The leaflet went on to explain court proceedings against the club to evict them from land behind the West Stand, that the massive East Terrace was unsafe to use (the largest terrace in the country) and 'we have had no alternative but to make other arrangements'. Those other arrangements were to ground share with that day's opponents Crystal Palace at Selhurst Park.

A Charlton spectator recollected, 'And then it happened. There I was given the piece of paper that would change the history of Charlton Athletic and lead to the most hostile confrontation between fans and directors the club had ever known. Effectively, it was a notice of redundancy to a generation of loyalists who had survived 30 years in the wilderness.' (*Voice of the Valley*, Charlton Athletic fanzine).

It turned out to be a seven-year exile – Selhurst Park and later West Ham United's Upton Park providing temporary homes. At the end of the decade, football journalist Tony Pullein noted, 'Charlton accept that their ground-sharing arrangement with Crystal Palace has not been a success. Many old faithfuls were angry at the move and have boycotted their games.'

Norman Bettison makes this comment on those supporters who stood on the terraces in the 1980s in his book, *Hillsborough Untold*, 'The authorities that oversaw football in that era seemed blind to the discrimination that existed in the sport prior to the Hillsborough disaster. The cheaper standing tickets that were made available to the majority of supporters came with fewer, and rudimentary, toilets, inferior catering and other facilities and a mean and brutal experience that was made tolerable only by the community of others in the same situation.' (Biteback Publishing, 2016).

My observations on that searing assessment of conditions for standing supporters are twofold – standing supporters knew no different to the conditions they faced on the terraces in the 1980s, they had been like that for decades, supporters had grown used to them, and secondly, entry to the terraces at the vast majority of grounds was by queuing up for cash entry at the turnstiles – tickets for standing were unusual, reserved only for the biggest games of the era.

Major incidents continued to occur at grounds. As early in the decade as January 1980, a gate at Ayresome Park, Middlesbrough collapsed after a game with Manchester United. Two people killed and others injured.

In October 1984, disaster struck at Norwich City's Carrow Road ground – an early-morning fire struck and destroyed the central section of the main stand; in time it was replaced by a new 3,100-seater stand at a cost of £1.7 million.

With the increasing levels of hooliganism, clubs had progressively introduced segregated terracing, some with metal fences forming individual pens, the main purpose to prevent supporters entering the field of play or moving to other sections of terracing. These actions were generally seen as a realistic and necessary reaction by the authorities and clubs in the face of the rising tide of hooliganism.

By the early 1980s, most first and second division clubs had fences at the front of their terraces.

And the viewing experience through the fences ? – at best not good. Some fences were made up of small square holes – stand behind one of those and you're looking at players through a chequered metal grill. The trick was to stand towards the top of the terracing, enabling an uninterrupted view of the pitch with the fencing below … that was fine if the terracing was high enough. Small, shallow terraces and there was no chance – it really did feel as though you were caged in.

For the most part, clubs did not fence in the seated areas of their grounds – the thinking was that spectators in those areas of the ground were much less likely to be hooligans and there was little chance of them encroaching on the pitch.

Leicester City had cause for concern in September 1982, writing in their programme, 'Important Notice – During our game with Charlton Athletic two occasions arose when a spectator ran on to the pitch. Leicester City FC have been proud of the fact that for some years we have been able to operate with three sides of our pitch unfenced in the belief that those in the seating areas on two sides and the enclosures on the third would not try to get on to the pitch. If, however, events such as those at the last match prove that belief unfounded, we shall have no alternative but to fence such areas, thereby spoiling to some extent the view for many innocent spectators.'

In some grounds there were structural changes to assist the police, who decided where the 'no-go' areas were on the terracing and in the seats, introducing so-called sterile areas between groups of rival fans. Bramall Lane's capacity was dramatically reduced – every year between 1982 and 1990, the 'no-go' areas were extended and revenue lost. Ground capacity in 1985 was 44,000; in the wake of the Hillsborough disaster in 1989, it was reduced to 31,000.

At Fourth Division Halifax Town's Shay ground, following the Bradford fire and Heysel disaster, a safety limit of 1,775 was set by West Yorkshire County Council in August 1985.

Coventry City, led by their managing director Jimmy Hill, took the seated areas one step further – in 1981/82, they became the first club in England to introduce an all-seater stadium at Highfield Road, with higher prices for entry aimed at pricing out the undesirable element that attached itself to football. There was generally less hooliganism in the Highfield Road ground, although when Leeds United visited in that first season of the all-seater stadium, the hooligan element ripped out seats and used them as missiles. Three seasons later, Manchester City fans tore out 500 seats after their FA Cup defeat.

Watford had a different problem at their Vicarage Road ground. In the programme for the match against Wimbledon in September 1986, it was stated, 'An average of 25 seats get broken at every match because people use them as stepping stones in their impatience to leave the ground after a match. So please help the club and don't tread on the seats. They are intended for bottoms not feet!'

The continued problem of hooliganism led to an increase in CCTV (closed-circuit television) at football grounds to view and monitor crowd behaviour. In 1985, Sheffield United received a grant of £25,000 from the Football Trust to install CCTV. By the end of the 1989/90 season the police had insisted a new control room had to be built at Bramall Lane to allow further CCTV monitoring of the crowd, and until then no games would take place.

The keenness to attract families resulted in the creation of many family enclosures from the mid-1980s. Clubs were appealing to a 'specific demographic'. At Bramall Lane, this enclosure in the South Stand was promoted as a 'safe and well-segregated area' – a family enclosure card costing £2 was required to purchase tickets in this area of the ground. The enclosure was sponsored by Panini, with albums given free to all members.

But there is no doubt that at many football grounds facilities remained poor and arguably close to primitive ... at too many grounds men urinated against walls or into sinks at half-time because of the lack of toilets, and many of the women on the terraces would have struggled to find readily available toilets.

One example of poor facilities immediately springs to mind. The Den, Coldblow Lane, Millwall's ground. Wednesday the visitors in December 1988 – I'd taken my six-year-old son Tom to the game, choosing to stand with the home supporters on the terracing opposite the main stand. It was undoubtedly safer, provided we did not make our team allegiance known.

The concern came at half-time. Toilet facilities were needed. With some difficulty, we managed to find our way to the top of the terracing and the toilets. Long queue outside to gain entry. Once inside, we were 'paddling' in half an inch of liquid. The facilities had 'overflowed' and it was getting worse. Tom did what he had to do and we left.

I had no intention of letting Tom's mum know what had happened, but in the way of six-year-olds he had no hesitation in describing to his mum his splashing around in the toilets. My protestations that Tom was exaggerating and 'it was not that bad' fell on deaf ears. Coldblow Lane was now out of bounds.

There were improvements to facilities at some grounds and the Football Grounds Improvement Trust had a major impact – improvements included toilets, especially for female fans, accommodation for supporters with disabilities and a range of other improvements.

Many clubs carried information from the Football Grounds Improvement Trust in their club programmes – a typical example coming at Aston Villa in February 1989:

- Football Trust receives £9 million annually from the Spotting the Ball competition run by Littlewoods, Vernons and Zetters – spent on benefiting the game in the UK
- Providing close circuit television at grounds – 110 league grounds equipped with it – to increase safety and help the police in cases of disorder

- Almost every club assisted with essential safety work – in 1988 £2,254,723 in grants for this purpose; and £1.5 million to improve family and disabled facilities

The only new ground built for a league club in the 1980s was Scunthorpe United's Glanford Park – the motivation to move from their Old Showground home was financial. In the wake of the Bradford fire in 1985, the ground had been 'designated' – like many lower-division clubs, they needed work to be undertaken to achieve the required safety status for their ground. Initially, capacity was reduced from 25,000 to 5,000, raised to 10,000 after £45,000 worth of work had been completed. The ground then required additional work costing £300,000.

Cue the need for a new ground. The Old Showground was sold for £2.5 million (a supermarket took over the site) and a new out-of-town ground built. Opened in 1988, it cost £2.1 million – the author Simon Inglis comments, 'Glanford Park was clearly a cut-price effort ... it was a strictly budgeted Design and Build Package, with the external appearance of a DIY shed.' (*Football Grounds of Britain*, Collins Willow, 1996).

A different change at four grounds took place in the 1980s – the introduction of synthetic turf, artificial pitches. Queens Park Rangers the first club to make the move in 1981/82, followed by Luton Town, Preston North End and Oldham Athletic. Jon Culley of the (Sheffield) *Morning Telegraph* had these observations, 'The cost of the Rangers plan has been estimated at £350,000, which represents quite a gamble since the league has yet to give official approval. Artificial turf will have many advantages over a natural playing surface but it will change the way British football is played and many will say for the worse.'

The obvious advantages included never having to postpone a game because of the state of the pitch and being able to rent the facility to local clubs knowing the surface would not be damaged. The commercial advantages of the artificial pitch were high.

It had an immediate impact on the game – players wore flat soles, not studs, tackles were less frequent and intense but skin burns from contact with the surface quickly became a concern. No doubt the surface gave an advantage to all clubs that installed it – they trained on it week in week out, played all their home games on it, their opponents did not.

My recollection of the pitch at QPR's Loftus Road when Wednesday played there at the end of the 1981/82 season was of a much slower game, more ball to feet. In particular, the bounce of the ball on the artificial pitch was much firmer, it bounced higher than on a grass pitch. It lacked the intensity and tackling of the game on a natural surface. I didn't like what it had done for the game and many shared that view.

John Burridge – 'Budgie' – the much travelled goalkeeper was custodian at Loftus Road when the artificial pitch was introduced. 'The first time I went out on to the pitch, it was like concrete … The ball used to bounce ridiculously high. When you dived on it, your body used to ache. I would be scarred and gashed to pieces. I had carpet burns all over the place from the synthetic surface. It wasn't much fun for outfield players, but for goalkeepers it was brutal.' (*Budgie: The Autobiography of a Goalkeeping Legend*, John Burridge, John Blake, 2013).

His counterpart at Sheffield Wednesday, Martin Hodge, observed in his programme notes, 'I found Oldham's pitch exceptional, and Luton's is good too. I don't like QPR's pitch. All I can do is pad up to reduce the jarring to elbows and knees. Not many players I've met actually like the surface.'

Trevor Francis, who joined QPR in March 1988, noted, 'The trouble was that it was not the best playing surface as some of the seams were splitting, which meant that sand was leaking out from under the AstroTurf. This was because the contract was coming to an end and the pitch was being allowed to deteriorate.' (*One in a Million: The Autobiography*, Trevor Francis with Keith Dixon, Pitch Publishing, 2019).

A spectator's perspective is provided by Roy Hattersley, Sheffield Wednesday supporter and Labour MP, after Wednesday's 2-0 loss at Loftus Road, 'The iniquity of forcing a proper football team to play on plastic turf rather than proper grass. Why the Football Association and the league allow QPR to take advantage of visiting teams by laying Omniturf where the pitch ought to be I shall never understand … No doubt synthetic soil suits the southern temperament, for it avoids the risk of wearing muddy shorts.' (*The Guardian*).

The Loftus Road artificial turf was replaced by natural grass in 1988/89, the three other clubs continued with their artificial surfaces into the 1990s before they were banned by the Football League. The unnatural bounce, the ball roll and concerns over long-term injuries to players were the primary reasons for their demise. Few spectators were disappointed.

# Chapter 6

# Crowds

THE LEVELS of attendance at Football League games fell alarmingly during the 1980s. The difference in the attendance figures at the start and end of the decade is stark:

1979/80 – 24,623,975

1989/90 – 19,445,442

The lowest attendance figure in a season: 1985/86 – 16,488,577. This is a reduction in overall attendances by a third in six seasons.

At club level, Manchester United had an average home league attendance of 36,488 in 1988/89, their lowest since 1961/62. They had not won the First Division championship since 1967/68. The highest average home league attendance in 1988/89 was Liverpool's 38,574.

The reduction in attendances affected all clubs. The average attendance figures for each club in Appendix 1 provide a stark reminder of those reductions.

And what caused them? Many will point to the seemingly incessant rise of hooliganism in and around grounds, the devastating Bradford fire in May 1985, followed weeks later by the televised disaster at the Heysel Stadium in Belgium. Another factor may have been the first regular live television broadcasting of Football League games, introduced in 1983/84.

The editorial in the *Rothmans Football Yearbook 1981/82* opened with, 'The slump in league attendances of almost 2.75 million during the 1980/81 season to a new post-war low of 21,907,569 is not due solely to the economic recession … many of the genuine followers of the sport, especially those of an older generation, have tended to disappear from active participation at grounds for a variety of reasons. They have been driven away by modern annoyances, including hooliganism, obscene language, the spiralling cost of attending matches and the realisation that the game probably no longer represents the one they once knew.'

Other reasons put forward for the decline in attendances included poor facilities at grounds and a lack of attractive football. For many, the real issue was hooliganism – at the ground, around the ground, on the way to or returning from a ground.

For my part, I'd attended games in the mid-1960s with my dad and on my own – from the age of eight – with little thought of hooliganism. In the 1980s, we had three young boys – Ben, Sam and Tom – who had all been to games by the end of the decade. At every game they had been to, it had been with me. No way would they have been allowed to go on their own.

Many parents refused to let their sons go to games in the 1980s because of the threat of hooliganism. And in my circle of friends and family, it was sons. If hooliganism stopped sons going to games, it most definitely acted as a greater deterrent for daughters, and women generally.

Not everyone agreed on hooliganism. In his programme notes at the start of the 1985/86 season, Aldershot manager Len Walker stated, 'The majority I have spoken to fear that the hooligan element are making it too dangerous to go to football matches. I feel that the whole thing is out of proportion as trouble of any sort is minimal at 90 per cent of football grounds, and although we must eradicate the hooligan element completely, I feel that football arenas have been tarnished showing them as battlefields.'

David Pleat, the Luton Town manager, had a different view on the problem of declining attendances, opining in his manager's notes in the club programme in September 1986, 'Surely the English game has not sunk so low that its most successful teams need no greater virtues than the ability to run, chase, close down space and play the offside game as though it was an article of faith.' For Pleat, this meant, 'Forget hooliganism; possibly the greatest cause of the public drifting away, is the chaotic restricting of space on a football field. We need width and length for skill to flourish.'

Six months earlier at Luton Town's Kenilworth Road ground, some of the worst hooliganism ever seen was broadcast to the nation, and here was Pleat saying, 'Forget hooliganism.'

My view is that hooliganism was the biggest issue preventing people attending games.

But the single biggest concern I've ever had at a game occurred in January 1985 – it focused on safety. I was genuinely frightened. I was at Stamford Bridge for a League Cup second-round replay, Sheffield Wednesday at Chelsea. Terrace admission pay on the night at the turnstiles. I was at the Shed End – with the home supporters.

The turnstiles situated in a block on the Fulham Road. I arrived at the ground about 20 minutes before the 7.45pm kick-off. Busy. People thronging, particularly around the turnstiles, no evidence of any queues, milling around the area, pushing forward, lightly at first, in an effort to move closer to the front and access the turnstiles.

More people arrived, more people behind me, more pushing, becoming insistent, heavier pushing, it was starting to feel uncomfortable. The crowd surging in from the left, then the right, trying to narrow in on the centrally located turnstiles ahead. It was everyone for themselves as the weight from behind increased relentlessly.

Two small, teenage girls in front of me were feeling the pressure from behind. Can't move. They talked. Can't hear. One of the girls' legs nearly buckled. More pushing. They were in trouble now.

A mounted policeman on horseback – shouting at the uncontrolled, milling throng to push in and get off the road. This was crazy. Some people shouted back, 'We're getting crushed here.' There was no audible reaction from the policeman. He went to the other side of the crowd, repeating his instruction. The girls in front struggling. I was conscious of my weight against them. With all my strength, my arms held horizontally, palms against the back of a guy in front of the girls, I pushed hard to take more weight on my back. Some movement back from the crush, girls had some space, they could breathe. They wanted out. There was no way. Hemmed in. Crushed, squashed – whatever the word there was only one way – forward, slowly, in the direction of the turnstiles.

My hands in the horizontal position were loaded against the guy's back all the way to the turnstiles. We made it. It took a good ten minutes. There had been no control, no order, no organisation. I felt more than once as though I would pass out. The police were seemingly more intent on keeping the road clear. It was frightening.

That experience, I'm sure, would have deterred many from attending a high-profile game.

To underline the decline in attendances, and unlike all previous decades, no club set an attendance record in the 1980s.

A detailed breakdown of attendances at Football League games is provided in Appendix 4.

Reduced attendances meant reduced revenue for clubs and this had an impact – it meant significant financial problems for most clubs, a smaller number of professional players and more top players moving abroad – particularly to Italy – to earn greater rewards.

The progression of season ticket prices over the decade for Sheffield Wednesday supporters at Hillsborough is interesting. All the prices below are based on an 'early bird' discount for early purchase:

| Season | | North/South Stand Centre Seats | Ground Terrace | Division | Games |
|---|---|---|---|---|---|
| 1980/81 | Adult | £57.10 | £26.80 | 2 | 21 |
| | Juvenile/OAP | £41.00 | £19.60 | | |
| 1983/84 | Adult | £63.00 | £31.50 | 2 | 21 |
| | Juvenile/OAP | £30.00 | £15.00 | | |
| 1984/85 | Adult | £80.00 | £40.00 | 1 | 21 |
| | Juvenile/OAP | £45.00 | £25.00 | | |
| 1989/90 | Adult | £116.00 | £64.00 | 1 | 19 |
| | Juvenile/OAP | £79.00 | £43.00 | | |

From season 1984/85 family season tickets were introduced, providing further discounts and encouraging families to attend.

Two further observations – the significant increase in prices after promotion to Division One in 1984/85, and the decrease in prices in 1983/84 for juveniles and OAPs.

On two occasions during the 1980s, there were no increases to prices from the previous season – 1983/84 and 1987/88 – a reflection of declining attendances, the local economy and unemployment levels.

For Sheffield Wednesday's away games, with the threat of hooliganism prevalent and seemingly ever present – I usually went to areas of the ground earmarked for home supporters. I did not wear any Wednesday colours – to have done so would have meant singling myself out as a target.

Hooliganism seemed almost inevitably focused on the away support – either within their ranks or those so-inclined amongst the home support seeking out away supporters for violent confrontations. I wanted none of that. And given that very few of the games had capacity crowds, I had no problem getting into the games. I did have a problem with keeping my football allegiance quiet on more than one occasion, and that was the real problem being amongst home supporters.

Admission prices for standing on the terraces at Wednesday's away league games in the First Division in 1986/87 are interesting:

Oxford United – £4.50; Leicester City and Chelsea – £4; West Ham United, Nottingham Forest, Wimbledon and Tottenham Hotspur – £3.50; Arsenal, Aston Villa, Coventry City, Newcastle United, Norwich City and Southampton – £3; Manchester City and Manchester United – £2.80; Everton and Liverpool – £2.60.

These were the prices for adults – no concessions to the adult price were offered for away supporters.

Tickets were required for admission at Manchester City, Manchester United, Everton, Liverpool and Nottingham Forest – for the game at Manchester United, only Wednesday season ticket holders could apply. At all other clubs, admission was pay on the day at the turnstiles.

Luton Town are missing from the list of clubs for away games – because they banned away supporters from their Kenilworth Road ground from 1986/87. This followed the

appalling scenes inside and outside their ground at their
FA Cup game with Millwall in March 1986. Only home
supporters were allowed, with a requirement to be a member
of the club and living within 20 miles of the ground. Guests
could be brought to games by home supporters.

Graham Mackrell, the Luton Town secretary, commented,
'Luton's policy has aroused great controversy within the game
… Kenilworth Road is not really suited for top-class football.
The Millwall riot in 1986 was the final straw.'

Banning away supporters generally worked well as far
as Luton Town were concerned. There were exceptions.
Some away supporters were very resourceful. Chelsea's visit
in January 1987 saw that club refuse the allocation of away
directors' and guests' tickets (15). Those tickets and the
away team's complimentary players' tickets (50) meant there
could have been 65 away team supporters in the ground – the
local Bedfordshire police estimated there were 600 Chelsea
supporters in the ground. They had found a way around the
membership scheme rules – registering their details with the
club with a local address or obtaining tickets through local
friends or relatives.

Banning away supporters was spearheaded by Luton Town
chairman David Evans, a Conservative MP and an acolyte of
Prime Minister Margaret Thatcher. As a result of increasing
hooliganism at home and abroad – particularly abroad – the
government had taken an increasing interest in clubs and how
they were addressing the problem.

The government introduced a White Paper, the Football
Spectators Bill – it planned to control behaviour by legislating
that fans' entry into grounds would be by identity cards only,
which would be confiscated if an individual misbehaved. It
was intended to be passed and brought in for the start of the

1990/91 season. Ultimately, the plan was dropped as the sheer mechanics of administering and operating it were considered unworkable.

It was the perceived threat of the Bill and its potential impact on clubs that caused football authorities to address issues and try to put their own house in order. In 1987, the Football League told all clubs that 50 per cent of grounds should be reserved for those supporters who had joined 'membership schemes'. At Bramall Lane, Sheffield United had the South Stand and John Street as members-only areas. A completed application form – warning of the consequences of misbehaviour – and £1.25 secured a membership.

# Chapter 7

# Hooliganism – The Spectre Fully Formed

THE SPECTRE of hooliganism had grown inexorably over the previous decade – inside and outside football grounds. Incidents had increased, their severity more marked. The oft-quoted 'small minority' of football supporters involved in acts of hooliganism were increasing in number. There was little evidence of any meaningful control being exercised by the authorities.

The first large-scale example of hooliganism in the 1980s took place at Hampden Park in May 1980, an outbreak described as the most violent disorder at an Old Firm game for over 70 years – at the Scottish FA Cup Final.

Trouble started immediately after the final whistle – Celtic had won the game with a Danny McGrain goal in extra time. Celtic supporters climbed over the perimeter fencing to get on to the pitch to celebrate the win with their players. One ran towards the Rangers end and kicked a ball into the empty net … it was too much for some of the Rangers fans and they came over the perimeter fencing.

All this shown live on Scottish television – BBC Scotland's Archie Macpherson, at the microphone, 'From both ends, supporters are storming on. The police have been nowhere in this, where are the police? For heavens' sake … These are sad and disgraceful scenes.'

Live coverage of the riot on the pitch interspersed with presentations to the players. But they were secondary. It was the scenes on the pitch that held the attention.

Macpherson continued, 'This is like a scene now out of *Apocalypse Now* … We've got the equivalent of Passchendaele and that says nothing for Scottish football. At the end of the day, let's not kid ourselves. These supporters hate each other … It is scandalous that this should be allowed to happen. People are limping away bloodied from Hampden Park.'

Charging, drunken supporters from both sides throwing missiles, assaulting opposition supporters. Apparently, only 12 police present in the ground when the pitch was invaded, with hundreds deployed outside the ground in readiness for supporters leaving.

In time, mounted police with batons appeared on the pitch and gradually restored some semblance of order.

Donald MacLeod, photographer for *The Scotsman*, commented, 'I'd never seen anything like this. But who had? I was stood near the dugouts when it all kicked off. People were getting stuck in. Lots of punches, but mostly kicks. And there were cans flying everywhere … The swoosh of a beer can going over your head and this trail of what you could only hope was lager coming out of it. Every time I think about that match, I hear noise. It starts off as a low roar – and then you hear the horses. I can still hear the hooves going across the pitch.'

More than 200 fans were arrested in the Hampden area.

The Scottish Football Association held an inquiry. Both clubs fined £20,000. It condemned sectarianism, which it claimed to be 'the root cause of the hatred and bitterness which has existed between the two sets of supporters for decades'. Consumption of alcohol was identified as a major element in the crowd trouble. The Criminal Justice (Scotland) Act 1980 was passed as a result, forbidding the consumption of alcohol at sporting events.

In England, major outbreaks of hooliganism came to the fore throughout the decade. At many clubs 'hooligan gangs' formed, becoming more organised and giving themselves identity with a collective name – these included Zulu Warriors – Birmingham City, Headhunters – Chelsea, Red Army – Manchester United, F Troop – Millwall, 6.57 Crew – Portsmouth, Owls Crime Squad – Sheffield Wednesday, Blades Business Crew (BBC) – Sheffield United, Inter-City Firm – West Ham United.

Much of the literature on and by football hooligans stems from their activities in this decade. It may come as no surprise that the same incident can be seen quite differently by the respective hooligans on both sides.

Desmond Morris produced his seminal work, *The Soccer Tribe*, at the start of the decade (Jonathan Cape Ltd, 1981). He asserted, 'Trouble on the terraces takes place at set times with a huge crowd watching and under the eyes of both press and police ... there are a few unstable, genuinely brutal individuals at a soccer match.' He goes on to list a range of proposals to address football hooliganism after first noting, 'It is certain managers who have responded with the most demented suggestions, demanding drowning, shooting and whipping, in moments of extreme anguish. One quoted as saying, "I think capital punishment is a great deterrent." Another exclaimed, "Get flame-throwers and burn the bastards. These people aren't human."' Morris wrote before hooliganism became more widespread and insidious in the 1980s.

In his book *Life's a Pitch: The Groundsman's Tale* (G2 Entertainment, 2019), Ian Darler, groundsman at the Abbey Stadium, Cambridge United's ground, describes the visit of Chelsea and their followers for a Second Division game in September 1980. He comments, 'The areas behind the goals had eight-foot high metal mesh fences designed to prevent fans from getting on the pitch. But a group of forty or fifty Chelsea supporters, gathered in the middle pen of the away terrace at the Allotments End, had other ideas.'

He goes on, 'For starters they set to work on some crush barriers. Held together by Allen keys [they] didn't stand a chance when the fans worked them backwards and forwards until they snapped ... the gang then hurled the barriers over the fence onto the running track ... followed by a number of fans removing some of their clothing and weaving their garments into the welded security fence at the front of the terrace. They then set their handiwork on fire and set about pulling at the fence, backwards and forwards, until the welds failed and it peeled open like a can of beans. Out they poured on to the pitch.'

Darler goes on to describe player-fan confrontations on the pitch, a 'massive fight' on the home terrace, fans mounting floodlight pylons, taking over the Anglia TV cameras at the game, and a terrace toilet flooded after a WC was ripped out and so it went on ...

The following season Chelsea supporters were associated with major incidents of hooliganism at away games – as a result of trouble at Derby the previous Saturday, the programme for the next home game in December 1981 noted, 'The headlines for the following three days were once again occupied by hooliganism – a word that is now all too readily associated with the once good name of Chelsea Football Club. This state of affairs cannot continue.'

A full-page article followed headlined, 'An Appeal by Chelsea FC'. It read, 'Football generally has suffered over recent years by continual falling attendances and whilst this can be attributed to many reasons, one major factor must the behaviour of a small minority of spectators inside and outside football grounds. Incidents such as those witnessed last Saturday at Derby and at other away matches are a disgrace to football.'

In conclusion, and in block capitals, the final paragraph read, 'IF THIS LUNATIC FRINGE IS ALLOWED TO CONTINUE THEIR DESTRUCTIVE WAYS THEN THIS CLUB COULD POSSIBLY GO OUT OF EXISTENCE IN THE NOT TOO DISTANT FUTURE. WOULD ALL GENUINE SUPPORTERS MAKE EVERY EFFORT TO DEFEND OUR GOOD NAME AND HELP TO KEEP THIS GREAT CLUB ALIVE.' The appeal is 'From the Directors, Players and Staff.'

Within four seasons Ken Bates, owner of Chelsea, had a new solution to pitch invaders at Stamford Bridge – prior to the London derby between Chelsea and Tottenham Hotspur in April 1985, Bates had installed a 12-foot high barbed electric fence all around the pitch. The intention to pen in the fans and keep them off the pitch. The 12-volt current in the fence was scheduled to be switched on for the home game against Spurs.

The effectiveness or otherwise of this barrier was never tested – days before the game, the Greater London Council stepped in and threatened legal action. The electric fence was never switched on.

In that same month I'd joined my new employer, ICL, based at Putney in south-west London. I recollect a conversation with the window-cleaning contractor at work – we passed the time of day and confirmed each other's football clubs; his was Chelsea:

'Who've you got Saturday?' I asked.

'Watford down here [Stamford Bridge]. We'll give 'em a good kicking.'

And he meant it. Not the Chelsea players involved on the pitch – he was referring to the 'welcome' he and his mates had planned for the Watford supporters. I found it astonishing and disturbing. He was looking forward to 'a good ruck on Saturday'. For the record, Chelsea lost the game 5-1. How much angst that would have caused the window cleaner I have my doubts – the game's result was not his primary interest.

Two years on and Chelsea had this notice in their home programme for the 1987/88 season that read, 'Warning TV Surveillance. This ground is equipped with Closed Circuit Television. Installed with the help of a grant from the Football Trust. It is there to increase crowd safety and to help the police. Recording facilities enable film and photographs to be taken of disorder, which may subsequently be used in a court of law.'

CCTV or not, in May 1988 Chelsea played Middlesbrough in the play-off final for the right to play in the First Division the following season. These the days when the play-off final was contested between one First Division club (Chelsea) aiming to avoid relegation and the promotion hopeful from the Second Division (Middlesbrough).

These were two-legged home and away games. Boro won the first leg 2-0 on Teeside. Everything rested on the second leg ... a 1-0 win for Chelsea. Middlesbrough were promoted, Chelsea relegated.

At the final whistle, hordes of Chelsea fans ran on to the pitch charging towards the away end – violent scenes inside and outside the ground. The images in the ground were captured on television. Bottles and missiles thrown at the away supporters in the stands.

The Middlesbrough MP Stuart Bell was reported as saying, 'Faces of the fans were contorted with hate' and they were 'like the hordes of Genghis Khan'.

Few clubs escaped the scourge of hooliganism in the 1980s.

Sheffield Wednesday's game at Oldham Athletic in September 1980 saw Wednesday favourite Terry Curran involved in an incident with home player Simon Stainrod (an ex-Sheffield United man) that led to Curran receiving his marching orders from the referee.

Curran's recollection is that he wanted to take a throw-in quickly, 'but was stopped from doing so as he [Stainrod] pushed me in the chest. I then brought up my knee with the idea of getting him where it really hurts. We were close together but I had time to stop and avoid making contact with him. Next moment, Stainrod was rolling around on the ground as if I had caught him … the referee walked towards me and brought out a card from his pocket. When we both saw it was red, Stainrod jumped to his feet and started laughing. The fans went ballistic. I shouted at Stainrod that he was a "f*****g cheat."' (*Regrets of a Football Maverick: The Terry Curran Autobiography*, Terry Curran with John Brindley, Vertical Editions, 2012).

Concrete and stones were hurled on to the pitch from behind the Wednesday goal, Wednesday fans came on to the pitch. Wednesday manager Jack Charlton came onto the pitch and attempted to restore order – to little avail. Charlton apparently in tears at the incident and the behaviour of his club's supporters. It took half an hour to restore calm and resume the game. The riot shown on the television news later that evening.

Jimmy Frizzell, the Oldham Athletic manager, commented on the hooligans, 'I'm not saying chop off their hands or stone them to death. But when you look at Saudi Arabia, a few lashes like that might do a bit of good.'

Events at Oldham took centre stage in the first home programme after the riot. Manager Jack Charlton stated, 'There is no condoning the actions of the lunatics who have disgraced our club ... I won't let hooligans destroy this club.' Under the headline, 'Are we really this kind of people?', chairman Bert McGee observed, 'It was a sad day, indeed a day of shame for Sheffield Wednesday Football Club. Some 200 or 300 of our supporters behaved as hooligans of the worst kind and bring disgrace to our club.' The editorial in the programme railed against the perpetrators, 'These morons are not football supporters and should be outlawed from society. Their behaviour is disgusting in the extreme.'

The Football Association punished Wednesday by closing all standing areas at Hillsborough for four games and placing restrictions on away travel. It had the unintended consequence of increasing revenue for the club as spectators had to purchase the more expensive seats to attend a game. And the more resourceful supporters found a way round the restrictions on away travel by purchasing tickets in person from the home club in advance of the game.

Trouble at other clubs. In May 1981, the London derby at Highbury between Arsenal and West Ham United was stopped for 12 minutes because of fighting on the terraces. The Arsenal manager Terry Neill commented, 'It makes you wonder what sort of parents produce mindless morons like this.' His opposite number John Lyall said, 'There seems to be nothing we can do about it.' After the game, a man was fatally stabbed outside the ground.

In its review of the 1981/82 season, the *Rothmans Football Yearbook* observed, 'Overriding all else, however, is the problem of crowd violence and mindless hooliganism ... streams of hooligans appear in court almost daily.'

The Birmingham derby – Aston Villa v Birmingham City – at Villa Park in October 1983 produced headlines. The *Sunday Mercury* front page read 'The Horror Show', the Birmingham *Evening Mail* called it 'Brum's Day of Shame'. Eighty fans were arrested and one stabbed.

And the players made their contribution to an ill-tempered game, with six players booked and Villa's Colin Gibson sent off. After the match, City's Noel Blake head-butted Villa's Steve McMahon, subsequently receiving a six-game suspension after the television cameras picked it up. More than 50 free kicks awarded in the game and as the players left the field at the end some of the Blues' players went into the Villa dressing room and a fight ensued.

An FA Cup game at Ipswich Town's Portman Road in February 1985 attracted trouble. Wednesday the visitors. I'd taken my place on the home supporters' terrace – the length of the penalty area from the away supporters' end. No more than 30 or so home supporters – lads in their mid to late teens – congregated on the same terrace in a tight cluster in line with the six-yard box. Without warning, a round red missile was thrown from that group at the Wednesday supporters, then a round yellow missile, then a blue one ... the missiles were snooker balls. Snooker balls. Hard, dangerous and readily capable of causing serious injury. What lunatic(s) would throw these missiles at unsuspecting football spectators? There were no police anywhere.

There was no telling – or seeing – who threw the snooker balls. A hand suddenly appeared from within the congregation and the projectile was on its way, the hand disappeared immediately. Did they hit anyone? I don't know. What became clear after the third missile was thrown was that the home supporters responsible suddenly disappeared – a large gap appeared on the terraces. The reaction from police in the ground? Nothing – and it was patently obvious something was happening.

One of the most violent and widely reported outbreaks of hooliganism occurred at Kenilworth Road, Luton in March 1985. The home club were hosting Millwall in an FA Cup quarter-final replay. Before, during and after the game, there was major disorder.

John Motson was the commentator for BBC Television. He announced there had been 'considerable crowd disturbances before the kick-off'. Spectators were seen walking along the touchline whilst the game was in progress. In the 14th minute Motson exclaimed, 'People are coming on to the pitch.'

The referee blew his whistle – the game suspended. A 24-minute delay before it restarted.

An appeal from Millwall manager George Graham over the ground's loudspeaker had no effect. It was only when Graham appeared on the side of the pitch that the spectators finally returned to the Kenilworth Stand. Even after this, some managed to find their way into the main stand, where isolated fights broke out and more seats were removed. The arrival of police dogs helped to clear the playing area.

Theo Foley, coach of the Millwall team, commented, 'We were embarrassed to be part of it and it really affected the club, which had been trying to make progress.' (*Theo Give Us a Ball*, Theo Foley with Paul Foley, Apex Publishing Ltd, 2018).

The game played, a 1-0 win for the home team. The final whistle. Then mayhem.

On the television screen, fans streaming on to the pitch from the away end, seats ripped up and thrown from the stand, confrontation with police on the pitch, seats thrown at the police. It was lawless.

Motson's commentary on the events reflected the pictures: 'unfortunate and ugly background ... scenes still going on ... a major inquiry needed here ... it's getting uglier and uglier out there ... they're outnumbering the police, horrible dreadful scenes at Kenilworth Road ... just look at this absolutely disgraceful..." Broadcast direct into living rooms across the country.

The numbers tell most of the story: 47 injured, 33 of them police officers; 31 arrests made, leading to 29 charges; £15,000 of damage done inside the stadium; and £45,000 of damage done on a train going back to London.

Wednesday, 13 March was, according to *The Guardian*, 'a night football died a slow death'. Luton's stadium was stripped, houses and cars smashed, and the image of the national game – already bruised by a battery of hooligan incidents – given another going over. The following day, England, who had been favourites to host the 1988 European Championships, lost out to West Germany. The Football Association chairman Bert Millichip blamed the violence, adding: 'The scenes at Luton were the most disgraceful I have seen ... and I have seen a lot.'

David Pleat, the Luton Town manager, observed, 'There were people being carried away on stretchers, fans on the edge of the pitch and players constantly looking up at their families because billiard balls were being thrown at the directors' box. I can't tell you much about the football, because there was so much else going on. It was completely out of control ... The great sadness was Luton lost one-third of their season ticket holders. Most of them left and never came back.'

The scenes triggered a national debate led by then Prime Minister Margaret Thatcher, who wanted English clubs to bring in a membership card scheme.

Millwall were fined £7,500 by the Football Association and Luton were told to erect fences around supporter areas. The fine levied against Millwall was subsequently quashed on appeal.

Arrests were made on the night of the game and in the days that followed as individuals were identified from TV footage. Posters showing the culprits were put up around Millwall's ground, The Den.

Incidents of hooliganism were not confined to the top divisions or to certain clubs' followers. In the Fourth Division at Wigan Athletic, playing for Walsall in an end-of-season game in 1980, Roy McDonough recalls, 'They tonked us 3-0 among chaotic scenes at crumbling Springfield Park. The referee took us all off the pitch for ten minutes as violence broke out around the ground. A massive lump of concrete was launched at the players from one of the stands, supporters were trading blows on the terraces and one fan ran towards the opposition spectators armed with a flag stick and started hitting people round the head with it.' (*Red Card Roy*, Roy McDonough with Bernie Friend, VSP, 2012).

In the last game of the season at St Andrews in 1985, Birmingham City v Leeds United, a 14-year-old boy died after a wall collapsed following crowd violence. The judge described the fighting as 'more like the Battle of Agincourt than being at a football match'.

New Year's Day 1986 – Wednesday away to Liverpool. I'd not been to Anfield and I fancied seeing my team play at the famous ground, this time watching from the away end. I travelled by car with Dad and my 14-year-old sister Jill – her first away game. We parked the car in one of the terraced streets close to the Anfield Road end.

The game a good one – finishing 2-2 thanks to a late equaliser by Wednesday's Gary Thompson.

A loudspeaker announcement to the away supporters near the end of the game had made it clear that Wednesday supporters would be held back from leaving 'to allow the ground and surrounding streets' to be cleared. The announcement was repeated at the end of the game. Waiting now, looking around, ground emptying. The time was ticking by. It was probably a good 20 minutes before the Wednesday supporters were released from their enforced enclosure at the away end.

It was clear to me, and others, that by controlling the dispersal of away supporters in this way that anyone in the vicinity of the ground would immediately know that people leaving at that time were Wednesday supporters – readily identifying them as targets for anyone intent on mischief.

Dark and dimly lit streets, we made our way to the car. Shouting, running and fighting was in our midst. We could see small groups of lads – teenagers as best we could see – running at separate groups of Wednesday supporters leaving the ground, we saw assaults from a distance. A group came running towards us – shouting, Scouse accents. They stopped, looked at us, and moved on. Why? I don't know. Maybe seeing an older man, an adult and young girl was not a group they wanted to engage in fisticuffs with. Off they went and attacked a group of Wednesday supporters down the road.

Lawlessness writ large, no evidence of any police, these groups causing mayhem as they pleased. My thoughts? As they approached, that they were going to threaten and attack us, how to protect Dad and my young sister … after the troublemakers had gone, make for the car and get out of the area as fast as we could. A very unpleasant experience.

Once in the car and out of immediate danger, I checked Dad and Jill were OK. They were although my sister was understandably a little shaken.

I thought more about the events as we drove back to Sheffield – what does Dad feel? What does he think about these groups of teenage thugs running amok around a football ground and seemingly threatening and attacking away supporters as they pleased? Dad – who had seen active service in the war and seen people killed in foreign lands, fighting with millions of others for the cause of freedom for their country. Whatever he felt, he said nothing save that he was OK, and he certainly showed no fear. But it was fundamentally not right – going to a football game and this happening.

And what particularly hit me was this had all taken place little more than seven months after the events at the Heysel Stadium in Brussels, where 39 people had lost their lives after a wall had collapsed following a charge by Liverpool supporters.

I wrote to Merseyside Police – and had a reply from Chief Superintendent Bob Blackburn. He thanked me for contacting the police and highlighting my concerns. He commented that at the time of writing there had been no incidents reported to the police in the area I'd referenced. Nonetheless, they intended to take on board the points I'd raised and would make some alterations to their deployment of officers after a game at Anfield. Hopefully that had a positive effect.

There were bans from grounds for some convicted football hooligans – Wednesday supporters convicted after the Oldham riot were banned as well as named and shamed in the club programme and local media. In the Derby County programme in November 1986, the club said, 'Derby County have practised for 18 months now the banning for life of anyone arrested in the Baseball Ground, and then found guilty by the courts as charged. We regret to record that former Rams photographer John Grainger, convicted by Derby Magistrates Court following the Doncaster game on May 3, 1986 and fined £50 with £250 costs, has been banned from the ground for life.'

Games in Europe with English clubs were scarred by football hooliganism.

West Ham United returned to European football after their FA Cup win in May 1980 – drawn against Castilla Club de Football in the European Cup Winners' Cup – the first leg in Madrid. Mayhem, hooliganism, violence in the Spanish capital and at the ground – supporters of the London club judged responsible. UEFA's sanctions swift – the ground closed to spectators for the return leg at Upton Park.

Reports of what happened highlighted 'large-scale crowd disturbances emanating from the away end. At least 50 West Ham fans were thrown out, and in an after-match melée, one was killed when a bus ran over him just outside the ground. Total and utter chaos reigned.'

The club were fined a then hefty £7,750 and after an appeal allowed to play at their home ground – without spectators. The official attendance at the home game – including officials, balls boys and photographers – 262, the lowest in the club's history.

And the national team playing abroad also resulted in consistently lurid headlines, including:

May 1981 – 'England fans violence in Basle' – the FA wanted, but failed, to ban fans travelling abroad.

September 1982 – Copenhagen – 'Fans totally out of control ... game delayed'.

November 1983 – 'England fans rampage in Luxembourg' – 'England supporters raced through the city centre overturning cars and smashing shop windows. About 500 policemen and 150 soldiers were on duty.'

And it went on inexorably.

Looking back on those times, *When Saturday Comes* editor Andy Lyons underlines that football was in a completely different place in 1989. 'Fences were seen as a good thing. It was a law and order issue. But football violence was highlighted more than any other violence.' The *Sunday Times* commented that football was 'a slum sport played in slum stadiums increasingly watched by slum people'.

If I had seen the quote at that time, I would have railed against it – me and the vast majority of people passionately supporting our teams being classed as 'slum people' – utterly wrong, offensive and very wide of the mark.

Nonetheless, it has to be readily acknowledged that in some circles football was seen increasingly in the 1980s as a pariah sport … not one that significant numbers of people wanted to be associated with. Hooliganism at the core of this perspective.

At work it became more unusual for people to volunteer that football was their passion. It didn't stop me – my first question on meeting someone, 'Which football club do you support?'

There's an interesting comment on the times from well-known Sheffield artist Joe Scarborough, who said, 'In 1984 I was exhibiting in London and was told, "Joe, we don't want any more smokey chimneys. Can you do sport instead? But we don't want football; it's a hooligan sport."' (*Yorkshire Post*, 10 August 2019).

And that hooliganism in the 1980s was increasingly, though not exclusively, moving outside grounds, on routes to venues or at transport hubs. Some of the confrontations between opposing clubs' fans became much more organised rather than spontaneous. Press reports from the time give an insight.

On 27 May 1988, four hooligan followers of Millwall, reportedly part of a 50-strong gang who attacked passengers on a train carrying Arsenal and Charlton Athletic supporters at New Cross station in London, were jailed for a total of 29 years (*The Guardian*, 28 June 1988).

Superintendent Appleby, head of the National Football Intelligence Unit, formed in 1989, noted, 'I think there is organisation and ringleaders. Spontaneous hooliganism occurs a lot less than planned hooliganism. It is purely for the joy of combat, of hurting people.'

Somewhere in the middle of this is a football game – to which the great majority of people wanted to travel in peace, watch without interruption or fear, and return home safely.

Hooliganism was not just a major issue for supporters. In his autobiography (*Life in a Jungle*, de Coubertin Books, 2018), Bruce Grobbelaar, the Liverpool goalkeeper for much of the 1980s, commented on issues he faced as the player positioned closest to the supporters – coins thrown at him at The Dell, at Turf Moor a dart thrown lodged in his back – the culprit's punishment a year's ban from football, which Grobbelaar described as derisory. At Old Trafford, there were coins, a billiard ball and a potato embedded with razor blades.

To underline how all-pervading the threat of hooliganism was in the 1980s, I recollect a game I went to with my ten-year-old son, Ben, a fourth qualifying round FA Cup game at Wokingham, the hosts were playing Woking – a typical non-league venue, a small number of seats, most supporters looking to get a view of the game from a standing position at ground level.

No police present, a small number of elderly male club stewards were in the ground. The enthusiastic roar as the teams emerged on to the pitch – followed quickly by about 20 youths purporting to support Wokingham charging down our side of the ground, where the main group of Woking supporters stood. Shouting, threats, stand-offs – the intent of the unruly 20 to cause physical damage to whoever wanted to take up the challenge from the visitor numbers.

Most spectators just wanted to watch a football match. We'd travelled some distance, managed to find a place where we both could see. But the plans and intentions of the civilised majority were abruptly spoiled by an uncontrolled and unruly rabble. It was threatening and at one point quite frightening with this mob close by.

As quickly as the threat appeared, it disappeared – simply because there was a similar unruly mob supporting the away team who took the challenge head-on and ran straight at their opponents, shouting and swearing, their arms flailing. The Wokingham 20 turned tail and ran as quickly as they could, away from the scene of mayhem they had been intent on creating.

We saw no more trouble – we had no idea where the 20 from Wokingham had gone. They may have left the ground without seeing any football. But this was a fourth qualifying round game in the FA Cup, with less than a thousand people in the ground. And we'd had to endure that. It was all too typical of the 1980s at a football ground – it was a microcosm of the times writ large.

# Chapter 8

# Racism

INCIDENTS AND examples of racism in the 1980s were widespread, although my direct experience of it was limited.

Theo Foley, involved in football for over six decades as a player, coach and manager, highlighted Millwall's FA Cup fourth-round tie against Chelsea at Stamford Bridge in January 1985. 'The Chelsea fans gave Fash [John Fashanu] stick all game, including some awful racist abuse. I won't go into all of it but it's the worst I think I've ever witnessed at a football game.' (*Theo Give Us a Ball*, Theo Foley with Paul Foley, Apex Publishing Ltd, 2018).

Tommy Tynan, at Plymouth Argyle, observed, 'I've called a player a black bastard – as an insult, not out of hatred – and they've come back with, "Yeah, your wife loves one, doesn't she?" I've also had a coloured centre-half call me white trash. It's intimidation, not racism, and goes on in football. I'm not a racist.'

Tynan commented further, 'We played Stoke once and they had two coloured lads called Carl Saunders and Tony Ford playing for them. The Plymouth fans jeered them and threw bananas and everything. All the time Calvin [Plummer] was standing on our right wing. They don't realise, they are too stupid to realise, that when they were having a go at the opposition's black players, they were having a go at Calvin too. It's the same in reverse when we play away. I've noticed it especially at Stoke and Leeds.' (*Tommy: A Life at the Soccer Factory*, Tommy Tynan with Richard Cowdery, Bud Books, 1990).

Ricky Hill, Luton Town and England international, and the fourth black footballer to play for England, said he often detected entrenched racism that was allowed to pass unchallenged. This, he said, was evident in Sir Alf Ramsey's verdict on England's options at the World Cup in 1986. 'He said I was a talented player, but you might not want to go to war with me. I thought, "You won the World Cup, but you don't know me, and you don't know what I've been through to get here." It was hurtful and no one disputed the inference. The word was black players didn't have the acumen to play in central midfield where I played. Ron Noades [Crystal Palace chairman] said he signed black players for flair and speed but needed white players around to add brains.'

Hill goes on, 'No one attempted to dispel the notion. Even the abuse we suffered early in our careers, very little of it was ever mentioned in the press at the time about the abhorrent behaviour of certain fans.' (*Daily Mail*, 29 March 2019).

Howard Gayle, of Liverpool, details his most important appearance for the Reds in the European Cup semi-final second leg away at Bayern Munich in April 1981. He was a substitute and introduced in the ninth minute of the game before being substituted 61 minutes later. He recalls his exercises on the running track at the Olympic Stadium prior to joining the game. 'I stretched my hamstring, stretched my calf and tested my groin before setting off on the claret-coloured asphalt.

'That's when the monkey noises started. I didn't realise what was happening at first because all my concentration was with the warm-up … And then I looked around, away from the pitch. More monkey noises; a few grown men making Nazi salutes. Great …' (*61 Minutes in Munich*, Howard Gayle, de Coubertin books, 2016).

Evidently, Hillsborough was not immune from racism. An article in the programme for the game against Wrexham in November 1980 stated, 'Another ignorant pursuit is that of singling out coloured players for special treatment … so come on, you true supporters, put the Owls back on the map for true sportsmanship.'

The two examples of racism I recollect took place outside the Boleyn Ground, West Ham United's ground, and at the Recreation Ground, Aldershot.

At West Ham it was close to the football ground, in the Green Street market, an open-air market with covered stalls packed tightly together. A group of four or five Hammers followers, dressed in claret and blue colours, and a good two hours before the Saturday afternoon kick-off against Sheffield Wednesday in December 1980, ran through the market stalls shouting and abusing women and young children of Asian appearance. The women and children – some in pushchairs – were just going about their business browsing the market stalls.

They ran at the women shouting racist abuse peppered with foul language. The essence of their 'message' was that they weren't welcome in this country. The abusers' appearance was startling and aggressive – and one that would not have been out of place ten years earlier. They were all skinheads with shaven heads, Doc Marten cherry-coloured boots and braces, their West Ham scarves tied around their wrists. These youths were a fearsome sight.

It shocked me. It came out of nowhere and was over almost as soon as it had begun, taking no more than a minute. The youths pressed their hostile, enraged faces right into those of the women, who stopped, stood motionless until the tirade finished. The children cowered and moved closer to their mums, a couple of them starting to cry.

Their foul deed over, the youths ran out of the market towards the football ground.

The impact it had on the women and their children I can only imagine – both mental and emotional. It affected me.

There were no police in Green Street market at 1pm that Saturday afternoon, so nothing and no one to stop the youths. I'd seen nothing like it.

Outside the ground, leaflets were being handed out to anyone who was interested – leaflets that few spectators seemed to be taking, and for those that did, a fair few ended up discarding them around the ground. The leaflets displayed the words 'National Front', the far-right political organisation, prominently on one side.

Interestingly, *The Spectator* magazine of 10 January 1981 referred to this game at Upton Park, the author C. Price noting, 'The ambience was nauseating – a sea of dirty denim emblazoned with union jack and swastika, imitation Heil Hitler salutes, pounding violence in the verbal obscenities, menace in patches of the home crowd on its way home.'

Six years later, in November 1986, at the Recreation Ground, Aldershot, there was racism inside the ground during the game against Rochdale. We were in the covered terracing close to the players' tunnel. There were a small number of away supporters on the terracing – maybe a dozen at most. But they were loud and vocal.

Rochdale losing the game and more than half the away supporters were crudely abusing their own striker – the number 10. They were giving him 'dog's abuse'. Worse still, they were focusing on his colour, the 'N' word used liberally, foul language used at will, as they accused their own striker of not trying and being useless.

The player looked in the direction of his own supporters as the abuse rained down on him – he made no gesture towards his racist 'accusers' and mouthed no words towards them. Maybe he was incredulous at what he was hearing. We were. His own team's supporters unleashing a torrent of abuse.

One of the Aldershot supporters turned around and shouted at the away supporters, 'Leave him alone, he's trying his best.' I would say he looked as if he was trying even harder than his team-mates. I started to watch him more closely given the abuse he was getting.

The home supporter's request had the opposite effect. No response to his plea albeit the away supporters increased the invective aimed at their own player. The player was later 'subbed' and as he made his way to the tunnel, the vitriol and racist abuse increased to a crescendo. Their satisfaction at his departure clear to everyone. And the player did not react at all as he departed.

There were no police present in the area of the ground the abuse came from. How the player felt, I don't know. I felt for him but it did not cross my mind to seek a police officer or steward to complain about the vile and racist language used. Looking back 30 and more years later, it is clear to me I was at least complicit – as were others – in doing nothing and allowing the racist abuse to continue.

These are the only two examples of racism I had personal experience of in the 1980s.

But racism inside and outside football grounds throughout the decade was evident. Black players had only just begun to establish themselves in the English game in the previous decade, and much has been written about the difficulties that players of that era encountered.

Leroy Rosenior describes the racism he endured in his autobiography (*It's Only Banter*, Pitch Publishing, 2018), commenting on a game at Elland Road in 1984, when he was playing for Fulham against Leeds United. He highlights an incident in which his team had a throw-in towards the large home Kop end. He recalls, 'Paul Parker and I were closest and looked to get our attack back on track. As we got to the corner flag, any thought of launching that attack went from our minds as we were met in the corner by thousands of fans with hate in their eyes, intent on unsettling these two young black footballers who had dared to come to their town to play a game of football.

'Usually there were the monkey chants, the "ooh-ooh-ooh" noises that all black players had been subject to at the time. There were the chants about shooting n*****s and the bananas that fell from the terraces of 1980s football stadiums with increasing regularity.

'What happened was none of the above. Instead, Paul and I were greeted with 5,000 or more Leeds fans with their right hands, erect to the sky, shouting "Sieg Heil" as if not attending a Second Division football match but a 1930s Nuremberg rally … Hatred was in their eyes and it showed just how deep the Far Right had sunk their dirty nails into the national game.

'Paul Parker and I were shaken by what happened at Leeds, but it wasn't spoken about in the dressing room. That wasn't football's way.'

The atmosphere at Elland Road at that time has been described as 'rancorous and rancid' – an ideal place for the National Front, the white nationalist party, to spread their ideas and sell their newspapers *Bulldog* and *The Flag*, looking to recruit people to their cause. A *Daily Mirror* investigation in 1988 was headlined, 'Fascist, racist and violent – club branded a breeding ground.'

Apart from Upton Park, the only other ground I saw evidence of National Front activity was Stamford Bridge, at Wednesday games there in the early 1980s. Leaflets were handed out promoting that group – with little interest shown by the intended recipients.

Paul Canoville, the first black player to play for Chelsea's first team, recounts his experience at Selhurst Park while warming up as substitute for his debut in April 1982. 'It was supposed to be my special time … supporters were baying, hooting like mocking monkeys and throwing bananas at me from the stands. I was on for three minutes and it seemed like the longest torture of my entire life.'

He goes on, 'At the final whistle I ran off straight down the tunnel as soon as possible. I was so glad none of my family was there to hear my magic moment disgraced. I was shocked and distraught. What happened there? Did I just hallucinate all that? I made my debut but a banana landed in front of me … they chanted, "We don't want the n****r!" and I was that "n****r" they didn't want. That's what really hurt me above all. It wasn't the away supporters. It was our own fans.' (*Black and Blue*, Paul Canoville, Headline, 2008).

Brendan Batson, the West Bromwich Albion defender, has said, 'What shocked me when I joined West Brom was the volume. The noise and level of abuse was incredible. At times, it was almost like surround sound in the grounds. But it was such a regular occurrence you almost got used to it.

'We'd get off the coach at away matches and the National Front would be right there in your face. In those days, we didn't have security and we'd have to run the gauntlet. We'd get to the players' entrance and there'd be spit on my jacket or Cyrille Regis's shirt. It was a sign of the times. I don't recall making a big hue and cry about it. We coped.' (*Backpass*, Issue 56).

Regis was at the centre of a more sinister incident just prior to his England debut against Northern Ireland at Wembley in 1982. He received a letter at the West Brom training ground that contained a bullet and the warning, 'You'll get one of these through your knee if you step on our Wembley turf.'

Evidently, Regis took the incident in his stride. He wasn't intimidated and even had 'a good laugh' about it, observing that black players used to get a lot of hate mail, particularly Laurie Cunningham, who had a white girlfriend.

In the Albion dressing room, the trio had unanimous and unequivocal support. Former defender Ally Robertson commented, 'We talked about it, but we also laughed about it. The three lads were our mates and we all used to stick together, so it was nothing to us. If they were being called anything, the rest of us would just tell them to try harder to win the game and shut the crowd up.

'I used to say to each of them, "If people call you a black so-and-so, then so what? How many times have I been told I'm a Scottish twat?" I didn't give two hoots. The thing was we never, ever allowed anyone to call them n****r. That's derogative. Anyone that did, I'd be the first to punch them.' (*Backpass*, Issue 56).

Racism was rife in the 1980s, and it was truly shocking.

# Chapter 9

# The Bradford Fire

SATURDAY, 11 May 1985 – the last league game of the season for clubs in all four divisions. Roots Hall my destination for the Fourth Division game between Southend United and Torquay United. An important game, it could determine which club had to seek re-election to the Football League at the end of the season. I watched from the East Stand – on wooden seats attached to a wooden structure.

That same date has much greater resonance for supporters of Bradford City. It was that afternoon, during a game against Lincoln City at Valley Parade, that a fire started in the main stand, quickly engulfing the whole structure and leading to the loss of life of 56 fans.

It is sadly ironic that the tarred and timbered roof of the main stand was due to be dismantled after the game – the local newspaper, the *Bradford Telegraph & Argus*, carried an article entitled, 'Spit and Polish for the Parade ground' in that morning's edition.

The game only 35 minutes old when the main stand caught fire – from a lighted cigarette discarded amongst piles of accumulated litter in the stand. A fireball quickly took hold and intensified in large part as a result of the design and construction of the old roof. The stand was built in 1909.

The consequences were devastating. As well as those killed, more than 200 were injured and many more were traumatised by what they'd seen. The pictures on the television news later that evening horrific – spectators struggling to get out of the stand on to the pitch, one man with his coat on fire, others running to help him, dousing the flames.

In his excellent book on football grounds published in 1983, the author Simon Inglis made these observations about Valley Parade and its main stand, 'Imagine watching football from the cockpit of a Sopwith Camel. That is the view from City's main stand. There are 22 thin verticals at the front with cross struts in between each, plus more supports further back.' And more tellingly, he observes, 'Underneath the seats are flaps which open to reveal piles of accumulated litter.' (*The Football Grounds of England and Wales*, Simon Inglis, Collins Willow, 1983).

Yorkshire Television were covering the game, with Bradford-born commentator John Helm positioned in the gantry opposite the main stand. 'We've actually got a fire on the far side of the ground, and that looks very nasty indeed … The heat is now becoming tremendous. I'm sitting immediately opposite the main stand and I can feel the heat. It's almost beginning to burn me over here, quite honestly … this was supposed to be a day of utter joy, triumph and celebration and it's turning into a nightmare.'

People started jumping over the perimeter wall to escape the fire. The linesman noticed what was going on and let the referee know. The game was stopped three minutes before half-time.

Helm went on with his commentary, 'The roof is caving in. The black pall of smoke is rising hundreds of feet in the air and the whole place is scorching. They've been talking about having a new ground at Valley Parade. They might soon have to have one because this is the day that Valley Parade football ground is burning down.'

In his autobiography, Terry Yorath, a coach at Bradford City and in the dugout that fateful day, recollects his frantic efforts to establish where his parents, wife and children were in the midst of the burning inferno – all had been sitting in the Directors' Box in the centre of the wooden stand. He was running and shouting to everyone in the rooms and offices beneath the stand to 'get f*****g out'.

He found his wife and children – they were out. He could not find his parents. 'It was complete confusion. By this time, the fire had reached the roof and wood and molten felt were raining down all over the place. Then it hit the tunnel [a 10ft-wide pathway at the back of the stand]. The fire went whoosh right along the tunnel, so anyone in its path would have stood no chance. It had taken just four and a half minutes for the whole stand to go up. It was an inferno – the flames had spread faster than a person could run ... In the end, I had to throw a chair at a window in the players' lounge and then jump through it to escape myself.' (*Hard Man Hard Knocks*, Terry Yorath with Grahame Lloyd, Celluloid, 2004).

Yorath's parents were safe. They were creatures of habit and had left their seats before half-time to have a cigarette – they were well away from the fire in the stand.

Others were not. Yorath remembers, 'After checking my parents were alright I went back into the ground, where I saw all sorts of dreadful things. Dead people were lying on the terracing – they had simply been burnt to death.'

Martin Fletcher, a 12-year-old Bradford City supporter, was at the game with his family and seated in the main stand. He has written a book about his experiences, the fire itself and the aftermath. He describes horrendous scenes and running for his life from the stand. 'As I'd made it through the inferno, molten tar from the burning roof had dripped on to my jacket, scarf and cap. By the time I'd reached the front paddock, I was on the brink of becoming a human torch.' He was the only member of his family to survive the fire – his dad, brother, uncle and grandfather all lost their lives. (*56: The Story of the Bradford Fire*, Martin Fletcher, Bloomsbury, 2015).

The pictures of the fire were horrific, with the flames gathering pace at an alarming rate. In his book, *Four Minutes to Hell* (Parrs Wood Press, 2005), Paul Firth explained, 'Because the stand was open to the elements at the front and side, the fire behaved as it would have done in a Dutch barn. The conditions held the heat in, caused it to rise up to the top until it hit the underside of the wooden roof and then it bounced back toward the tip of the roof pointing downward ... Those early moments of the blaze show a mass of smoke and flames curling out from the front edge of the roof and moving rapidly along the roof towards the Bradford end.'

The impact of the Bradford fire was immediate – it dominated the news that weekend on television and radio, and in newspapers. The images were vivid and horrifying.

On the Monday evening, I went to White Hart Lane; Sheffield Wednesday were playing Tottenham Hotspur. The bright new stands with their gleaming blue plastic seats. The contrast with the vision of Valley Parade could not have been greater. People talked about the horrors of the fire – their overriding thoughts were ones of disbelief, utter disbelief. A football match, a celebration of promotion for the home supporters ... and then the fire.

Before the game, a minute's silence was held to remember the victims of the Bradford fire – the first time I recall being in a crowd where such a remembrance had taken place. The silence was observed impeccably.

Subsequently, the Bradford Disaster Appeal was launched in aid of the victims' families. A benefit game was played at Leeds Road, Huddersfield Town's ground, between Bradford City and Manchester United on 6 August 1985. The programme carried a message from Bradford City's chairman Stafford Heginbotham. 'Following that terrible day, Manchester United were the first club to contact us with this offer of assistance. It is little wonder, after such acts of generosity, that they are considered by many to be the biggest club in the world.'

This was underlined by City manager Trevor Cherry, who commented, 'Ron Atkinson was the first manager to telephone me after the Valley Parade fire tragedy and offer to play a match against us for the disaster fund.' The fund eventually raised over £3.5 million.

Home Secretary Leon Brittan announced an inquiry into the disaster. The hearing, conducted at the City Hall in Bradford from 5 June 1985, saw statements from 77 witnesses heard by appointed High Court judge Oliver Popplewell (sitting as Mr Justice Popplewell) following a preliminary session on 23 May 1985.

The inquiry focused on the Bradford fire and additionally the events at Birmingham City's St Andrews ground, where a 14-year-old boy lost his life after a wall collapsed following violent disturbances amongst supporters. There was criticism about the two events – one a large-scale disaster caused by fire, the other a loss of life caused by football violence – being linked. The government was not for turning on the terms of the inquiry.

Much has been said about the inquiry, with some criticising its speed, its conduct and its outcome. A thousand fans were interviewed – not one was female. Of the 56 victims, 11 were female.

The hearing lasted five and a half days, after which Popplewell concluded, 'I am quite satisfied that the cause of the fire was the dropping of a lighted match, cigarette or tobacco.' Verdict: death by misadventure.

Popplewell's blueprint on the findings was published on 24 July 1985. Its recommendations had far-reaching consequences. Those recommendations included banning smoking in combustible stands, training stewards in fire prevention, manning exits at all times, training in evacuation procedures, and in grounds holding more than 5,000 people fire authorities were given the power to restrict the use of a stand they considered a risk.

The fire and its impact brought about an unprecedented community spirit. It was buoyed by worldwide messages of condolence and monetary contributions from a host of public events towards the Bradford Disaster Appeal fund, with the aim of returning to a new Valley Parade stadium. The club had to play all their home league and cup fixtures for the 1985/86 season and the first half of the following season at various other grounds – Bradford Northern RLFC (now Bradford Bulls) at Odsal Stadium, Huddersfield Town (Leeds Road) and Leeds United (Elland Road).

The new ground was first used on 14 December 1986 with a commemorative fixture against an England X1 before a capacity crowd of 15,000.

At Valley Parade, the new entrance to the redeveloped Sunwin Stand has a memorial with the names of the 56 people who lost their lives.

# Chapter 10

# Heysel

I'D JOINED ICL in April 1985. A month later, the European Cup Final was taking place at the Heysel Stadium – the King Baudouin 111 Stadium – in Brussels.

The game was due to start at 7.15pm. For reasons I don't recollect, I was staying at The Novotel, Hammersmith in London on the night of the game on 29 May. Leaving the office by car at 6.30pm for the three-mile journey from Putney to Hammersmith, commuter traffic near-gridlock. Radio on to listen to the preview of the game.

Odd. Talking about crowd trouble. Peter Jones, the lead football commentator for BBC Radio, describing scenes from inside the stadium. Supporters had apparently charged at one end of the ground, from one section to another. It had caused panic. A wall had given way. Supporters had fallen, and others had fallen on top of them.

It seemed scarcely believable. The reporting continued … the most chilling report came with news that one of the reporters had been outside the stadium and seen lifeless bodies. The words 'death at a football match' soon followed. Horrendous.

I made it to the hotel, straight to the room and switched the television on immediately. Awful. Scenes of the stadium and one end in particular – supporters running and one section empty of spectators. As pictures broadcast the reality of what had happened, Jimmy Hill introduced coverage on BBC1 with the words, 'The news is very bad from Brussels. Hooliganism has struck again and I'm afraid the scenes are as bad as anything we've seen in a long time.'

A discussion followed about what appeared to have happened. Seemingly, Liverpool supporters had run from their section of terracing over the wire fence into Section Z and ran at the Juventus supporters. The report said people had been killed – numbers unknown at that point.

The commentator Barry Davies said from the ground, 'It was the pressure of movement down towards the running track which resulted in the wall giving way and people being pinned underneath.'

Retreating Juventus supporters had put pressure on the perimeter wall, which caused its collapse. Thirty-nine people lost their lives, a further 600 were injured. On the day after the game UEFA's official observer at Heysel, Gunter Schneider, said, 'Only the English fans were responsible. Of that there is no doubt.'

The talk on television moved on to whether the game should be played or not, given what had occurred. No decision had been made by the authorities at that stage, although the scheduled kick-off time would have to be put back if the game went ahead. The commentators focused on how the players – from both teams – could possibly concentrate on the game given the events in the stadium.

Writing later about events, Liverpool supporter Chris Rowland recalled, 'Forged tickets were being used successfully. We witnessed cash being handed over to turnstile operators, who then allowed them in.' He reflected there was little official information about what was happening in the hour before scheduled kick-off. 'Outside in the darkness, helicopters buzzed angrily, their lights twinkling in the sky, and sirens wailed. The PA system continued to babble indecipherably. Apparently the two team captains broadcast an appeal for calm, but nobody I have ever spoken to – during or since – even heard Phil Neal's voice.' (*From Where I was Standing: A Liverpool Supporter's View of the Heysel Stadium Tragedy*, GPRF Publishing, 2009).

The decision was made to play the game later that evening. The authorities were apparently more concerned about how the crowd would react if the game was not played that night.

When the game started, it seemed surreal to me given the events of hours earlier. Players seemed to lack the intensity normally associated with a European Cup Final. And the commentators appeared to some degree distracted and not fully focused on the game. Juventus won the match 1-0. The goal came from a penalty given for a foul generally acknowledged to have been committed outside the area. But no one seemed too concerned. The game needed to be over and done.

For some Liverpool supporters on the terraces, there was a feeling that with a Juventus win they had more chance of getting back to their coaches outside the ground safely – the Italian supporters focused on their victorious team.

Alan Hansen, the Liverpool player and later a TV pundit, commented after the game, 'You came into the dressing room afterwards and it's horrific, horrific, and it's like so sad.' (BBC TV documentary).

Hansen had seen problems before the game, observing that when Liverpool players had gone out on to the pitch to warm up more than an hour before the scheduled kick-off time, missiles had been thrown at them by Juventus supporters. Some were bricks from the crumbling stadium.

For Liverpool manager Joe Fagan, it was his last game in charge. He'd decided to retire in February that year and his decision was announced on the day of the game. At the press conference after the match, he said, 'I won't be able to forget my last game of football for the rest of my life. It is tragic. It was really horrific. I broke down and cried. Tonight upset me very much but it wasn't over the result. What's a game of football when so many are dead?'

Ian Ross in the *Daily Post* reported, 'Liverpool's dream of bringing the European Cup back to rest at Anfield for all time perished in Brussels on a night of shame for both football and Merseyside.'

*The Mirror*, 'Mobs of Liverpool supporters brandishing flag poles and sticks and lighting fires broke down a flimsy wire fence separating them from Juventus fans. A wall and metal crash barriers collapsed as thousands fled in panic on to the pitch.'

In *The Guardian*, it noted the game went ahead 'alongside hideous scenes, as corpses in green plastic shrouds were carried to a makeshift tented mortuary outside the main entrance.' David Lacey, commenting in the same newspaper, said, 'Professional football as a spectator sport lay mortally wounded.' The *Daily Express* described it as 'the most horrifying outbreak of soccer violence the world has ever seen'.

The Liverpool squad arrived back home the day after the game – the BBC news report captured the solemn mood. 'The Liverpool squad arrived home after the most disastrous European tie in history to more media attention than had they won the Cup for keeps in front of peaceful crowds. Flags were flying at half-mast [in Liverpool] out of respect for the dead and it seemed in shame as well.'

How had it happened? The stadium was in very poor condition, not fit for purpose to host a European Cup Final. Crumbling walls, bricks on the terracing – evidently used by supporters of both clubs as missiles – and an outer perimeter wall with a large hole enabling supporters to pass through it at will. One Liverpool supporter at the game said, 'It was a wreck.'

Many viewed the sale of tickets on the day of the game in Section Z of the stadium – supposedly for neutral Belgian supporters and purchased by many Juventus fans – as extremely ill advised. Liverpool supporters were in Sections X and Y. Missiles were thrown between the Liverpool and Juventus supporters. Only a small chain-link fence – described as no more than chicken wire – separated the Liverpool sections from Section Z and the Juventus fans. It was no deterrent. A group of Liverpool supporters charged at the Italians, creating panic. Juventus supporters ran away, putting pressure on the wall, which collapsed. There were 39 fatalities and over 600 injured.

This was the latest – and by far the worst – incident of hooliganism in continental Europe involving supporters from England. Prime Minister Margaret Thatcher put pressure on the Football Association and Football League to withdraw English clubs from European competition. UEFA felt compelled to act. The Football Association withdrew all its clubs from European competition for the forthcoming season – 1985/86. UEFA reinforced their initial action by confirming English clubs (not Scottish clubs) would be banned from all European club competitions indefinitely, and Liverpool would be banned for an additional three years if and when the ban was lifted.

The message was stark, the impact direct and immediate.

Everton had qualified for the European Cup in 1985/86 after becoming league champions in 1984/85 (only the league champions of each country qualified for the competition). The events at Heysel and their consequences prevented Liverpool's Merseyside neighbours from competing in Europe's premier club competition.

Seventeen clubs missed out on the chance to play in the three European club competitions as a result of the ban, among them Norwich City, Luton Town, Coventry City, Derby County, Sheffield Wednesday and Wimbledon.

In the event English clubs were banned for five years and readmitted in 1990. Liverpool served an additional one-year ban, not three. And whilst the ban was lifted in 1990 it took clubs a further five years before they had earned all the places they held in European competitions prior to Heysel.

There was great consternation at the negative impact the ban would have – including concerns that clubs would fall behind in their tactics, skills application and development as a result of not being tested by the best of the European clubs; that English clubs would necessarily become more insular – and that the England national team would suffer as a result of domestic competition only.

Additionally, top clubs lost revenue from games in the European competitions – both matchday and television income.

In its editorial for the start of the following season, the *Rothmans Football Yearbook* commented, 'On 29 May 1985, as witnessed on live television, there occurred the worst hooliganism-related tragedy in European football history. The reaction of the football authorities to the events of that awful night in Brussels was also, in its own way, tragic.'

The editorial criticised the hooliganism of some Juventus supporters and the fateful charge by some Liverpool fans that led to the deaths of 39 people. The police were criticised for their lack of action on the night and the selection of a ground with crumbling terraces was condemned, along with the sale of tickets to anyone who turned up at the various selling points in the stadium.

Following the Heysel disaster, the national Football Supporters Association was formed in Liverpool later the same year.

The trial of those supporters charged as a result of the tragedy was long and drawn-out. Verdicts reached in April 1989 – 14 Liverpool supporters were found guilty of manslaughter and sentenced to three years' imprisonment, with half of each term suspended. They were each fined £1,000.

Years later, Bruce Grobbelaar, the Liverpool goalkeeper on the night, commented, 'I said to myself after that game, "I don't want to be part of a club that caused death and destruction in a game or sport." I felt very, very strongly, and if that game had been the semi-final, I don't think I'd be playing today. But it was the last game of the season … I sat on the beach and thought, "If I knock it on the head and not play any more, then these idiots have won. If I've gone then they've won, they've destroyed me, and they're not going to destroy me." … That's why I decided to carry on.' (*Three Sides of the Mersey*, Rogan Taylor and Andrew Ward with John Williams, Robson Books, 1994).

# Chapter 11

# Hillsborough

SATURDAY, 15 April 1989. The date of the tragedy that unfolded at Sheffield Wednesday's ground, Hillsborough. A place where 96 Liverpool supporters lost their lives.

The day started for me as a normal Saturday. Both FA Cup semi-finals were being played at the same time – Liverpool v Nottingham Forest at Hillsborough, Everton v West Ham United at Villa Park. By the evening, it could be an all-Merseyside FA Cup Final, which at the time I thought was the most likely outcome.

Beyond those thoughts, I didn't dwell on the game being played in my home city. I'd been to five FA Cup semi-finals at Hillsborough in the 1970s – together with Villa Park, it was an almost automatic choice for a neutral ground FA Cup semi-final.

I'd stood on the Leppings Lane terrace directly behind the goal for the 1972 FA Cup semi-final, Leeds United v Birmingham City. It was crowded, it was tight, it was full of atmosphere. But it was not uncomfortable; if it had been too tight, the crowd would have spread out to fill the full width and depth of the terrace. There were no constraints on movement. Very different to 1989, by which time fences and pens restricted movement to the side and to the front.

None of those thoughts came to mind that morning – our football-watching plans that day were focused on the Recreation Ground, Aldershot.

For the Shots, it was the biggest game of the season, a Third Division fixture against league leaders Wolverhampton Wanderers, with future England international Steve Bull, Andy Mutch and all. There were plenty of away supporters in attendance in their old gold and black colours – segregated as best they could be.

We took our position down the side terracing close to the Flowerbed End. It was the biggest gate of the season, 5,465. It was a good game, lots of atmosphere and the league leaders deservedly ran out 2-1 winners.

Early in the game, a spectator standing close to us with a radio held next to his ear had told anyone who wanted to hear that the semi-final at Hillsborough had been stopped – there were 'crowd problems'. That was the term he used, 'crowd problems'. People drew their own conclusions. The initial reaction from those few who proffered a view was that hooliganism was the likely cause. In the context of the times, it was an understandable thought.

Getting back to the car after the game and listening to the radio, the full horror of the afternoon in Sheffield unfolded. Peter Jones, the football commentator, his voice authoritative but despairing, said the game had been abandoned. People had died at the ground. Jones had been a commentator at Heysel and had described those horrific scenes.

Back home and the events from Hillsborough were being broadcast live on television. The main BBC News led with the catastrophe.

John Motson, the television commentator, was at the ground to cover the game, with recorded highlights to be shown on *Match of the Day* later that evening. But there was no match – his role changed from football commentator to live news reporter for the *Grandstand* sports programme on BBC1 that afternoon.

The facts were that innocent Liverpool supporters had been crushed to death on an overcrowded terrace. They had no way of escaping the horror.

For me, what had happened at Hillsborough that afternoon was almost incomprehensible. It was a football game. It was a football game at 'my ground' – the ground where I'd first gone to watch football as a lad. I'd stood on those self-same terraces that had been the scene of such carnage and tragedy. The sense of disbelief overwhelming. But it was all too real.

The Liverpool goalkeeper, Bruce Grobbelaar, was at the end of the ground in front of the Leppings Lane terracing when the game started. 'One shot went over the bar. I went to pick up the ball. All they said was, "They're killing us, Bruce, they're killing us." Voices through the fence. I looked round and I could see the fright on people's faces through the fence, and I said to the policeman, "Is there any chance you can open the gate here?" The ball was away in the corner. I went to retrieve it, and I said to the policewoman, "Get the effing gate open. Can't you see that they need it?" And there were screams coming at the time. I kicked the ball upfield and I went back and said, "Get the f*****g gate open." ... The ball went out, and that's when I shouted to the referee. The policeman came on to the field, and the game stopped.' (*Three Sides of the Mersey*, Rogan Taylor and Andrew Ward with John Williams, Robson Books, 1994).

The game stopped at 3.06pm and did not restart. Hundreds of people came on to the pitch from the Leppings Lane terrace, frantic efforts were made to save people from the terrible crush in the central pen of the terrace. Television footage of the scenes and news reports are harrowing. The tragedy was unfolding on television screens. Makeshift stretchers made from advertising hoardings were used to carry people. A lone ambulance made its way across the pitch ten minutes after the game had been stopped to where people lay. Ninety-six people lost their lives at Hillsborough.

Steve McMahon, the Liverpool player, observed, 'There was precious little conversation in our dressing room, which is usually alive with banter, but on this occasion no-one had anything to say ... John Barnes was in a terrible state ... He was inconsolable, he was in tears. The full impact of what had happened just seemed to hit Barnsie right away.' (*The Day of the Hillsborough Disaster*, Rogan Taylor, Andrew Ward and Tim Newburn, Liverpool University Press, 1995).

John Aldridge, one of the Liverpool forwards in that game, recalled, 'I didn't take it in until that night, when we come home, me and the wife. We were just watching the telly and it come on the news, and we just broke down, the two of us, we just broke down. We couldn't believe it, what we'd seen, what had happened. We were crying all night, couldn't get to sleep.' (*Three Sides of the Mersey*, Rogan Taylor and Andrew Ward with John Williams, Robson Books, 1994).

Evertonian Peter Reid, who had joined Queens Park Rangers along with Nigel Spackman, who had played for Liverpool, said, 'I'll never forget that day. We were playing Middlesbrough and Don Howe, the coach, pulled Nige and me at half-time to say, "It looks like there's been fatalities at Hillsborough, do you want to carry on?" We finished the game then took in what was happening on TV devastated ... In the week afterwards, Nige and I went up to Anfield to see Kenny Dalglish and Alan Hansen. What I saw was heartbreaking, the messages, the flowers and what hit me was the number of blue scarves tied across the ground.' (*Daily Mail*, 27 March 2019).

Once Liverpool and Forest had been drawn together for the semi-final, the Liverpool chief executive – mindful of events and ticketing arrangements at the Hillsborough semi-final in 1988, where Liverpool had been allocated the Leppings Lane end – asked the Football Association to allocate the Spion Kop to Liverpool fans and the Leppings Lane to Forest fans. Liverpool supporters would outnumber Forest fans and that allocation would best suit the demand. The request was turned down. The police considered that Liverpool supporters approaching the ground from the M62 motorway would find it easier if they were situated at the Leppings Lane end.

On the day, there were 1,112 police on duty at Hillsborough – about one for every 45 supporters – with 34 mounted police from Liverpool and Nottingham utilised to marshal their own supporters.

In his seminal work, Professor Phil Scraton highlighted, 'Twenty-one officers were given responsibility for policing the perimeter track ... They were instructed to "pay particular attention to prevent any person climbing the fences to gain access to the ground." The gates in the perimeter fences were to remain "bolted at all times ... with no one allowed access to the track from the terraces without the consent of a senior officer."' (*Hillsborough The Truth*, Phil Scraton, Mainstream Publishing, 2016). As Scraton referenced in his book, the last instruction 'was in capitals and underlined'.

Additionally, the police had an inexperienced match commander, David Duckenfield, who had been appointed to the role only three weeks prior to the game.

Focusing on the ground, 'the south and east sides of the ground accommodated some 29,800 whose access on the day was through 60 turnstiles. The other two sides of the ground, north and west, with a capacity of 24,256, were fed solely from the Leppings Lane entrance, where there were only 23 turnstiles.' (Lord Justice Taylor, interim report, para 31 and 32). Worse still, of the 23 turnstiles for Liverpool supporters only 7 of those were used for the 10,100 supporters in possession of standing terrace tickets.

To compound the issue, the flow rate through stadium turnstiles is 750 per hour, identified in the *Green Guide*, which in the late 1980s was regarded as the bible for safety at sports grounds. The ground, the section capacity, the number of turnstiles and the flow rate all added up to a major problem.

In addition, at the previous year's semi-final, supporters recalled a police cordon positioned some distance from the Leppings Lane turnstiles, checking tickets, before they were allowed to proceed. No recollection of such a cordon this time.

The build-up of supporters at that end of the ground increased as time ticked towards kick-off. Growing numbers of people filled the small area immediately outside the seven turnstiles at the Leppings Lane end – their focus getting to and into the ground. There was little organisation and even less control of the crowd. By 2.30pm, there was a crush and it was getting worse.

With real fears there could be serious injuries or worse outside the ground, the decision was made to open the gates to let the crowd through to ease the crush. Once that decision was taken, the key problem was that no one was directing supporters inside the ground. Many of them made for the central tunnel leading to the central pen that was already overcrowded. The pressure of those supporters coming into that fenced pen led to the crushing of people further down the terrace and the disaster unfolded.

Graham Kelly, the FA chief executive, was at the game and stated, 'Chief Superintendent David Duckenfield, the match commander, told me that a gate or gates had been forced, showing me a picture from a video camera which purported to represent this.' (*Sweet FA*, Graham Kelly, Collins Willow, 1999). Kelly went on television and radio to relay these comments – that supporters had effectively broken down the gates to obtain entry into the ground.

Except it was not true. Duckenfield had given the order to open the gates as he was confronted with a potential catastrophe outside the turnstiles. He had lied to the FA Chief Executive. 'David Duckenfield was not a match commander worth his salt because he now says so himself. He tried to mask his failings in the aftermath of the disaster. He told an infamous and ignominious lie suggesting that Liverpool fans had forced their way into the ground.' (*Hillsborough Untold*, Norman Bettison, Biteback Publishing, 2016).

Subsequent investigations would establish beyond doubt the sequence of events that led to the tragedy:

- A significant build-up of spectators outside the turnstiles at the Leppings Lane end of the ground which had been allocated to Liverpool supporters – only seven turnstiles for 10,100 spectators.
- As time progressed towards kick-off, supporter numbers increased substantially in this area – there were concerns for the safety of the supporters outside the ground.
- To ease the crush, the police made the decision to open a metal gate allowing spectators into the ground without the need to go through the turnstiles.

- They poured through the gate and made for the narrow, dark 30-yard tunnel in the centre which offered them their first view of the pitch.
- Going through the tunnel, they went straight into the central fenced-in pen, already overcrowded, thereby crushing spectators further down and at the front of the pen – the individual pens either side had room to accommodate latecomers but there was no one to show or guide supporters in the direction of these pens.
- Spectators were trampled underfoot, some crushed into the perimeter fencing at the bottom of the terracing.
- Fencing which had been erected to prevent hooligans invading the pitch prevented people from getting out of the pens.
- The game was stopped after six minutes – the first ambulance arrived ten minutes later.

No one can know what the victims and their families went through – except the families themselves. People watched and saw the horrors broadcast on television. Families with friends and relatives at the ground did not know what had happened to their loved ones, these the days before mobile phones. Much later, when supporters were let out of the ground, some found a public telephone box, others able to use a residential telephone offered by householders near the ground.

The Hillsborough tragedy was the centre and focus of all news for weeks. Prime Minister Margaret Thatcher and Home Secretary Douglas Hurd visited the scene of the disaster and were shown, with Wednesday chairman Bert McGee amongst others, walking on the terraced steps at the Leppings Lane end.

Joe Ashton, MP for Bassetlaw and a Wednesday supporter, was asked about the tragedy and the crowd at the Leppings

Lane end. He highlighted the position of the individual pens and how the crowd had nowhere to move as it became overcrowded and then dangerously overcrowded. There was no room to the side and no room to the front. The pens fenced the crowd in.

On the Monday after the tragedy, the front pages of all the national newspapers had the Hillsborough disaster as their lead story – as did those of many foreign newspapers. The image most used was that of bodies crushed against the fencing at the front of the terracing at the Leppings Lane end, their faces pressed against it. It was a dreadful and heartrending image.

Headlines in the national newspapers included: *Daily Star* – 'Shut the Terraces Now'; *Today* – 'Tear Down Cages of Death'; *The Sun* – 'The Truth'. Except from *The Sun*, it was anything but the truth – it was outrageous lies, which I will not deign to repeat, concerning actions the newspaper claimed had been undertaken by some Liverpool supporters.

An inquiry into the events at Hillsborough, led by Lord Justice Taylor, was announced. The Hillsborough ground was closed for weeks after the disaster.

I felt moved to write to the local sports paper *The Green 'Un'* – it was the featured letter on the letters page the following Saturday. The headline, 'Soccer tragedy an anthem for doomed youth'.

The letter printed is reproduced in full below, with the title, 'What passing bells for those who die as cattle?' (a line from Wilfred Owen's First World War poem 'Anthem for Doomed Youth'). That's how I felt about the events. The Liverpool supporters had not been treated as human beings at the ground; they had suffered appallingly. The letter read: Tragically it is all too redolent of the appalling events at Hillsborough last Saturday.

Of course we must establish the cause of the catastrophe – examine the organisation, the role of the police and stewards, the motivation and effects of ticketless Liverpool fans close to kick-off outside the ground, crowd control inside the Leppings Lane end, and the effect of the so-called "safety fences".

Most of all, the lessons must be learned, recommendations must be implemented; no price can be too high for the lives lost.

I doubt whether Hillsborough can be quite the same place again. In my view, Sheffield Wednesday should:

- Remove the fences.
- Never again use the central section of terrace at Leppings Lane; it should be replaced with seats at the earliest opportunity – but the front section should not be occupied by spectators ever again.
- Place a suitable memorial to those supporters who lost their lives at the Leppings Lane end of the ground.
- Above all to demonstrate their remorse, compassion, sensitivity and concern to ensure that appropriate measures are thoroughly implemented.

Football supporters are not cattle, their dignity and that of the game in general must be restored. Sheffield Wednesday Football Club has a major part to play – please play it.'

Were there ticketless fans outside the turnstiles? In the media immediately after the tragedy, this question had been raised. It would appear there were some. A turnstile operator, 19-year-old Stephen Copeland, said that fans who came prior to 2pm came 'early enough' but that 'it went from calm to mayhem' after around 2pm.

He estimated that 150 to 200 fans passed through his turnstile without tickets, had tickets for the wrong end, or jumped or 'tailgated' in. He acknowledged these numbers were a guess and overestimated by 65 per cent when questioned at the inquest. (*Liverpool Echo* report of the Hillsborough inquest, 16 September 2014).

In his autobiography, Martin Edwards, Manchester United chairman, commented, 'Alex [Ferguson] and I made a special point of visiting Anfield shortly after the Hillsborough disaster to show our grief and personal support for Liverpool Football Club on behalf of everybody associated with Manchester United. We arrived quietly to pay our respects, away from the media glare, and brought with us a sizeable donation for the Hillsborough Disaster Appeal fund. This terrible tragedy could have befallen any team's supporters.' (*Red Glory*, Martin Edwards, Michael O'Mara Books, 2017).

Across the country, football clubs held a one-minute silence before games took place the following Saturday, 22 April, in memory of the Liverpool supporters who died at Hillsborough. Deepest sympathies were extended to the relatives of the victims and to the injured.

In the Chelsea programme for that day's game against Everton, chairman Ken Bates said on the page devoted to his normal column, 'In Memoriam, Hillsborough, Saturday 15th April 1989'. His stark words were in large white lettering on a black background.

Immediately underneath in bold black lettering on a white background, it read, 'The people deserve a full inquiry – not a whitewash.'

Club supporters' fanzines shared that view. *A Kick Up the Rs* (Queens Park Rangers) had a 'Hillsborough Special', the front cover a graphic of a tearful QPR player and the words, 'We've witnessed your triumphs and envied them, now we've witnessed your sufferings and we share them.'

The front cover of the magazine *When Saturday Come*s had the headline, 'Hillsborough: Unanimous Verdict' with four photographs immediately below: Graham Kelly, FA chief executive; Prime Minister Margaret Thatcher; Chief Constable of South Yorkshire Police, Peter Wright; and a crowd of supporters standing on the terraces.

The first three images included a speech bubble, 'It wasn't our fault'. The speech bubble for the crowd read, 'Oh well, it must be our fault again'. It was anything but. The point made that the authorities appeared to be distancing themselves from responsibility.

Fences were removed, in time seats replaced the terracing at the Leppings Lane end, the central section used like any other part of the ground. A memorial was eventually erected nearly ten years after the event and placed away from Leppings Lane, positioned on the Parkside Road side of the ground.

The outpouring of grief, the flowers and tributes outside the Leppings Lane end of the ground, the carpet of flowers and tributes that covered the pitch at Anfield. It was overwhelming.

Liverpool manager Kenny Dalglish ensured the club was represented at all 96 funerals. Dalglish went to many himself, including four in one day, along with players from the club.

Thirty years later, Dalglish said, 'I never, ever forget what happened. But if it was difficult for us, imagine what the families are going through. They sacrificed their lives.' (*Daily Mirror*, 15 April 2019). The newspaper commented, 'It is the way he carried a club and city through their darkest hour which remains his greatest achievement.'

Dalglish acknowledged that Hillsborough and its aftermath had been a major factor in his surprise decision to leave the manager's job at Liverpool in February 1991.

The first game at Hillsborough after the disaster was against West Ham United – an evening kick-off on 9 May. I had to go. During the walk to the ground, you could have heard a pin drop. No one was talking, just looking at the stadium where the tragedy had unfolded more than three weeks earlier. It was silent except for three away supporters who were shouting their team's songs – they shouted rather than sang. They were unresponsive to requests asking them to show respect. Unbelievable.

For me, the whole impact of the disaster was one of disbelief. It had occurred at my ground, I'd stood on those terraces, I'd enjoyed watching football there. But it had happened. Before the game, I had to walk round outside the ground from Penistone Road before we went into the North Stand. It felt unreal as I walked to the Leppings Lane end.

Arriving at the Leppings Lane entrances, I stood and looked at the scene – at the turnstiles, at the gates. I have little doubt I must have shook my head – I know I was lost in the moment. Or rather the minutes, and my eyes welled up. I said a prayer before I moved away and walked to the North Stand entrances.

The game? I recollect it being played in a subdued, almost sombre atmosphere. Wednesday did not play well. I'm not sure that West Ham played much better. I think the occasion may well have got to the players. In the end, the visitors won 2-0. So what.

The programme cover for that game had a photograph of the many flowers and mementoes laid at the Leppings Lane gates in the aftermath of the tragedy. On the inside page, 'A message from the Reverend Gordon L. Wilson, Sheffield Wednesday FC Club Chaplain', with club chairman Bert

McGee stating on the following page, 'What happened here at our beloved Sheffield Wednesday's ground on Saturday 15th April was a horror we can never forget. I find it difficult now to consciously accept those terrible happenings.

My thoughts and heartfelt feelings are with the bereaved who lost their loved ones – many so young as not yet to have enjoyed the flower of their youth.'

The Hillsborough Disaster Appeal was highlighted in the programme. By the time it closed, it was reported to have raised over £12 million.

That first game at Hillsborough after the disaster had to be played. In the games that followed, the normal matchday atmosphere started to return. But the disaster could not be forgotten. I'm sure the Sheffield Wednesday board of directors have never forgotten, and will never forget, the events of that Saturday, although it took more years than many had hoped for the creation of a memorial to those who lost their lives at the ground.

Liverpool won the rearranged semi-final against Nottingham Forest, setting up an all-Merseyside FA Cup Final. In the programme for that game, FA chairman Bert Millichip commented, 'The Football Association was faced with the choice of calling off the competition or continuing in what would clearly be difficult circumstances. We believe that we made the right decision, not only as a memorial to those who died but as a means of providing concrete support for those left to grieve their passing.'

The next time Liverpool played at Hillsborough was the following season against Wednesday in November 1989. An evening kick-off. The away supporters in the upper tier of the West Stand at the Leppings Lane end. I felt I needed to be there to pay my respects.

Before the game, Alan Hansen, representing Liverpool, and Chris Turner, representing Wednesday, walked to the centre circle to lay wreathes. There was a minute's silence to honour the memory of those who had died. It was observed impeccably – except from the away end part way through that minute, there was a loud, plaintive, heart-wrenching shout and scream from a lone voice. I couldn't decipher the words. I could feel the emotion that came with it. It was raw and heartfelt.

It was clear following the tragedy that the way fans watched football had to change – the time-honoured ritual of standing on the terraces had become outdated. The Taylor Report made recommendations that included all major stadiums (Divisions One and Two) converting to all-seater; fences being removed; the required number of turnstiles installed in each section of the ground; the number and testing of crush barriers made mandatory; and alcohol sales restricted. Costly recommendations to implement but undoubtedly necessary.

The search for justice for the grieving families has been a long and difficult road. The headline in the *Liverpool Echo*, 'Hillsborough: The shameless smears, lies and cover-ups' (26 April 2016) encapsulates in a few words what had been done from the day of the disaster, through the decades that followed, to prevent the truth from being told.

Writing in the *Daily Mail* (29 November 2019) – the day after David Duckenfield, the match commander at Hillsborough, was cleared of the manslaughter of those supporters who lost their lives, under the headline 'Is No One to Blame', chief sportswriter Jeff Powell, who was at the game, reflected on being in the gymnasium where the bodies were taken. 'Still. Silent. Heads bowed … We were struggling to comprehend the scale of the disaster we had just witnessed. It defies belief that now, 30 years later, relatives of the 96 victims are still bereft of the closure which might apply some spreading of balm upon their grief. The memories live on. Vivid. Haunting. Indelible.'

# Chapter 12
# Players

AT THE dawn of the 1980s, the age-old way of starting a career in football – being taken on as an apprentice, learning your trade, as well as undertaking menial jobs at the club – was well established. The usual route involved being 'spotted' by a scout while playing boys' football for a representative team and then invited for a trial at the professional club. It was the tried and tested method.

From 1983, the introduction of YTS (Youth Training Scheme) provided clubs with the opportunity to take young players on using a new method. The government paid a training allowance as part of the scheme.

There were exceptions to the rule – not least Eric Nixon. In 1985, whilst working at a Ford dealership in Manchester, Nixon dreamt of being a footballer. His shift finished at 3pm on a Friday afternoon, he headed home, the route taking him by Manchester City's Maine Road ground. Impulsively, Nixon stopped his car at the ground and decided to go for it.

'I suddenly decided that I would go in and ask if they would give me a trial. No one else was going to do it for me … so I had to do it myself. It took a lot of balls. Once inside, I walked across the plush carpet and climbed up about 15 steps to a reception area where Julia and Libby, the secretaries, worked.

'Julia looked at me with surprise, clearly not expecting a fit, 6ft 4in, 15 stone young man in an Auto-Cleanse t-shirt at that time of day. I stood in front of them and announced that I wanted a trial with Manchester City. 'I'm a local keeper. Any chance of you watching me?'

After a few moments, Julia replied, 'No one asks for a trial like that!'

My response was to the point, 'Well, I just have. I'm Eric, I'm a goalkeeper and I'm here!' (*Big Hands Big Heart*, Eric Nixon, Trinity Mirror Sport Media, 2012).

Three men emerged – Ken Barnes, Tony Book and Denis Law, each of them a City legend. They talked with Nixon, asked questions. He couldn't quite believe it. He played for his local team the following day and on Sunday morning. On Monday morning, he got a call asking him if he could play for Manchester City reserves that evening.

From there, his career took off. He amassed over 650 first-team appearances for 13 clubs, including Manchester City, Tranmere Rovers and Sheffield Wednesday.

Transfers of players between clubs were an integral part of the game – not all were straightforward. In March 1985, Alan Ball, then manager at Portsmouth, signed Mickey Quinn from Oldham Athletic. Ball later recalled, 'Quinn's arrival came after I rejected the offer of a £25,000 bung for another player. The lad had been playing for us on loan and had done quite well. Mr [John] Deacon [the chairman] called me into the old boardroom and said he had agreed a £75,000 fee with the player's agent. I just said, "Mr Chairman, I don't wish to take him."

'The agent suggested we have a talk outside. He said my chairman was happy, the player was happy and there was £25,000 for me. It was the first time I had encountered agents.

I turned it down. My heart was set on Quinny.' (*Playing Extra Time*, Alan Ball, Sidgwick & Jackson, 2004).

In the close season of 1983, Bob Bolder, then Sheffield Wednesday's goalkeeper, described how he left the club. 'Times were different then. We didn't have agents in those days, so players could ring around the clubs and see if they wanted you. You had to do it all yourself.

'It was all new to me and I was quite naive on that side of things. I was out of contract and Liverpool came out of the blue and Wednesday didn't offer anything substantial anyway to keep me there or make me feel wanted. If Wednesday had offered a good bit of money and a signing-on fee, I would probably have signed.' (*The Star*, 14 October 2019).

Barry Venison's move from Sunderland to Liverpool at the start of the 1986/87 season was secured in similar circumstances. The Liverpool programme for the first game of the season had a page on their new player, revealing, 'When his contract was up at Sunderland, he wrote to every First Division club and received replies from Sheffield Wednesday, Luton Town, Oxford United, Coventry City, Watford and Liverpool.' Venison had no hesitation in joining Liverpool.

The agent Eric Hall, who readily acknowledged he knew nothing about football, became involved with the game and its players during the 1980s. His first client was Steve Perryman at Tottenham Hotspur. Initially, Hall's involvement was in obtaining outside commercial deals for his clients before it extended to taking on negotiations of players' contracts.

For Perryman, Hall had an idea for the player to host a programme on the commercial station Radio Luxembourg, where a big-name guest talked about a specific year and records were played from it. Hall persuaded Braun Electronics to sponsor the programme. For a 12-week series, Perryman received £50,000 – a substantial sum in 1983.

On his dealings with players and club chairmen, Hall makes specific reference to Robert Chase (Norwich City) and Irving Scholar (Tottenham Hotspur), not because they were difficult negotiators – the reverse. 'I could deal with men like Scholar and Chase forever,' Hall said (*Monster!*, Eric Hall, Boxtree, 1998).

It was reported that until the end of the 1970s, most players at Manchester United would talk directly with the manager about contracts and wages. By the end of the following decade, it was common practice for players' agents to deal directly with the club's chief executive on such matters.

Commenting on football agents, Manchester United manager Alex Ferguson observed, 'It's a rat race and the rats are winning.'

Chris Waddle's career is interesting. Whilst working in a small seasoning factory in the North East, he joined non-league Tow Law Town at the end of the 1970s.

Having impressed, Newcastle United expressed interest in signing Waddle and were quoted a fee of £30,000. Knowing Waddle's one-year contract expired at the end of the season, the Magpies decided to wait and sign him for the start of the 1980/81 campaign – paying their non-league neighbours a total of £1,000.

After five seasons at St James' Park, Waddle was keen to move on. Tottenham Hotspur expressed an interest in signing him. In these pre-Bosman times, a tribunal determined the transfer fee. A three-man tribunal sat at Preston North End's ground, Deepdale, listening separately to each of the three parties involved (Waddle, Newcastle and Tottenham) before calling the parties in to advise of their decision on the fee.

Waddle said he wanted to move to a club that offered him the chance to play in European games. Newcastle had highlighted Waddle's talents to the tribunal and were looking for a fee of £2 million. Tottenham contended that Waddle was not the finished article and was only worth £200,000.

The tribunal determined the fee for Waddle should be £595,000. On hearing this assessment, Newcastle manager Jack Charlton stood up and said, 'You three haven't got a clue' and walked out. ('The Owl Sanctuary' – Chris Waddle Podcast – 6 December 2018).

Waddle played for the north London club for four seasons, then signed a seven-year contract that would have kept him at the club until he was 36. Within months, in July 1989, he was at the Wimbledon tennis championships with team-mate Paul Walsh. The latter received a call from agent Dennis Roach, who wanted to talk to Waddle. Roach said Waddle should 'be at White Hart Lane tomorrow morning at 10am'.

Not convinced, Waddle wanted to know what it was all about. Roach said a club had put in a bid that had been accepted by Tottenham Hotspur. More would be revealed the following morning.

Waddle arrived at the ground with his agent and met with chairman Irving Scholar, manager Terry Venables and Roach. He was told Marseille had come in for him and had offered £2 million, which had been turned down by the club. Marseille came back and asked how much they would have to pay for Waddle's transfer. They were quoted £4.5 million – and within ten minutes were back on the telephone to confirm the deal. Waddle was transferred to Marseille.

Marseille was a great experience for Waddle, albeit with significant cultural differences. In England, it was the norm for players to go out for a night together and enjoy drinking

*Floral tributes cover the pitch at Anfield following the Hillsborough disaster,*
*April 1989*

*Kenny Dalglish,
Liverpool manager,
Hillsborough, 15 April
1989*

*Bent and twisted
fencing at the foot
of the Leppings
Lane terrace in the
aftermath of the
Hillsborough disaster,
15 April 1989*

*A police officer attempts to shield the heat from his face as he runs in front of the blazing Main Stand, Valley Parade, Bradford, 11 May 1985*

*A cross made from charred timbers provides the backdrop to a memorial service at Valley Parade, Bradford, 21 July 1985*

*Riot police and fans clash, Heysel, 29 May 1985*

*Supporters leave flowers at the Heysel Stadium to commemorate the first anniversary, 29 May 1986*

*Liverpool's coaching team of Chris Lawler, Roy Evans, manager Joe Fagan and Ronnie Moran celebrate winning the European Cup, Rome, 30 May 1984*

*Everton celebrate winning the FA Cup, Wembley 19 May, 1984*

*Coventry City striker Keith Houchen scores with a diving header to level the score at 2-2 during the FA Cup Final against Tottenham Hotspur, 16 May 1987*

*Aston Villa's Gary Shaw (8) and Gordon Cowans celebrate with goalscorer Peter Withe, European Cup Final, Rotterdam, 1982*

*Naranjito mascot for the 1982 World Cup finals*

*England's Bulldog Bobby mascot for the 1982 World Cup in Spain received criticism for its aggressive image*

*Argentina's Diego Maradona scores his 'Hand of God' goal against England goalkeeper Peter Shilton, World Cup quarter-final, 22 June 1986*

alcohol. This was not the way in France. If they went out, it was water and coffee on the menu. They did not understand how players could train the morning after a night drinking alcohol.

At the club was an eight-foot-high fridge crammed full of bottles of water for the players after a game. This was not what Waddle was used to. 'Any chance you can just fill it up with lager and Guinness, just once?' he asked Marseille boss Bernard Tapie.

After the next home game, Waddle found a fridge full of Heineken and Guinness, and players enjoying a drink in the Jacuzzi. Tapie approached,

'Mr Waddle.'

'Yes.'

'You happy now?'

'Very happy.'

'One week only!' ('The Owl Sanctuary' – Chris Waddle – Podcast – 6 December 2018).

Interestingly, many of the French players smoked cigarettes, which they did not consider to be as bad as drinking alcohol.

Waddle acknowledged it was a great learning curve in France. He considered Marseille ahead of their time in a range of areas such as diet, including yoghurt for breakfast (instead of the sausage and bacon he'd been used to), taking regular blood samples and even highlighting the ice cream that should be eaten – coconut because it 'gives you more energy'.

Highlighting his own transfer, Trevor Francis observed, 'My move from Nottingham Forest took place right at the end of 1979/80 and I couldn't understand why I was being sold. I realised that only one voice [Brian Clough] mattered at the City Ground. When any manager decides it is time for you to go, then it's time to go.' He signed for Manchester City on a three-year contract worth £100,000 a year plus bonuses (*One in a Million: The Autobiography*, Trevor Francis with Keith Dixon, Pitch Publishing, 2019).

Carlton Palmer, the West Bromwich Albion midfielder who joined as a YTS trainee, commented that after five years with the club he turned up for training as normal one day when he and two other players – David Burrows and Steve Bull – were told to go to the main ground. He had no idea the purpose of the summons. 'None of us knew what was happening ... David Burrows was the first one into the office. He came out about five minutes later.

"What happened?" I said.

"I'm out," he replied.

"Out?"

"Transferred."

"Why?"

"We're skint."

"Who are?"

"We are. Albion are. They need to sell us for the money."

"F*****g hell. Where are you going?"

"Liverpool, I think."

"What about us?"

"F**k knows."

"You're next CP. Better go in."

'I went in and was told Chelsea and Sheffield Wednesday had put in offers for me.' (*It is What it is: The Carlton Palmer Story*, Carlton Palmer with Steven Jacobi, Vertical Editions, 2017).

Palmer had no thoughts of a transfer at that time. Financial circumstances at West Bromwich Albion dictated a move. Palmer chose Sheffield Wednesday, Bull moved to Wolverhampton Wanderers.

Ricky Hill, the Luton Town player and England international, reflected on the circumstances of his departure from Kenilworth Road after 13 years' service in 1989. When Luton boss Ray Harford promised him a free transfer he set up a move to France, ' … only to find chairman David Evans demanding a fee of £115,000. Evans refused to leave his office and greet the delegation from Le Havre. Hill settled the impasse by using £50,000 of his own money to buy out his contract, waiving a £30,000 signing-on fee. 'The deceit hurt,' said Hill, 'To do this to me after I'd given my best years to this club. If I'd been penniless, I didn't want to work for those people again.' (*Daily Mail*, 28 March 2019).

On the other hand, there are examples of clubs providing payments to players they transferred – at Aston Villa, Mark Walters was transferred to Glasgow Rangers in December 1987 – a fee of £575,000 payable within seven days by the Scottish club and a further £20,000 payable after Walters's first five full international appearances for the England team. As part of the transfer, Villa agreed an *ex gratia* payment to Walters of £25,000.

A month later, Simon Stainrod was transferred to Stoke City – a fee of £100,000, payable with £57,500 on the signing of the transfer agreement and 12 monthly payments of £3,541.66. Villa agreed an *ex gratia* payment to the player of £15,000.

Operating at the other end of the scale as manager of Orient, Frank Clark reflected on his time trying to bring players to the club and the difficulty of doing so with very little money available. He pointed to the case of Northern Ireland striker Colin Clarke, given a free transfer by Peterborough United, who Clark wanted to sign. The Orient manager persuaded Clarke not to take a signing-on fee but the stumbling block was the weekly wage. Clarke wanted £220 a week, Orient would only offer £200 a week. No deal. The player went on to enjoy great success at club and international level, later transferring to First Division Southampton for £800,000.

Some reported information about other players – future England international Tony Cottee, an apprentice at West Ham United in 1980, was on £20 a week, three years later, as a professional, it increased to £110 a week. In October 1980, Manchester United signed Garry Birtles from Nottingham Forest for a reported fee of £1,250,000, wages of £800 a week and a signing-on fee of £75,000. Neville Southall joined Everton from Bury in 1981 on £300 a week and Paul Gascoigne moved from Newcastle United to Tottenham Hotspur in 1988 on a reported £4,000 a week.

One transfer stood out. Danish international Allan Simonsen joined Second Division Charlton Athletic from Barcelona for a reported £250,000 in November 1982, with the player on a reported £82,000 a season for two years.

In the other direction, there were high-profile players leaving England to ply their trade abroad, most notably in Italy. These included Mark Hateley and Ray Wilkins (AC Milan), Liam Brady and Ian Rush (Juventus), and Graeme Souness and Trevor Francis (Sampdoria). These transfers came at a time when English clubs were banned from playing in European competition.

At a lower level, Tommy Tynan, who played for Sheffield Wednesday, Lincoln City, Newport County and Plymouth Argyle, amongst others, has an interesting perspective. 'Players' wives and girlfriends cause a lot of problems within football. A lot of backstabbing comes from players' wives. Players tell their wives certain things; players tell other players something different; and wives tell other wives the original version again. My missus has always told me more about my team-mates than

I have learnt from them myself. Women tend to be a lot more open and honest than men when they chat among themselves. When wives find out that other wives' husbands are on more money, it causes problems, rifts, because certain wives want to outdo certain other wives.' (*Tommy: A Life at the Soccer Factory*, Tommy Tynan with Richard Cowdery, Bud Books, 1990).

The nature of football in the 1980s meant that the hardmen in each team could make their presence felt and indeed flourish. The Everton team that won the First Division title in 1984/85 was a first-rate, quality footballing side. But they could look after themselves.

Reviewing the film *Howard's Way*, which focused on Howard Kendall's Everton in the 1980s, Simon Hart comments, 'Younger viewers might shudder at the tackles and even [Adrian] Heath is taken aback when reviewing the force of Sheffield Wednesday midfielder Brian Marwood's challenge which did severe damage to his right knee ligaments, ending his season in December 1984. [Peter] Reid's revenge "tackle", which led to Marwood being carried off in turn, draws a wince too.' (*When Saturday Comes*, January 2020).

Keith Hackett, the FIFA international referee, comments, 'The more renowned iron men have usually been either defenders or midfield players – Jimmy Case, for example. He can be a fairly violent player. That can be seen by the number of cautions he has received ... Gerry Gow was a mighty hard man. But that was his role – to put himself about and put the fear of God into opponents. But I do not think they were cynical. Clumsy maybe, but not cynical. They invariably had the ball in mind.' (*Hackett's Law*, Keith Hackett, Collins Willow, 1986).

You'd complain readily when the hard men transgressed against your own team, albeit took a different view if they played for your team.

My hard men XI:

Ray Clemence – Could look after himself in goal, no liberties taken by forwards

Stuart Pearce – Had the tag 'psycho' – no prisoners

Kenny Burns – Enjoyed preventing an attacking player passing him

Brian Kilcline – 'Killer' – fearsome tackling, swashbuckling

Keith Stevens – 'Rhino' of The Den, fearless

Mark Ward – Terrier-like, very much up for the physical challenge

Jimmy Case – Strong, determined and very capable in the tackle

Graeme Souness – Has been described as 'the hardest player of his generation'

Vinnie Jones – Took no prisoners, made his presence felt

David Speedie – Referred to as 'a firebrand', kept defenders on their toes

Roy McDonough – Felt every crunching challenge

Subs: Ron Harris, Mark Dennis, Terry Hurlock, Gerry Gow, Julian Dicks

Apprentices, YTS players, hardmen and transfers were all part of the game.

For some players, at what they thought was the start of a dream career, there was a problem – an horrendous problem that only reached public attention in 2016 ... some men involved in youth coaching or scouting took the opportunity to abuse boys in their charge.

It was an outrageous and flagrant breach of trust.

One individual who was convicted was former youth coach Barry Bennell, who faced 43 charges relating to 12 former junior players between 1979 and 1990 during his time working with Manchester City and Crewe Alexandra.

Bennell has been described as one of the country's most prolific paedophiles and was jailed for 31 years. It was his fourth conviction for abusing boys. Since his conviction, another 86 people have come forward to make complaints against him.

There have been more allegations since those first raised. Some of the accused have died, some are being investigated and some are going through the justice system.

The impact on the boys concerned is difficult to imagine. The details that came out from former professional footballers were harrowing, the emotional distress and mental impact stark.

Coming towards the end of a career, for one-club men in particular, testimonials could provide an important source of income – Brian Little of Aston Villa had to retire from the game and his testimonial against an England team at Villa Park in May 1982 made £25,000 from a crowd of 9,229. Three days later, an England team provided £17,000 for Fulham's Les Strong at Craven Cottage.

In May 1984 at Old Trafford, Lou Macari's testimonial between his current and previous clubs – Manchester United and Celtic – drew a crowd of 40,140 and record receipts of £85,000 for a testimonial in this country.

Mark Smith's testimonial at Hillsborough in 1987 against Sheffield United attracted 10,800 with receipts of £20,000.

Other testimonials were less well attended. A reported 1,007 spectators were present at Alan Warboys's testimonial game between Doncaster Rovers and Sheffield Wednesday at Belle Vue in May 1982.

And once football careers were over? Players went into a myriad of different occupations. A small number stayed in the game as scouts, coaches or managers and some became agents. Peter Springett became a police officer, Neil Webb and Brendan Ormsby postmen, David May a wine importer, Eric Gates ran a farm, Larry Lloyd became a publican and some had a spell in prison – Mickey Thomas and Mark Ward.

# Chapter 13

# Managers

KEITH HACKETT, the former top referee, provides an interesting insight in his book (*Hackett's Law*, Keith Hackett, Collins Willow, 1986), recalling an exchange with then Arsenal manager Terry Neill in the 1980 FA Cup semi-final against Liverpool. Both Neill and Reds boss Bob Paisley had come to hand in their teamsheets to Hackett before the game. 'As the pair were leaving, I wished them luck and hoped they would enjoy the game. "Enjoy the game?" said Neill, who was always immaculately dressed, "We'll be dying out there. It's a bloody semi-final. How can we enjoy it?"'

The manager's job was undoubtedly tough and challenging, and starting to come under increasing media scrutiny as the decade progressed. And the job was insecure. For Stan Ternent, manager of Blackpool, then in the Third Division, the beginning of the decade proved a difficult time, with growing rumours he would be sacked and replaced by 1966 World Cup hero Alan Ball. The rumours became reality, the Blackpool board even allowing Ball to conduct business more than 5,000 miles away while he was still at Vancouver Whitecaps. In *The Sun*, reporter John Sadler could not contain his anger at how the club was being run. 'The Blackpool board have betrayed Stan Ternent by bringing in Alan Ball behind his back. At one point, Ternent had to remind the players his contract was valid until June 1980.'

The most successful manager in English football history, Bob Paisley, retired from Liverpool at the end of the 1982/83 season, the club having won six league championships, three European Cups, one UEFA Cup and three League Cups.

In his obituary of Paisley, Ivan Ponting commented, 'A meticulous planner, clever tactician and shrewd judge of a player, he never stopped preaching to his charges the traditional Shankly gospel of passing and movement, controlling the ball and finding space to receive a return dispatch, always supporting the man in possession and, above all, working until they could barely stand ... Though undoubtedly hard when the occasion demanded – as plenty of former Liverpool stars could testify – Paisley was essentially a kind, caring man who, as Brian Clough remarked, proved the fallacy of the myth that nice guys win nothing.

'As he had promised so self-effacingly, Bob Paisley had done his best – and it turned out to be better than anyone else's.' (*The Book of Football Obituaries*, Ivan Ponting, Pitch Publishing, 2012).

Joe Fagan replaced Paisley as manager from within the club – the famous Boot Room. Further success followed, including a treble in his first season – European Cup, league championship and League Cup. Kenny Dalglish succeeded Fagan in 1985/86, again from within, and maintained the success of his predecessors with three First Division titles, two FA Cups and the double in 1985/86.

Brian Clough at Nottingham Forest was the only manager to remain with the same club in the Football League throughout the decade, all of it in the First Division. His tenure at the club lasted 18 years (1975–1993).

Overall, clubs continued to change their managers at a significant rate during the decade – the average number of managers per club in the First Division was four in the 1980s. Clough was the obvious exception, although both Southampton and West Ham United had only two managers during the decade – John Lyall leaving Upton Park in 1989 after 16 years in charge.

At the other end of the scale, both Queens Park Rangers and West Bromwich Albion made eight changes in the 1980s. In Albion's case, Ron Atkinson had two spells in charge of the club during that decade.

Brian Clough's most successful period at Nottingham Forest came in the late 1970s and early 1980s. The departure of his right-hand man, Peter Taylor, had a major impact in 1982, when Taylor left the club with a £25,000 golden handshake. Taylor returned in the summer of that year to manage Derby County, the club that brought the Clough-Taylor partnership their earliest successes.

Clough was a man apart, idiosyncratic in many ways. This exchange with Chris Cattlin, manager of Brighton & Hove Albion, illustrates the point. Cattlin wanted to purchase Danny Wilson from Nottingham Forest. He called Clough one Sunday and was met with:

'Do you know what day it is?'

'I said, "Yes, and it's a Sunday in Brighton as well."

'He said, "What do you want?" and I said, "I want to buy Danny Wilson."

'He goes, "I've told you, I paid Chesterfield £250,000 for him."

'I said, "Well, I've only got £30,000." And it went silent. Then he said, "Get forty-grand over in the morning or clear off and never speak to me again."'

Cattlin managed to persuade his chairman Mike Bamber to get the additional £10,000 and Wilson was on his way to the Goldstone Ground – 'and he was terrific for us.' (Brighton & Hove Albion programme, 4 January 2020).

Mark Crossley, the Nottingham Forest goalkeeper, reflected on a pre-match incident between Forest and Wimbledon at the City Ground. The Dons changing room was becoming increasingly noisy with their 'ghetto-blaster' volume turned up. Clough told Alan Hill to ask their visitors politely to turn the volume down. Two requests were made, both times the volume was turned up higher. 'The gaffer could stand it no longer. He knocked on the door, brushed past Vinnie [Jones] and, to the astonishment of the Wimbledon lads, picked the ghetto blaster up and smashed it on the floor. He said, "Now try and play your f*****g music" and left. The Wimbledon lads were all stunned to put it mildly. We won 4-1.' (*Big Norm Looking After No. 1*, Mark Crossley, 2011).

In his book of *Football Obituaries*, Ivan Ponting comments, 'He specialised in taking unfashionable clubs and unconsidered players by the metaphorical scruff of the neck (actually in the case of certain individuals it wasn't so metaphorical) and inspired them to undreamed-of heights. Clough transformed Derby County, then Nottingham Forest from comparative nonentities into league champions before, incredibly, leading the latter to two European Cup triumphs … throughout the pomp of his headline-hogging, ceaselessly stormy career, soccer's most celebrated maverick.' (Pitch Publishing, 2012).

Ron Saunders, the tough disciplinarian manager at Aston Villa when they won the First Division championship, was interviewed on a Saturday night football highlights show on ITV on the evening of 2 May 1981, hours after he led his club to the title. Known for his stern personality, Saunders was asked if he would give the viewers a smile. No chance. 'Life's not just about laughing, football is a serious business,' was his response.

In an era of increasingly high-profile and media-friendly football club managers, Saunders was the antithesis. 'Saunders carried the aura of the barrack room. He drove his players hard: pre-season training was built on hours of running up and down sand dunes and he demanded absolute loyalty to the team cause.' (Obituary, *The Times*, 11 December 2019). Illustrating Saunders's uneasy relationship with chairman Doug Ellis at Villa Park, for an away game at Old Trafford, 'he instructed the team coach to leave Villa Park for Manchester on the stroke of 10, even though Ellis had not arrived. When he turned into the car park at 10.05am to discover the coach had left, he was furious. Saunders had made his point – the players knew who was in charge.'

Saunders resigned on a point of principle in 1982 and within days was appointed at city rivals Birmingham City. Four years at St Andrews did not produce success and after leaving the Blues in 1986, Saunders joined West Bromwich Albion. He is the only manager to have taken charge of all three clubs in the second city.

Frank Clark reflected on his managerial experiences in the early 1980s as assistant manager to Ken Knighton at Sunderland. He reflected that Knighton and he had clashed with chairman Tom Cowie, the latter apparently focused on containing costs at the club. For a big Boxing Day fixture, the manager wanted the players to stay in a hotel on the night before the game. Cowie said the club couldn't afford it. Knighton found a local hotel at £10 a room and leaked the story to a local journalist that the manager was having to pay for the players' stay at the hotel, hoping to shame the chairman into picking up the bill.

'It was a big mistake and the whole thing backfired. Cowie went along with it and just said, "Ken, that's a great idea. If you want to pay for the hotel then you go ahead and do it." For the want of a bit of common sense on both sides, they ended up having a big row played out in the pages of the press.' (*Kicking with Both Feet*, Frank Clark, Headline, 2000).

Knighton and Clark were sacked in April 1981, their pay stopped immediately and their cars taken off them. They had 15 months left on their contract but the club offered them a 'pitiful amount'. They took the case to a tribunal but the club paid up in full the day before the hearing.

In August 1981, Knighton and Clark were appointed to similar positions at Third Division Orient. Clark pointed out that as assistant manager at a lower-league club with very little money available, 'assistant' meant 'general dogsbody' – looking after kit, hiring a minibus for the team and acting as co-driver to and from games.

Clark's differing experiences at Sunderland and Orient prompted him to think about the way clubs treated managers, ultimately leading to the formation of the League Managers Association. Clark pointed to himself, Howard Wilkinson, Lawrie McMenemy and Graham Taylor as the prime movers in its formation, which came about in 1992.

There was a different development for a small number of managers in the 1980s – becoming a director as well as manager of their football club. In the programme for the Bristol derby at Ashton Gate in September 1987, it stated, 'Gerry Francis (Rovers) shares with Terry Cooper (City) the benefits of being a manager with director status. Any doubts about his commitment to the Club have been dispelled by him putting his own money into what can hardly be termed a shrewd investment.'

Managers had different motivation techniques with players. Allan Clarke, then manager of Barnsley, took it upon himself to take his players to a local colliery 'to show them how hard their supporters work for their wages'. There was no immediate dividend on the field as they lost their next game.

Jock Stein, the legendary Celtic manager of the 1960s and 1970s, was manager of the Scotland national team in the 1980s, having been appointed in 1978. He was in charge and in the dugout – along with his assistant Alex Ferguson – for the momentous World Cup qualifying game against Wales at Ninian Park in September 1985. The game was broadcast live on television. It ended 1-1, with Wales knocked out and the Scots progressing to an eliminator to qualify for the 1986 World Cup tournament in Mexico.

But it is the tragedy of Stein's collapse in the tunnel at the end of the game and his subsequent death that is remembered most.

Alex Ferguson's managerial career was in its early stages at the start of the 1980s. He was manager at Aberdeen, where he had unprecedented success. It attracted Manchester United's interest and Ferguson succeeded Ron Atkinson at Old Trafford in 1986. His first domestic honour south of the border came in 1989/90 with the FA Cup. Ferguson went on to dominate football, winning trophies like no other manager before or since.

# Chapter 14

# Referees

REFEREES HAD to deal with a myriad of issues in the 1980s – not least the potential threat of hooliganism, pitch invasions and missiles thrown from the terraces. The game, the safety of players and officials were at the forefront of their minds.

Ray Lewis, the referee at the 1989 FA Cup semi-final at Hillsborough, had the most difficult and harrowing experience of them all. Some years later, he was a guest of honour at the end-of-season awards at our boys' football club, Onslow Boys in Guildford.

Before the event we were told he would not talk about Hillsborough … nor should he. That experience and its impact had to be his own. On the evening, Mr Lewis was perfectly amiable and took part in the awards in the same efficient and friendly way he refereed.

Well before the 1980s, there had been a push for the introduction of 'professional referees' – Norman Burtenshaw, an ex-FIFA referee who retired in the 1970s, made the observation that a better description would be 'full-time' referees. The thinking was that the fitness of referees would be more likely to increase if they were focusing on it full time. Professional referees or full-time referees. Not in the 1980s.

On the same theme, Keith Hackett said that if the game had moved to full-time referees he would have had to have given it careful consideration, looking in particular at the financial implications and what he would have done after his refereeing days were over (referees retired from the Football League aged 47).

Referees had full-time jobs and fitted their officiating around their primary source of income. A list of Football League officials from that decade contained referees who were policemen, teachers, accountants, bank managers, personnel managers, newsagents and many others. Accountants made up the greatest number of referees, including Joe Worrall, David Scott, Brian Hill and John Lloyd. One of the more unusual occupations was that shown for Ken Redfern – jewellery importer.

At the age of 27, Mark Halsey, who later went on to become one of the top referees in the Premier League, was considered young when he first embarked on a refereeing career. In 1987, he took the decision to sit the referees' exams to start at what was then the lowest level – Class 3.

Because Halsey had played the game to a reasonable standard, the Mid-Herts Referees Association waived the eight-week training course he would otherwise have had to attend. He said the cost of a referee's kit was £50. For refereeing a Sunday League game, he was paid £15, for being a linesman in the Premier Division of the Herts County League, he was paid £12.50. When he was promoted to referee for a game in the Herts County League, the pay increased to £25.

It was not that much higher at top level – just £35 to referee the FA Cup semi-final in 1980. By 1984/85, it had increased to £43 for Football League and FA Cup games, plus travelling expenses and an overnight stay at a hotel if necessary.

Graham Poll, who in time would become a prominent FIFA referee, was also in the early stages of his career in the 1980s. He reflected on his early days in the Football League as a linesman, a role in which he was inclined to be a little showy. This came to the attention of John Goggins, the Football League Referees' secretary. For the last game of the 1987/88 season, Goggins appointed Poll to run the line for the experienced Neil Midgeley. It worked. Poll learned if he wanted to progress, his showy antics had to end.

The case of Clive White of Harrow, Middlesex is interesting. He made the Football League referees' list in 1973 at the age of 33, the FIFA list in 1978, refereed the FA Cup Final and replay of 1982, and officiated at the World Cup Finals in Spain the same year. A top referee, things looked to be on the up until it was reported he was convicted of deception and he subsequently resigned from the referees' list on 31 July 1982. Interestingly, White's pen portrait in the 1982 FA Cup Final programme was shorter and pithier than any of the pen portraits of his colleagues who refereed in other FA Cup Finals during the decade. It omitted to mention his occupation too.

The decades-long tradition of referees and linesmen wearing predominantly black with white trim was maintained through the 1980s. In 1986/87 the linesmen's flags changed, as noted in a Watford programme in September 1986, 'Flags of the linesmen are of a different design this season. Instead of the red and yellow flags, both flags are now yellow, but upon close inspection, you can see they are made of an "airtex" material, which is like a close-knitted string vest. One of the flags has a solid (i.e. not 'airtex') yellow trim and the other a solid red trim. This is part of an experiment by the League to improve visibility and identification of the flags and so aid the match officials in their duties.'

Red and yellow cards were dropped as a means of sending off and cautioning players in 1981, having been introduced in 1976. They were reintroduced in 1987 after pressure from FIFA.

It's interesting to note the level of women's involvement in officiating started to increase in the 1980s, albeit from a low base. Elisabeth Forsdick ran the line in an FA Cup qualifying match in 1981 and by 1989 Kim George had refereed an FA Cup preliminary-round game, telling *The Times* that she was 'not a strident feminist carrying the banner for women in sport'.

And FIFA President Joao Havelange made this observation about referees, which was a little odd to say the least, after the 1982 World Cup in Spain. 'There were no complaints [about referee selection] before the tournament started, so why complain now?'

On the theme of commenting on referees, under the headline 'Well Done Ref', an article appeared in a Sheffield Wednesday programme in 1987 observing, 'Often the poor old ref is criticised from all sides and ignored if he has a good match. Well done, then, Ray Lewis of Great Bookham, Surrey, who handled the Owls' match at Southampton with great competence.'

But the article did not stop there, adding, 'Wednesday players felt they were very hard done by at Norwich. Ref Alf Buksh upset the Owls with his performance.'

The loudspeaker announcer Keith Valle had his own way of remarking on the referee's performance as the Bristol Rovers and Wigan Athletic players left the pitch after a game in 1989. 'The referee is available for Christmas pantomime or cabaret,' Valle joked.

Observing how Neil Midgeley refereed, Keith Hackett complimented his fellow official over the way he sought to bring players closer to referees. Midgeley had an excellent way of communicating, often with a smile, which paid dividends in his control of a game.

To enhance knowledge and communicate with younger football supporters, Hackett had a feature called 'Whistle Stop' in the popular magazine *Shoot*. Typically, it had illustrations of possible scenarios on the football pitch that a referee might face, and asked what decision should he make. An example: 'During a game, a dog runs on to the pitch and chases the ball. Do you (a) allow the game to continue, or (b) stop play and have the dog removed? Answer – Stop play and have the dog removed.'

One further observation regarding referees focuses on a boys' football game, more precisely an under-eights six-a-side tournament in Surrey. At that time, there was a plethora of such tournaments held in the so-called close season for boys in junior football. In this one, the 'Guildford Saints' tournament, my youngest son Tom played for Onslow Boys, a Guildford-based team. The team made it through to the final of the tournament, where they met Old Coulsden Jets.

Little was known about Old Coulsden Jets, primarily because the Jets were outside the area our teams played in. For reasons I don't recall, it was the visitors to Guildford who were clear favourites for the tournament.

It's worth reflecting on the nature of under-eights football. Many of the boys tend to swarm around the ball like bees, their enthusiasm for the game undeniable, their effort and energy in chasing the ball there for all to see, but the organisation of the team a little lacking.

Much to the chagrin of the Old Coulsden Jets manager and more particularly their players' dads, Onslow Boys had taken the lead with an opportunist strike from distance. This wasn't in their script.

Part way through the second half, the frustration of the Jets contingent at the side of the pitch was becoming increasingly evident. It culminated in one of the dads bellowing across the pitch, 'You've lost control, ref', after a decision went against their team. The eight-year-old lads looked bemused. Some craned their necks backwards and looked up at the referee, who was at least twice their size. The game continued with the referee unruffled by any distractions from self-appointed secondary officials by the side of the pitch.

In truth, the Onslow Boys' dads just laughed – how could a referee lose control of an under-eights six-a-side game? By no stretch of anyone's imagination had the referee done anything other than keep the game flowing and well under control. The real source of amusement for the dads was that the referee was Alan Robinson from Waterlooville. Robinson was wearing his referee's top, adorned with the Football Association badge on its breast pocket. He just happened to have refereed the FA Cup Final at Wembley four seasons earlier between Everton and Liverpool.

And he'd 'lost control' of an under-eights six-a-side tournament final?!!

## Chapter 15

# Control of the Game and Economics

CRISIS. IT is against the backcloth of crisis that football authorities – particularly the Football League – operated for much of the 1980s. A crisis in attendances, a crisis of hooliganism, a crisis of economics, more pressures and regulations from government, costs increasing. No fewer than 15 league clubs had to be rescued from the brink of extinction between 1981 and 1985, including famous names like Wolverhampton Wanderers and Charlton Athletic (twice).

The *Rothmans Football Yearbook* diary entries provide snapshots of the problems faced by clubs in the 1980s:

'6/11/81 – Birmingham City losing £5,000 a week ... reveal liabilities of £1.2 million

27/11/81 – Leicester City announce a loss of £319,000

2/12/81 – Norwich City announce a loss of £327,000. 'I'm afraid there will be hundreds of players on the dole at the end of the season,' says chairman Arthur South. The club sack seven members of the backroom staff

25/1/82 – Darlington *will* fold unless they receive £10,000 within six weeks – Bristol City call in the PFA to thrash out the club's plan to give eight leading players immediate transfers to cut the £350,000 annual wage bill

18/2/82 – Chester announce loss of £137,000 a week

25/2/82 – Hull City with debts of £35,000 call in the receiver

1/3/82 – Halifax Town's playing staff go up for sale

2/4/82 Aldershot announce a loss of £92,000 – Rochdale say they will close unless the next five home matches double their attendance

21/4/82 – Chester have the lowest gate of the season, 1,034, the lowest in their history'

A season on and the same editorial had a more sobering theme, 'The professional game may be on the gallows with the noose of insolvency around its neck, but it has cried wolf so often to threats of financial ruin that its critics remain unimpressed.'

And so it went on. Times were bleak for clubs.

All First and Second Division clubs were affected by the requirements of the Safety of Sports Grounds Act 1975. By 1985, 50 clubs had been 'designated' – requiring them to undertake costly safety work at their grounds, leading to reduced capacities.

A sign of the difficult economic times was reflected in the number of professional contract players registered with the Football League. In 1979, there were 2,025 contract players with Football League clubs. By 1983, the lowest number of 1,575 had been reached. To underline the problems, by 1982 the number of free transfers had increased to 442 – more than 20 per cent of the players registered with the Football League.

The precarious nature of football's finances in the early 1980s seemed at times a weekly concern presented in the pages of the newspapers – the size of debts, a reduction in income as attendances fell and club staff sacked. Even Liverpool were not immune – in May 1982, under the stewardship of Bob Paisley, the club won their 13th league championship. Even so, gates at Anfield were down 25 per cent over two seasons. Winning the league championship in 1983/84, their average attendance had fallen to 31,998.

All this against a background of difficult economic times in the country. There was a deep recession in 1981 as the government tried to control inflation (at 16.4 per cent in 1980). The recession was particularly bad in manufacturing. Unemployment rose to over three million and did not fall below that figure until late 1987 (the jobless rate stood at 11.9 per cent in 1984).

Football clubs operated in this environment – and many did not operate well.

The Professional Footballers' Association came increasingly to the fore, aiding their members and clubs in the process. 'For three or four hectic seasons, the PFA secretary Gordon Taylor seemed to be the chief surgeon of football, dashing around the country to administer the kiss of life and bandage up clubs wounded by debt and despondency. Meanwhile, club chairmen seemed to spend as much time in the courts as they did in the boardrooms, pleading their cases, or begging for a stay of execution.' (*League Football and the men who made it*, Simon Inglis, Collins Willow, 1988).

Clubs tried initiatives to reduce their debts and costs:

– Leeds United, Wolverhampton Wanderers and Preston North End sold their grounds to their local councils.

– Land was sold for redevelopment – for supermarkets at Burnden Park (Bolton Wanderers), Boothferry Park (Hull City), Selhurst Park (Crystal Palace), Old Showground (Scunthorpe United); for flats at Griffin Park (Brentford); houses at Dean Court (Bournemouth); and a pub at Prenton Park (Tranmere Rovers).

– Bristol Rovers and Charlton Athletic were forced to leave their grounds because of escalating costs – moving to Bath City and Crystal Palace respectively to ground share.

– Proposals to combine clubs were made – Fulham and Chelsea; Thames Valley Rangers combining Reading and Oxford United proposed by Robert Maxwell.

Some clubs appeared oblivious to what was going on – at Manchester City, Malcolm Allison was in spend mode, buying Steve Daley from Wolverhampton Wanderers for £1.4 million, Kevin Reeves from Norwich City for £1 million and Michael Robinson from Preston North End for £765,000. City had substantial debts.

At the Football League, Alan Hardaker, the long-standing authoritarian Director General, died of a heart attack in March 1980. The newly elected President of the Football League, Jack Dunnett, described the organisation as a 'beleaguered garrison'.

Following a 'Save our Soccer' consultation with clubs, the Football League passed important resolutions in September 1980:

- From 1981/82 three points for a win instead of two points – to encourage more attacking play – a change that Jimmy Hill, in particular, had been championing.
- The limit on fixtures scheduled for Friday night and Sunday to be raised – this was focused on increasing attendances and reducing crowd violence. The first Sunday game since 1974 was staged in February 1981 at Feethams, a Fourth Division game, Darlington v Mansfield Town, with 5,932 in attendance, trebling their average league gate. By 1987/88, excluding live televised games, in the Football League 27 games were scheduled for Sundays and 102 for Friday nights.

- No club official or secretary to have control of management of more than one league club.
- Each club to have one paid director – each one to be vetted by the Football League and Football Association. The specific point was that a fully professional director/chief executive was needed to handle the increasing responsibilities of individual clubs. Queens Park Rangers, Fulham and Liverpool were the first clubs to appoint a paid director. By the end of 1986, 30 clubs had followed suit.

The Chester Report on the State of Football, requested by the Football League, was published in March 1983. The main recommendations were a reduction of clubs in the First Division and a reorganisation of clubs in the Third and Fourth Divisions to form four regional leagues of 16 clubs. Additionally, it recommended that home clubs retain all the gate money from a game.

That last recommendation was endorsed and implemented at the Football League's AGM in June 1983 – inevitably, the recommendation for home clubs to retain their gate money favoured the bigger clubs with larger attendances, to the detriment of smaller clubs that previously enjoyed a share of large gate receipts generated by bigger crowds.

A reduction of clubs in the First Division was implemented from the end of 1986/87 and completed by the start of 1988/89 – a reduction to 20 clubs in the top flight and an increase to 24 clubs in the Second Division.

There was no change to the organisation and structure of Divisions Three and Four.

Furthermore, the existing system of seeking re-election to the Football League for the bottom four clubs in Division Four continued, a vote taking place at the Football League's

AGM in June each year that also included aspirant clubs from the non-league. The nearest a non-league club came to achieving election to the Football League was in June 1980, when Alliance Premier League club Altrincham polled 25 votes, one fewer than Rochdale, who were re-elected.

This system remained unchanged until the Football League AGM of 1986, when the principle of automatic relegation from Division Four was agreed for implementation at the end of the 1986/87 season, with the relegated club replaced by the non-league club finishing top of their league at the end of each season.

That change was a key one among many agreed at the AGM. The others included:

- The reduction in clubs in the First Division.
- The implementation of a play-off system affecting promotion and relegation at the end of the season.
- Television money – a change in the distribution of the pool of money received from the television companies – Division One – 50 per cent; Division Two – 25 per cent; Division Three and Four – 12.5 per cent.
- Sponsorship money for the Football League – a change in the distribution: Division One – 50 per cent; Division Two – 25 per cent; Division Three and Four – 12.5 per cent (before this change, each of the Football League's 92 clubs received an equal share of sponsorship money).
- Changes to the monies distributed from the pool of receipts from League Cup and FA Cup games.

The changes were to the benefit of First Division clubs, amongst whom there had been agitation, particularly from the so-called 'Big Five', for an increase in monies for clubs in the top flight.

The 'Big Five' – Arsenal, Tottenham Hotspur, Manchester United, Liverpool and Everton – had been rumoured to be discussing setting up a Super League. In October 1985, the *Daily Mail* reported Everton chairman Philip Carter had hosted a meeting at Goodison Park for that purpose with representatives of those clubs. All this was taking place with attendances and gate receipts down, there was no European football, advertising revenue had fallen, alcohol sales were severely restricted and football clubs were under significant cost pressures.

On BBC Radio Sheffield, First Division Sheffield Wednesday's chairman Bert McGee stated he had no prior knowledge of those talks and in response to a question about why he had not been invited, he responded, 'You'll have to ask Philip Carter.'

At Crystal Palace, chairman Ron Noades observed, 'What they want is not a Super League, it's a Selfish League.'

The changes at the Football League AGM of 1986 delayed the Super League – for now.

## Chapter 16

# Clubs and The League Competition

LIVERPOOL, ASTON Villa, Liverpool, Liverpool, Liverpool, Everton, Liverpool, Everton, Liverpool, Arsenal, Liverpool. The sequence of First Division title winners from the beginning of the 1980s to the end of the decade.

The decade when one club, and one club alone, was pre-eminent in domestic league competition – Liverpool FC. No other club in the history of the Football League or Premier League has ever dominated the top flight in one decade as Liverpool did in the 1980s. The club enjoyed phenomenal success.

With good humour, Bob Paisley, the club's most successful manager, who retired at the end of the 1982/83 season, observed, 'Mind you, I've been at Liverpool during the bad times, too. One year we came second!' And it was not far from the truth.

Over the period 1979/80–1989/90, the club won seven league championships, were runners-up on three occasions and finished fifth in 1980/81. It was a magnificent achievement by the Merseysiders.

Reviewing the decade as a whole and considering the performance of league clubs over that period produces this consolidated league table for the 11 seasons – 1979/80–1989/90:

## CONSOLIDATED LEAGUE TABLE
### 1979/80 – 1989/90

| | Seasons in First Division | Highest Pos | Lowest Pos | Average Pos |
|---|---|---|---|---|
| Liverpool | 11 | 1st (x 7) | 5th | 1.6 |
| Arsenal | 11 | 1st | 10th | 5.2 |
| Manchester United | 11 | 2nd | 13th | 5.9 |
| Nottingham Forest | 11 | 3rd | 12th | 6.5 |
| Everton | 11 | 1st (x 2) | 19th | 7.1 |
| Tottenham Hotspur | 11 | 3rd | 14th | 7.1 |
| Southampton | 11 | 2nd | 14th | 8.9 |
| Aston Villa | 10 | 1st | 23rd | 11.4 |
| Coventry City | 11 | 7th | 19th | 14.3 |
| Norwich City | 9 | 4th | 25th | 14.6 |
| West Ham United | 8 | 3rd | 29th | 15.8 |
| Ipswich Town | 7 | 2nd | 29th | 16.2 |
| Luton Town | 8 | 7th | 28th | 16.6 |
| QPR | 7 | 5th | 30th | 16.8 |
| Manchester City | 7 | 10th | 30th | 19.3 |
| Watford | 6 | 2nd | 40th | 19.9 |
| Chelsea | 5 | 5th | 40th | 20.6 |
| Sheffield Wednesday | 6 | 5th | 47th | 20.6 |
| WBA | 7 | 4th | 41st | 21.8 |
| Newcastle United | 5 | 8th | 33rd | 21.8 |
| Leicester City | 5 | 15th | 35th | 24.5 |
| Stoke City | 6 | 11th | 44th | 24.6 |

- The number of clubs in the First Division – 22: 1979/80–1986/87; 21: 1987/88; 20: 1988/89–1989/90; in the Second Division 22, 23 and 24 clubs respectively for the above seasons.

- Position calculated by position in the Football League, eg. second in the Second Division, 1981/82 = 24th.
- Average position is the aggregate position over the period divided by 11 (seasons).

The decade saw Liverpool build on their achievements of the 1970s – five league titles in that decade and top of the consolidated league table for that decade, with an average position of 2.2. The Reds' league championship success of 1989/90 was their 18th title overall, the highest for any club.

Liverpool were involved in one of the most exciting climaxes to a season – 1988/89 – against Arsenal. The title depended on the last game of the season at Anfield. Unusually, the game was moved to a Friday night for live television coverage on 26 May (the season had finished later because of the Hillsborough disaster). Arsenal needed to win the game by two clear goals to take the title. Any other result and the trophy remained at Anfield.

For the Gunners, the game was all they could have wished for. Alan Smith scored after 52 minutes before Michael Thomas dramatically made it 2-0 in the second minute of added time, clinching the title.

With the backlog of fixtures as a result of the Hillsborough disaster, Liverpool played nine games from their resumption of football on 3 May up to that final game. In that same period, Arsenal played three games.

Four clubs started the decade in the First Division and played in the Fourth Division before the end of the 1980s – Bristol City, Wolverhampton Wanderers, Bolton Wanderers and Swansea City. Bristol City's relegations were particularly brutal for the club and its supporters – relegated in 1979/80, 1980/81 and 1981/82, by 1982/83 they were in the Fourth Division.

In total, 41 clubs appeared in the First Division in the 1980s. Eight clubs competed in that division in every season of the decade – Liverpool, Manchester United, Arsenal, Nottingham Forest, Southampton, Tottenham Hotspur, Coventry City and Everton.

Three clubs appeared in the top division for the first time in their history – Oxford United, Wimbledon and Millwall. Wimbledon's rise was meteoric – admitted to the Football League in 1977/78, they were promoted to Division Three at the end of 1978/79 then relegated the following season. Their rise to the First Division continued apace and they eventually joined the footballing elite in 1986/87.

Aston Villa's success in claiming the league championship for the first time in over 70 years in 1980/81 was achieved with only 14 players. Seven players appeared in every game, one missed two games and another missed three games.

No commentary on the decade can omit a reference to Crystal Palace. Labelled the 'Team of the Eighties' under manager Terry Venables at the start of the decade, they failed to live up to the billing and were relegated to Division Two at the end of 1980/81.

At the other end of the scale, Burnley came within a whisker of being relegated from the Football League on the last day of the 1986/87 season. They needed to beat Orient at Turf Moor in the last game of the season to retain their status. It had been a poor season for the Clarets, with an average attendance of 3,257. For that final game, 15,781 turned out to watch a 2-1 win for Burnley, ensuring league football continued. Lincoln City relegated from the Football League.

Goals scored in league competition were low in the 1980s. The introduction of three points for a win in the 1981/82 season was expected to produce more goals as teams strived to win games rather than settle for the draw. The overall increase in goalscoring was relatively small, a rise of 5.5 per cent – 5,277 goals scored compared to 5,002 the previous season.

In the context of three points for a win, Sunderland manager Alan Durban was quick to criticise the new points system after the game against Ipswich Town ended in a 3-3 draw. 'It is outrageous that the clubs should lose two points each for drawing after giving such a superb exhibition like that.'

Durban had form for eye-catching quotes. As manager of Stoke City in 1980/81, his team had lost 2-0 away at Arsenal and a journalist said there was no entertainment in watching his team's performance. Durban replied, 'If you want entertainment, go and watch a bunch of clowns.'

In 1986/87, the play-offs were introduced. For many clubs that previously had little interest in league games towards the end of the season, it meant there was something to play for. Play-offs were considered a positive introduction generating and maintaining interest right through to season's end.

There were dissenting voices – not least Brian Clough, then manager at First Division Nottingham Forest. The alternative view was that play-offs undermined the integrity of the league competition – the final standings – and that promotion and relegation were sacrosanct based on the performance of a club over the full season. However, those voices did not prevail.

In short, the play-offs were a success. Attendances at play-off games reflected their importance for the future of the clubs concerned.

The real boost to attendances came with the change to the one-game final for each of the divisions and the prestige of playing at Wembley in 1989/90. For the Division Two play-offs that season, North East rivals Sunderland and Newcastle United met in one of the two-legged semi-finals. At Roker

Park, the attendance was 26,641; at St James Park, it was 32,216. The final at Wembley between Sunderland and Swindon Town attracted 72,873.

By the end of the decade, with three points for a win, play-offs generating extra interest and attendances on the rise, things were looking more positive for the league competition.

# Chapter 17

# FA Cup

NINETEEN EIGHTY, the FA Cup semi-final replay at Elland Road – Monday, April 16th – Everton and West Ham United. Me? – not at the game, working at the Ford Dagenham Paint Trim and Assembly (PTA) plant as a personnel officer. And working late – often happened in those days. Industrial relations in the mass production motor industry were at a nadir and had been for several years. The Trade Unions were at their zenith and relations with management poor. Personnel officers played a key part in dealing with industrial relations issues – and there were plenty of them.

Precisely the reason for working late that night I don't recollect. The Ford works at Dagenham – 30,000 Ford employees on the site in 1980 – was West Ham United country.

Not quite so many people evident in the manufacturing plant as shift start time approached at 10pm. It took no time to realise that absentees would be focused on the outcome of the game at Elland Road. The game had gone to extra time – 0-0 at the end of normal time. And not having enough workers on the shop floor would put the shift's scheduled output of 700 'jobs' at risk. A 'job' was a completed, assembled car – the Ford Cortina Mark IV going through the full build process in one shift.

A roar within the plant – an outpouring from those listening to their radios. A goal for the Hammers … ten minutes or so later, a low dull noise. Everton equalised. Two minutes later, a bigger roar. Frank Lampard (Senior) scored for the Hammers to give them the lead. Minutes later, an even louder roar – the final whistle. The Hammers had won and through to the FA Cup Final. A buoyancy in the plant, a happy, jovial mood, and excepting the final shift before Christmas, this was all but unique.

Second Division West Ham United had made it an all-London final against Arsenal, the latter heavy favourites to retain the FA Cup after their win the previous season against Manchester United. But not so. An unlikely headed goal by Upton Park favourite and England international Trevor Brooking proved to be the winner and the cup travelled across London.

One other notable incident in the game saw Arsenal's Willie Young cynically fouling Hammers youngster Paul Allen from behind as he moved into the penalty area with a good chance to score. Only a booking, but in time the incident would spark a change in the punishment for such offences to a sending-off.

The final of the FA Cup was played on Saturday. At Ford plants, no production took place over a weekend. Come Monday morning, the start of the working week all was *bonhomie* and good cheer. The Hammers had won the cup and Dagenham was celebrating.

None more so than Gerry Warner – a shop steward on 'B' shift – he came into the personnel office that morning with a beaming smile as wide as the proverbial Cheshire cat. 'Our boys did it and deserved it. You'll have no issues from me this week.' His assertion turned out to be right. Gerry, a dyed-in the-wool Hammer, had been supporting his club 'since Adam was a lad'. To win the FA Cup was brilliant for him and his fellow supporters. They felt good about themselves and their club. For that week, industrial relations problems were greatly reduced.

There was no doubting the importance and impact of the FA Cup on football supporters. And no less important to businesses that benefited from the increase in productivity that cup wins produced.

In the 1980s, FA Cup Final day was a big event. At the beginning of the decade, it was the only domestic club game broadcast live on television. The networks – BBC and ITV – made it a big event, reporting live from the team's hotel, travelling on the team coach to Wembley, famous supporters of the two clubs interviewed, quite apart from pundits analysing before, during and after the game.

For the 1981 FA Cup Final, my father-in-law Eric had asked me whether I'd like to go to Wembley if he could get tickets. The invitation came out of the blue – tickets for the FA Cup Final were like gold dust. I'd never seen an FA Cup Final ticket, never mind been offered the chance to go to the game. Stan Flashman, a renowned ticket tout, is the only name I associated with getting hold of cup final tickets. To my father-in-law's invitation, I replied, 'Yes, of course.'

Tickets were obtained from Southend United, I assumed as a result of his long friendship with chairman of the club, Frank Walton.

We travelled to Wembley by car, a tobacco brown-coloured Ford Granada, and parked about a mile from the stadium, the car half on the road, half on a grassed area next to the kerb. A line of cars parked in exactly this fashion.

Three-quarters of an hour to kick-off as we left the car, not as many supporters heading to the venue as I'd anticipated –

most must be in the stadium or close to it. The noise emanating from inside the ground grew as we approached the turnstiles.

A decent position in the stadium almost opposite the royal box – evidently an area occupied by neutrals.

The game Tottenham Hotspur v Manchester City – the bulk of these clubs' supporters were positioned behind each goal. The game largely uneventful – certainly for the neutral – ending in a 1-1 draw with a replay to follow. Tommy Hutchison, City's Scottish international, scored for both teams – an own goal following one for his own team.

My father-in-law's disappointment was that we'd not seen the cup presented that afternoon. We would not be going to the replay. More tickets were available to supporters of each club for that game. Quite right too.

Back to the car. Arriving, we found it had been broken into, as had all the cars parked in that road. No car alarms, the biggest day in the football calendar, no doubt the thieves made hay. Ten pounds taken from the glovebox and a repair job needed on the driver's door too!

The replay at Wembley the following Thursday saw a great game – ultimately a 3-2 win for the London club. The game went into extra time and included the celebrated winner by Ricky Villa with his mazy run and finish in the City penalty area.

Years later, a quiz question came up: 'What is missing in the sequence, Sunderland, ********, Villa?' For the answer thoughts naturally turn to football clubs. The answer is 'Brooking'. The sequence is winning goalscorers in the FA Cup Final – Alan Sunderland (Arsenal, 1979), Trevor Brooking (West Ham United, 1980), Ricky Villa (Tottenham Hotspur, 1981).

The 1982 FA Cup Final saw Queens Park Rangers reach that stage of the competition for the first time in their history, where they played fellow London club, and cup holders, Tottenham Hotspur.

Reflecting on their 1-0 win in the semi-final against West Bromwich Albion at neutral Highbury, Rangers' Tony Currie noted, 'Getting to the cup final in 1982 was one of the highlights of my career. It was always my ambition to play in a cup final. It was incredible to think the dream was going to come true.' (*The Matador: The Life and Career of Tony Currie*, E J Huntley, Pitch Publishing, 2015).

Celebrations after the semi-final win were raucous. 'Rangers players mingled and celebrated with supporters and well-wishers such as Rangers' old boy Stan Bowles at the Crown and Sceptre pub. Currie and Ian Gillard even served drinks from behind the bar.'

Prior to the final, Rangers' manager Terry Venables commented, 'Win or lose, we'll have some booze.' The game was a cagey affair with little open football, ending 1-1 after extra time. In the replay five days later, Glenn Hoddle scored the only goal of the game for Spurs.

Wednesday's first strong showing of the decade in the FA Cup came in 1982/83 in a quarter-final tie against Burnley at Turf Moor. I had to go. A bit of a distance to travel from Essex but, no matter, the custard-coloured Vauxhall Chevette made it without difficulty.

I'd bought a ticket from the home club and sat in the stand behind the goal with the home supporters – the person sitting immediately to my right was Jimmy Adamson, a legend of Burnley, who had recently left the club as manager.

Before the game, there was trouble on the terraces – violence, running fights clearly visible. Within minutes, hordes of young men came over the barriers on to the track around the pitch. They were wearing blue and white colours

– Wednesdayites – and relocated to behind the goal intended for away supporters. It was a very unpleasant prelude to the game, delaying the start, and according to Les Comer in the next Sheffield Wednesday programme was 'caused primarily by the naive selling of tickets for the Burnley Kop to all-comers'.

The game was nip and tuck – a 1-1 draw and a replay. That game was one-sided at Hillsborough as the home team ran out 5-0 winners.

Wednesday played Brighton & Hove Albion at Arsenal's Highbury ground in the semi-final. Hope sprang eternal but to no avail. It finished 2-1 to the south coast club. The front-page headline in that night's *Sheffield Star Green 'Un* said it all – 'Heartbreak Wednesday'.

Interestingly, the *Daily Telegraph* described Brighton as 'virile dreadnoughts' in the FA Cup that season, the newspaper comparing their cup exploits with their league form. They were relegated from the First Division at the end of the season.

I recollect, and I am reminded of the 1984 FA Cup Final by an ex-work colleague, 'Chiv'. We worked at Warley, Ford's Head Office for Europe at the time, and she invited me to her wedding in May that year. Evidently, my response to the invitation was, 'We can come because it's not the day of the FA Cup Final.' Her response, 'that's very good of you', I took at face value, because of the importance in the calendar of the FA Cup Final.

The year 1984 was Watford's first FA Cup Final and they were pitched against seasoned cup finalists Everton. My primary recollection the tears in chairman Elton John's eyes as the crowd sang the pre-FA Cup Final song, 'Abide with Me'. It was a poor game, Everton deserving their 2-0 win. That meant nothing to 'Chiv'.

In 1985, Wednesday reached the semi-finals – drawn against Everton at Villa Park. No ticket. But again, I had to be there. Living in Leigh-on-Sea, Essex, there was no access to any black market tickets, Dad said some had been advertised in the 'For Sale' section of the classified ads in the Sheffield evening newspaper *The Star* – but there were more ads for tickets in the 'Wanted' section!

No choice but to get up there early on the morning of the game. I travelled by car and arrived at Villa Park at 10am. Parking close to the ground easy at that time of day, Villa Park no more than 400 yards away. The residential road appeared to have its own police constable, who helpfully said where I could and couldn't park. More helpfully, she had a few clear and sharp words with some young lads on the road who tried it on. 'Protect your car, mister?'

Where to get a ticket? Even at that time, there were people milling around the ground – all looking to buy not sell. The club shop opened at 10.30am. I'd try there first.

I approached the guy behind the counter. 'Good morning. Have you any idea where I might get a ticket for today's game?' Short, to the point.

The guy looked me up and down. He delayed responding. He seemed to be thinking. He looked at me again. 'I do have one ticket.' He looked at me again.

Play it cool. 'How much would you like for it?'

'I only want the face value. It's a seat in the Upper Stand behind the goal opposite the Holte End. It's in a neutral area.'

'That's fabulous. Thank you so very much. And I'd like to buy this book on the history of Aston Villa.' I'm not sure I did want to buy it really but that was the least I could do given I'd struck gold so early in my quest.

The game? Wednesday lost in extra time.

Peter Reid, who played in the game for Everton, noted, 'It was a tremendous game, they gave it their best shot, but we were that bit stronger ... The Wednesday fans gave their team fantastic vocal support. The atmosphere was tremendous. The tension was incredible ... In the players' room afterwards, a few of the Wednesday players were in tears. I'd thought on previous occasions how horrible losing in the semi-final must be. I felt a bit more for Wednesday than I had in the other two matches.' (*An Everton Diary*, Peter Reid with Peter Ball, Queen Anne Press, 1988).

The FA Cup Final of 1985, Everton v Manchester United, saw a first – a first sending-off in an FA Cup Final. United's Kevin Moran given his marching order by referee Peter Willis for a so-called professional foul. United won the game with ten men, 1-0.

One further aspect of that Wembley game is interesting. In an Aldershot programme in March 1986, there was an article entitled 'Back Handers'. It stated the official attendance for the FA Cup Final was 100,000 but went on, 'However, that figure isn't quite right; in fact an extra 7,672 watched the game thanks to numerous turnstile operators who in return for cash let extra fans into the stadium.' It quoted the outcome of trials at Acton Crown Court – six turnstile men pleaded guilty to 'corruptly receiving bribes' and were fined £750 each, with five receiving suspended prison sentences, one turnstile operator caught with £1,000 hidden in his jacket.

There was an historic first the following year. The cup final was an all-Merseyside affair – Liverpool v Everton. The result a 3-1 win for the Reds.

As well as being the first Merseyside FA Cup Final, it was a first regarding the organisation of a players' pool – the money generated from exclusive articles provided by players to the media, a record by the team and other commercial activities. The monies shared by all the players. One agent – Eric Hall – was given responsibility for the pool for both clubs. He'd organised the Everton players' pool for the FA Cup Final in the previous two seasons. This time, the captains of both teams (Kevin Ratcliffe and Alan Hansen) confirmed their players wanted Hall to run the pool and agreed the players' pool for both teams be combined. Evidently, it resulted in a very big pot indeed.

The 1988 FA Cup Final pitched the three-times cup winners and that season's league champions, Liverpool, against the 'Johnny come latelies' of Wimbledon. The odds were stacked heavily in favour of the Merseysiders.

As is often the case, the game did not go to plan for the favourites. Whether or not it had anything to do with what is alleged to have happened in the tunnel between the teams' respective players before the game, who knows? Allegations that Wimbledon players tried to out-psych their opponents, making a lot of noise in the tunnel,

The game was evenly balanced, and it took a header by Wimbledon's Lawrie Sanchez from a Dennis Wise free kick to settle it. In saving a penalty by Liverpool's John Aldridge, Dons' stopper Dave Beasant became the first goalkeeper to do so in a Wembley FA Cup Final. At the end of the game, he had another distinction – the first goalkeeper to receive the FA Cup as captain.

John Motson's commentary on BBC Television included the well-worked line, 'the Crazy Gang have beaten the Culture Club' – a reference to the 1950s music hall act and the 1980s pop music group featuring Boy George.

Having the opportunity to talk with John Barnes directly a couple of months later, I reflected with him how well his

Liverpool team had played at Hillsborough a week before their Wembley game. They beat Wednesday 5-1, looking every bit league champions. Barnes's comment was simply that 'we peaked a week early'. He had no excuses for Liverpool's defeat.

The 1989 FA Cup Final was the most emotional, following the disaster at Hillsborough – the fences had been removed at Wembley and for the second time an all-Merseyside game, a 3-2 win for the Reds after extra time.

# Chapter 18

# The League Cup

THE LEAGUE Cup was an important competition. For the winners, it carried the prestige of being the season's first domestic honour as well as guaranteeing entry into the following season's UEFA Cup. But the final was played during the season, on a Saturday, until 1984, when it was switched to Sunday. It was played at the same time as league fixtures were taking place. It had neither the history, tradition nor glamour of the FA Cup.

For Liverpool, the most successful club of the 1980s and the previous decade, it took an inordinately long time to claim their first League Cup success. It was not until 1981 that Liverpool claimed their first win in the competition, defeating West Ham United at Villa Park after a replay – 20 years after it was introduced.

As if to make the point 'it was about time too', the Merseysiders won the next four League Cups to make it five in a row, becoming not only the club to have won the cup most times, but most times in succession.

Aside from Liverpool's five wins, it was one apiece for Wolverhampton Wanderers, Norwich City, Oxford United, Arsenal, Luton Town and Nottingham Forest. All the wins took place in one game at Wembley except in the 1981 final and the final three years later, which Liverpool won in a replay against Merseyside rivals Everton at Maine Road.

As for Liverpool, one game from the 1983/84 competition stands out for me – against Wednesday at Hillsborough in the fifth round. It was a midweek fixture, with Wednesday in the Second Division and the Reds atop the First Division. The game had caught the imagination of the home club's supporters. Dad had managed to get tickets in the front row of the North Stand close to the arc of the penalty area at the Spion Kop end. We were amongst a crowd of 49,357, Wednesday's best crowd for a decade and more.

It was a game full of the proverbial blood and thunder. Liverpool captain Graeme Souness fouled Wednesday skipper Mick Lyons, ex-Everton, in the first minute. The incident incensed most of the crowd and the game's intensity reached another level. The flow of the game went one way and then the other, both clubs taking the lead before the full-blooded game ended 2-2.

Two incidents in the first half spring readily to mind. In the first, the ball went out of play directly in front of us for an attacking Liverpool throw. Their Australian-born midfield player Craig Johnston came running over to take the throw, his fully permed hair – the style for some footballers at that time – blowing in the wind as he did so. What was clear to us as he moved down the byline holding the ball was that one of his feet was partially over the line and in the field of play.

'Watch his feet, linesman – they're over the line. Mek sure you flag – it's on telly, you'll see it tonight.' Even in the general noise and hubbub in the ground, the linesman must have heard it – I'd shouted as loud as I could. Johnston ran four or five paces to deliver the ball from the throw-in. Ball released, the linesman's arm rose in a flash, his flag waving furiously. The referee saw the flag and blew his whistle. The linesman moved his leg forward over the line to imitate Johnston's offence. Splendid. Wednesdayites pleased, Johnston not so. He looked dumbfounded – his permed hair moving in every direction as he shook his head and mouthed words to the linesman.

'Well done, linesman – absolutely right. You'll see that tonight,' I shouted. The linesman merited words of appreciation and acknowledgement because he'd made the right decision. I was pleased with my small contribution for the home team. The linesman clearly alert and his mind on the job.

Ten minutes later, a Wednesday throw straight in front of us, Gary Megson comes across to take it. He runs and releases the ball ... the linesman again waves his flag furiously. Whistle blown, linesman makes the same gesture with his leg – foot over the line. 'Hang on a minute, linesman, you're not supposed to be flagging our players.' This observation (rightly) was of no consequence to the linesman but he smiled all the same. Fair play – 1-0 to him. Megson gave much the same reaction as Johnston minutes earlier, less the absence of permed hair moving hither and thither. There was now no point in encouraging the linesman's observations – he was on the ball.

The replay at Anfield a week later saw a 3-0 win for the hosts on their way to retaining the trophy against Everton in the final.

Liverpool's Mark Lawrenson remembered the 1984 final against Everton at Wembley. 'It was the first time the clubs had played each other for a trophy – and I think there were concerns in London about the mass movement of 100,000 coming down from the north. The people of Liverpool had been battered, cut adrift by the government, and the Met Police were braced for the two clubs being in

London. But there wasn't a murmur of trouble. Two proper clubs, two proper teams and one proper city.' (*Daily Mail*, 27 March 2019).

This final was the first played on a Sunday and the first to be broadcast live on television.

There was an interesting by-product of the following season's League Cup Final – won 1-0 by Norwich City thanks to an own goal by Sunderland's Gordon Chisholm – which was the creation of the Friendship Trophy. The trophy is contested by Norwich and Sunderland, with the trophy awarded to the winner of each competitive game between the clubs.

It dates from the friendship forged between the two clubs at the League Cup Final. Supporters of the Mackems and the Canaries mingled and drank together before and after the game. The Norwich manager Ken Brown noted, 'The Sunderland supporters were magnificent, and everyone seemed to mix. It was light hearted and very nice.' On the London Underground journey from Wembley Stadium, the Norwich City fans sang, 'We won the Cup.' Their Sunderland counterparts responded, 'We scored the goal.'

Perhaps Ken Brown talked a little in the heat of the moment when he said, 'And now I believe I can turn a little club like Norwich into a big one, just like Brian Clough did at Nottingham Forest, Bobby Robson at Ipswich and Lawrie McMenemy at Southampton.' The Canaries were relegated – as were Sunderland – at the end of the season.

The following season's final saw Oxford United defeat Queens Park Rangers 3-0. U's manager Maurice Evans sent 72-year-old trainer Ken Fish to collect the trophy. For his part, Rangers' manager Jim Smith did not mince his words. 'We were diabolical. We just froze – we were frightened of the occasion.'

The League Cup was the first domestic trophy to be sponsored, the National Dairy Council (NDC) signing a deal worth £2 million for four years from 1981/82. The Milk Cup was born. An everyday wholesome product, it was a gift for headline writers – 'Cream of the Crop', 'Gold Top' and more besides. The NDC had a new Milk Cup trophy made.

In the 1985 final, Sunderland's Shaun Elliott was named man of the match and received free milk for a year.

Littlewoods took over sponsorship of the League Cup from 1986/87 for four seasons, producing their own trophy for the competition. It was an impressive solid silver trophy made in 1895. The original League Cup, with three handles, which was 'rested' during the Milk Cup sponsorship, was also presented to the winners.

# Chapter 19

# Other Competitions

ASIDE FROM the three main domestic club competitions, the 1980s saw a plethora of additional tournaments – the Anglo-Scottish Cup, the Full Members' Cup, the Associate Members' Cup, the Screen Sport Super Cup and the Mercantile Credit trophy. All were intended to provide much-needed extra revenue for the participants.

The Anglo-Scottish Cup started in 1976 for invited clubs north and south of the border, 16 English clubs and 8 Scottish clubs taking part in that inaugural season and continuing into the early 1980s.

Season 1980/81 saw the involvement of Glasgow Rangers for the first and only time – the Ibrox club not involved in European competition that season.

A quarter-final tie saw John Greig's team play Chesterfield, then of Division Three. The pundits saw it as no contest, with the Derbyshire club making up the numbers. A 1-1 draw in the first leg at Ibrox added a little spice to the return game, with 5,000 travelling Rangers fans making the journey to Chesterfield. The local authorities instructed all the town's pubs to close for the day, and an additional 500 police were brought in.

The mighty Glasgow Rangers were humbled, suffering a 3-0 defeat at Saltergate. The opening goal was scored by

Spireites' legend Ernie Moss followed by a brace from Glasgow-born midfielder Phil Bonnyman, who started his career at Ibrox. To add salt to the wound, Chesterfield's participation in the tournament followed a last-minute withdrawal by Sunderland.

Victory for the Spireites against Bury in the semi-finals meant a meeting in the final with old foes Notts County – an East Midlands derby. After a 1-0 win for Chesterfield in the first leg at Saltergate, the Magpies pulled the tie level in the second leg. The game went to extra time, with penalties looming when Chesterfield's Alan Crawford backheeled the winner in the 120th minute. It was the only major piece of silverware in their history.

A postscript to the second leg of the final – Mike Firth, a young reporter on the *Derbyshire Times*, recollects their photographer, Doug, was down to cover a Chesterfield game. With Doug's knowledge and interest in football limited, he assumed the game was at Saltergate, 'so he sauntered across town with his camera and called in a couple of pubs en route. In the second one, he asked the barman why the pub was so empty given the Spireites were playing at home. He learnt he should have been down the road in Nottingham, where the club was just about to kick off the biggest game in their history. By the time he arrived at the ground, extra time had started. All the other photographers had been there for a couple of hours, but Doug took his place at the side of the goal just in time to photograph Alan Crawford score the winning goal.'

Mike reflected, 'Next morning we looked at his one strip of negatives from the cup final. He had a great shot of the goal, celebrations and presentation of the cup! All we needed! Doug was lucky like that!'

The Anglo-Scottish Cup ended that season. It was scrapped after the Scottish League withdrew its clubs as a result of the continued absence of English First Division clubs from the competition.

The competition limped on the following season as the Football League Group Cup, with little interest shown – 3,423 attended the final. For its final season in 1982/83, it was renamed the Football League Trophy, 3,142 in attendance at the final.

The Full Members' Cup was introduced in 1985/86 as compensation for the exclusion of English clubs from European club competitions following the Heysel disaster.

Jack Dunnett, president of the Football League, welcomed supporters to the inaugural final at Wembley for the game between Chelsea and Manchester City in March 1986. He noted the competition had been 'introduced at the specific request of a number of clubs who felt that the game needed an additional challenge'. Clubs in the First and Second Division – full members of the Football League – qualified for entry to the competition. That season, only 23 clubs entered. It consisted of a group stage followed by knockout games for the winners of each group.

Attendances were not high. The two-legged Southern Area Final between Chelsea and Oxford United attracted 6,081 to the Manor Ground and 8,528 to Stamford Bridge. In the Northern Area Final between Manchester City and Hull City, 5,213 saw the game at Boothferry Park and 10,180 the return at Maine Road.

In the programme for the final, Ken Bates, the Chelsea chairman, observed, 'Because of a commitment to entertaining football, Chelsea have not won the honours they might have done over the years and we have therefore won the tag of being the "alternative" London team to the more regular trophy winners, Arsenal and Tottenham. I have found the same feeling exists in Lancashire for Manchester City and [who] have often been described as the Chelsea of the north.'

Peter Swales, the Manchester City chairman, commented, 'The Members' Cup has been unfairly criticised and many people doubted that the final would be played at Wembley but I'm happy to say that those of us who supported the competition have got the last word and this should be a magnificent match. Ken [Bates] and myself were so determined that today's match should be played at Wembley that we personally guaranteed the financial security of the event.'

The attendance at Wembley for the final was 67,236, with receipts of £508,000, the game won 5-4 by Chelsea.

The appeal of a Wembley final and, from 1987/88, sponsorship from Simod – a renamed Simod Cup – increased participation, with 40 clubs entering the competition that season.

For Third and Fourth Division clubs, the Associate Members' Cup was introduced in 1983/84, financially enhanced with sponsorship and renamed the Freight Rover Trophy in 1984/85. For this competition too, the attraction of the final at Wembley was significant for players and supporters of the clubs concerned, with 59,000 in attendance at the 1986/87 final.

One new competition had a shelf life of one season, 1985/86, the Screen Sport Super Cup for the six clubs that were not able to compete in Europe after the Heysel disaster. The European satellite sports channel Screen Sport invested £254,000 in the competition – Liverpool the winners, defeating Everton over two legs, 47,000 attending the two games.

1988 was the centenary of the Football League, which held a tournament during the 1988/89 season, sponsored by

Mercantile Credit. The competition was played on a knockout basis between the clubs that finished in the top eight of the previous season's First Division. The final took place at Villa Park – Arsenal v Manchester United, the Gunners winning 2-1. Interest in the tournament was lukewarm at best, only the semi-final between Arsenal and Liverpool attracting a crowd of over 25,000.

In April 1988, a further tournament took place over two days at Wembley Stadium. Twelve clubs from all four divisions were selected to participate based on their goalscoring record. Mercantile Credit sponsored the Mercantile Credit Football Festival. Games were of 40 minutes' duration in the early group stages, 60 minutes in the semi-finals and final. Similarly, interest was low, 17,000 attending the second day, which included the final.

Sheffield Wednesday qualified for the tournament. I'd not seen my club at Wembley – indeed as we walked outside the Twin Towers a number of Wednesdayites said it was the first time they'd seen them there too, the more sceptical going as far as to say, 'It will be the only time I see Wednesday at Wembley.' The views of the more pessimistic Wednesday supporters were understandable if not uplifting!

In the final, Wednesday lost to Nottingham Forest on penalties after a 0-0 draw.

# Chapter 20

# Sponsorship

WITH THE financial challenges and ills facing the game in the 1980s, the opportunity to obtain sponsorship was never more welcomed by the Football League and individual clubs. At the same time, the economic climate meant many companies adopted a more prudent approach with their expenditure.

The first competition to be sponsored was the Football League's first domestic cup competition – the Football League Cup, launched in 1961. The major domestic competition – the FA Cup – was not available for sponsorship. The Football Association had made it clear that the oldest cup competition in the world would not be seeking sponsorship.

For the Football League, sponsorship was primarily focused on its main competition – the league itself. The first sponsorship came in 1983/84 through Canon, the Japanese firm that manufactured cameras, computers and photo-copying machines. It became known as the Canon League.

Financial arrangements for that first Football League sponsorship saw Canon put in £3.3 million from 1983/84. Prize money was awarded for success in the separate divisions:

Division One: 1st £50,000; 2nd £25,000; 3rd £15,000
Division Two: 1st £25,000; 2nd £15,000; 3rd £5,000

Division Three: 1st £15,000; 2nd £8,000; 3rd £4,000
Division Four: 1st £8,000; 2nd £4,000; 3rd £2,000; 4th £1,000

The teams scoring the most goals in each division were rewarded each month and for the full season.

Teams scoring the most goals in a month received:

Division One: £1,000; Division Two: £750; Division Three: £500; Division Four: £250

For scoring the most goals in a full season, teams received:

Division One: £6,500; Division Two: £5,000; Division Three: £3,500; Division Four: £2,000

Additionally, there were payments made to centres of excellence and for loyalty awards.

Canon ensured a clause in the contract that enabled it to withdraw sponsorship money if league games were not shown on television – in time this clause applied, resulting in a £10,200 reduction in prize money when football was off TV screens in 1984/85.

Their three-year sponsorship completed, Canon was satisfied its aims had been met – greater awareness of its brand name and products.

With Canon's exit, the Football League took more time than it would have liked to find a replacement. In October 1986, the replacement was announced – the *Today* newspaper, and the Today League. The newspaper was first produced in 1986 and the first to be colour printed. For such a new brand, the association with the Football League was a great opportunity to raise awareness.

The deal was worth £4 million over two seasons. As with the Canon deal, prize money was awarded. The First Division champions similarly received £50,000. Additional payments under the new deal included initiatives taken to attract families to games.

Within a year, it was clear the sponsorship deal had not worked as intended. From the *Today* perspective, other national newspapers were reluctant to highlight a rival when the Football League competition was referenced, including in the results of games and the tables of the four divisions. The newspaper was keen to extricate itself from the sponsorship deal and did so 11 days before the start of the 1987/88 season.

Every cloud has a silver lining – Barclays Bank came to the fore and signed a three-year agreement two days before the start of the season. The sponsorship was valued at £4.55 million – the largest single sponsorship deal in British sport. Prize money for the First Division champions was maintained at £50,000. The league was renamed the Barclays League – and for the Football League it was an excellent outcome.

One further sponsorship initiative the Football League had put in place earlier in the decade was with Mitre, worth £50,000. As well as receiving footballs, clubs using the Mitre ball received a share of the sponsorship fee.

Individual clubs were keen to maximise sponsorship opportunities – club sponsors, shirt sponsors, match sponsors, match ball sponsors, man of the match sponsors, players' kit sponsors and so it went on.

Liverpool were the first club to announce a shirt sponsorship deal in July 1979, signing an agreement with Japanese electronics firm Hitachi. In welcoming the sponsorship, Liverpool chairman John Smith said, 'The days have gone when clubs like ours can control their destiny in the financial sense by relying on the money that comes through the turnstiles. We are all desperate for money and we have to explore new ways of finding it.'

At that time, because football clubs were not allowed to wear sponsored shirts in televised games, Jimmy Hill, the

Coventry City chairman, suggested, to get round the ban, clubs could be renamed, as their name and emblem could only appear on the shirt. He suggested his club could be renamed Coventry Aspirin! It didn't happen.

Shirt sponsorship went from strength to strength. By the start of the 1983/84 season 59 league clubs were sponsored, although Sheffield Wednesday were not one of them, some supporters urging the club not to have a sponsor's name across their shirt. That season, sponsors' names on shirts included: Crown Paints – Liverpool; Sharp – Manchester United; JVC – Arsenal; Pioneer – Ipswich Town; Guinness – Queens Park Rangers; Saab – Manchester City; Hafnia – Everton; Ind Coope – Leicester City; Bedford Trucks – Luton Town; Findus – Grimsby Town. The local council backed Bradford City and Scunthorpe United, and the London Development Corporation supported Millwall.

The larger sponsorship deals focused on the bigger clubs. Liverpool, Manchester United and Arsenal had reportedly attracted sponsorship of £500,000 over three seasons, whereas Norwich City, for example, had a reported £150,000 deal. By 1987, every club had received some form of sponsorship.

Many clubs had sponsors for individual games. For the game against Cardiff City in December 1983, Sheffield Wednesday's sponsors, Whitbread & Co. Sheffield, welcomed all their guests by name in a full page of the matchday programme – all 41 of them, and all male.

As the decade progressed, sponsorship became an increasingly integral and necessary part of the game.

# Chapter 21

# Commercially

ASIDE FROM sponsorship, clubs looked at a range of ways to make money during the 1980s. Club lotteries were a big earner – in November 1980, Mike Hardwicke, commercial manager at Luton Town, noted, 'Lotteries are our prime source of income in these troubled times of inflation. Sponsorships, advertising inside the stadium and in the matchday magazine. We know that money is tight. Short-time working, higher prices have had an effect on our sales. In the last financial year, fund-raising efforts brought in £200,000.'

The Football League were keen to wrest money from the football pools industry – worth £550 million annually – and brought in a competitor in 'Top Score', with an eye-catching £600,000 available for the winner. It was introduced at the beginning of 1985/86 and survived three months.

In the second half of the decade, and primarily in response to government pressure to impose an ID card requirement on every spectator, clubs introduced membership schemes – initially to watch games from specified parts of the ground. In time, clubs saw the commercial benefits of a membership scheme. In one such scheme at Chelsea in 1989/90, costs were UK associate (adult) £18 and juvenile/OAP £16. Members were able to buy away tickets, enjoy reduced admission to the terraces, discounts at the club shop and receive personal Christmas and birthday cards, amongst other benefits.

At the end of the 1980s, the introduction of 'Clubcall' at many clubs brought all the latest news, interviews and match reports, 24 hours a day, seven days a week – a dedicated number for the supporter to call. Liverpool's 'Clubcall' was charged at 46p a minute 8am–6pm and 23p a minute after 6pm and at weekends in 1989/90.

Some clubs looked at other revenue streams, including rugby league. Fulham were the first club to host a rugby league club in 1980, followed by Cardiff City and Carlisle United the following season, entering teams into Division Two of the rugby league championship. Kent Invicta played at the Priestfield Stadium, Gillingham, and then metamorphosed into Southend Invicta playing at Southend United's Roots Hall.

The experiments were not altogether successful. At Southend, just 85 people turned up to watch the game against Huddersfield Barracudas. I went to one rugby league game at Roots Hall, against Whitehaven from Cumbria one Sunday morning, 11am kick-off. Two hundred people there, many of them from 'Haven'. The visiting supporters clearly keen.

For some clubs, their parlous financial position left them open to a potential takeover.

Anton Johnson, the fifth-generation owner of Johnson Butchers, had taken an interest in football clubs. He purchased Rotherham United, apparently on a whim when he heard on *Match of the Day* they were for sale. Don Megson, the ex-Sheffield Wednesday full-back and captain, worked with Johnson at Bournemouth, another club he bought, noting, 'He'd made quite a few enemies in the game because of his supposed reputation for ducking and diving.' (*Don Megson: A Life in Football*, Don Megson with Chris Olewicz, Vertical Editions, 2014).

Megson had been appointed manager at Bournemouth by Johnson, Harry Redknapp his assistant and Brian Tyler made managing director. Megson points out the aims of the two men differed. Megson wanted to improve the team and seek promotion, whereas Tyler's primary goal was to maximise profitability.

Anton Johnson turned his attentions to Southend United – the club were losing money, crowds were down. My father-in-law Eric and brother-in-law Ray were small-scale shareholders in the Shrimpers. I recollect both preparing to go to an extraordinary general meeting of the club, where the would-be purchaser's proposals would be set out. On returning from the meeting, my father-in-law was unconvinced. He doubted Johnson's motives.

No matter – purchase it he did.

Perhaps my father-in-law's misgivings were not misplaced – attendances at Roots Hall fell below 3,000 in 1984, and *The Rough Guide to English Football: A Fans' Handbook* (Dan Goldstein, Rough Guides, 2000) commented, 'Perhaps unfortunately for the club's long-term future, this did not deter local entrepreneur Anton Johnson from sinking his claws into United – in little more than 12 months he ran up debts of more than £1 million, before his labyrinthine network of share dealings involving several other clubs led to his being banned by the league.'

After selling Rotherham United and Bournemouth, Johnson said, 'I was still receiving adverse publicity in the press. The papers were saying I was the Mafia taking over football. Nobody had bothered to enquire – it was all speculation – but it made good reading. A [television] programme [*World in Action*] came out six months later painting a very black picture of me. Unfortunately, once it had been broadcast it was too late to defend myself. The programme said I was involved with the running of eight clubs; theoretically, they were right, but I was only trying to assist five of them.' (*King of Clubs*, Anton Johnson, Grosvenor House Publishing Limited, 2012).

Johnson identified another potential club, Queens Park Rangers. 'I had become close friends with Terry Venables [QPR manager]. I also got to know the QPR chairman Jim Gregory. Jim was thinking of selling Loftus Road for a property development and was prepared to sell me the club. My dream was to take them to play at Southend, where I could see football every week: First Division one week, Third the next.' The initiative did not progress.

By 1984, a Football League commission had undertaken an investigation and as a result Anton Johnson was effectively banned for life from any involvement with the league's member clubs.

In the top flight Tottenham Hotspur were £4 million in debt in November 1982, the directors struggling to retain control. It was time for change. The long-standing directors, led by the Wade and Richardson families, were replaced by a new group, led by Irving Scholar, a 35-year-old property developer, and a board of directors led by a solicitor, Douglas Alexiou.

Within a year, Tottenham Hotspur FC were changed fundamentally. In the summer of 1983, Scholar announced the club would become the first sports club to float on the stock market. The claim was it would allow new investment in the club, covering the cost of the over-budget West Stand and the increasing gap between static club income and spiralling transfer fees.

There was one significant issue to address to enable flotation – the Football Association's rulebook prevented paying part-time directors and unlimited dividends, and it restricted what could be done to a club's assets if it was wound up. The answer to the problem was simply that Tottenham Hotspur FC would be a wholly owned subsidiary of Tottenham Hotspur PLC, and this holding company floated on the stock market, not the football club. Once this approach had been successfully applied, it enabled other clubs to follow suit.

In September 1983, Tottenham Hotspur's 3.8 million £1 company shares were a complete sell-out as soon as they came to market.

In August 1984, at the first annual meeting, pre-tax profits of £902,000 were announced, compared to £168,000 the previous year.

Earlier that summer, perhaps one of the most telling observations was made following the surprise departure of manager Keith Burkinshaw. The club had won the UEFA Cup and seemed set fair to challenge for more trophies.

It was not a spur-of-the-moment decision for Burkinshaw. All reports indicated there had not been a meeting of minds with the new owners over how the club would operate in the future, with Burkinshaw's responsibilities reduced.

Meanwhile, Scholar had been looking for a new manager to take over from Burkinshaw and had identified Alex Ferguson, then manager at Aberdeen, for the role. That did not materialise.

Burkinshaw saw things were changing. It was reported that in discussion with journalist Ken Jones, the ex-manager purportedly said, 'There used to be a football club there.' The veracity of the comment has been questioned, but in the context of the times it was an interesting observation.

At Manchester United, chairman Martin Edwards was considering selling his stake in the club in the summer of 1989.

It was a particular low point for football after the Bradford fire, Heysel and most recently the Hillsborough disaster. Following the Taylor report, United knew they would have to self-fund ground improvements, with no grants available. Michael Knighton offered to purchase Edwards's shares, as well as rebuild the Stretford End at Old Trafford, and wipe out the debt (over £900,000) Edwards had been carrying.

Knighton's perspective was he wanted to revolutionise the club – enhance its commercial prospects and follow through on the redevelopment of the ground, exploiting the club's potential in a positive way for the benefit of the club, the manager (Alex Ferguson) and the team.

Knighton said he was offered the option to purchase the club – or at least Martin Edwards's shares (around 50 per cent of the club's shares) – at £20 a share, then trading at £5-£6 a share, a total cost of £10 million. The would-be purchaser saw that as a price well worth paying.

Before the first game of the 1989/90 season against Arsenal, Knighton was introduced to the Old Trafford crowd as the new owner of Manchester United. He was resplendent in United kit, making for the penalty area and juggling the ball before kicking it into the empty net. He was received well by the United crowd.

Martin Edwards acknowledged he himself wasn't a fans' favourite. He'd been at the helm for years and the club had won nothing since 1985. Knighton maybe offered greater promise for the fans.

So, why did Knighton's purchase of the club not materialise? Edwards said 'Knighton's credibility, along with his attempt to take over Manchester United, began to unravel. Just a week before Knighton was due to confirm the deal, Cohen and Thornton dramatically pulled out. Knighton was left with no choice but to find new backers. His accountants compiled a report on Manchester United, which was sent out to several investors.' (*Red Glory*, Martin Edwards, Michael O'Mara Books Limited, 2017). Edwards underlined this was confidential United information that could fall into the hands of competitors. The club took legal action to prevent the report from being released.

Edwards went on to say that as time progressed, 'not only was everybody at the club against him [Knighton], but now the fans didn't want the takeover to go through after the months of speculation in the media about whether the deal would happen or if he had the finance. I told him that events had now gone too far and I suggested he tear up the contract. If he did that, I was prepared to offer him a seat on the board.' Knighton agreed and stayed on the Manchester United board for three years.

Knighton's perspective was that he included more people in the deal. Questions were raised about who was intending to purchase the club, and about Knighton's finances. 'The press went mad for it. My name was mud, my motives questioned, my finances suspected. The notion was that I was now a front for others. Though all they needed to have done was call me for the truth, the smear was out there ... David Walker, a writer for the *Daily Mail* at the time, informed me that [Robert] Maxwell [owner of the Mirror Group, Oxford United and Derby County and failed purchaser of Manchester United] had told his journalists to "destroy this Knighton bloke ... let's destroy him."

'And that's what they tried to do. It was very intense ... I told Martin that we should talk and find a decent solution to end the frenetic media circus. After the talks, I told him the sale was off.' (*FourFourTwo*, Issue 306).

The football club sale that never was.

# Chapter 22

# Football in Scotland

ANY VIEW of Scottish football from outside the country almost inevitably focuses on the big two – Glasgow Celtic and Glasgow Rangers, the Old Firm – the clubs that have dominated the game north of the border.

The achievements of the Bhoys and the Gers in the domestic game dwarf those of any other club in Scotland. Since the Scottish League championship began in 1890/91, there have been only 14 seasons when the trophy has not resided at Celtic Park or Ibrox. Domination.

But not so in the 1980s. Celtic claimed four titles, Rangers three, Aberdeen three and Dundee United one (1979/80–1989/90).

In the cups there was a similar breach in the Old Firm's supremacy. The Scottish FA Cup – Celtic four wins, Aberdeen four wins (in five seasons), Rangers two wins and St Mirren one win; the Scottish League Cup – Rangers six wins, Dundee United two wins, Aberdeen two wins and Celtic one win.

Yes, the two Glasgow giants featured strongly in the domestic honours in the 1980s, but in relative terms there was a significant change that saw Aberdeen and Dundee United break up the duopoly.

In Europe too, the Old Firm were the only Scottish clubs to win European honours before the 1980s (Celtic – European Cup, 1967; Rangers – European Cup Winners' Cup, 1972). In the 1980s, no such honours for Glasgow's big two but Aberdeen defeated Real Madrid to win the European Cup Winners' Cup in 1983 and Dundee United reached the UEFA Cup Final in 1987 against Gothenburg.

And the men behind those achievements? Alex Ferguson at Aberdeen – eight domestic honours and the European Cup Winners' Cup in the 1980s; their players included Jim Leighton, Alex McLeish, Willie Miller and Doug Rougvie. At Dundee United, manager Jim McLean – three domestic honours in the 1980s; their players included David Narey, Paul Sturrock, Eamonn Bannon, Ralph Milne and Paul Hegarty.

The Old Firm continued to feature strongly in the decade, the derby game between the clubs to the fore.

Trevor Francis, transferred to Rangers from Sampdoria, said, 'Nothing compares to the Glasgow derby. The atmosphere that is generated is the absolute best and nothing rivals it. Playing in that atmosphere is something special, as you are subject to some intimidating tackles, a frantic pace and frantic challenges that could be dangerous.' (*One in a Million: The Autobiography*, Trevor Francis with Keith Dixon, Pitch Publishing, 2019).

Francis's observations were a prelude to the most hard-fought Old Firm derby of the decade – a fierce 2-2 draw at Ibrox on 17 October 1987. Three players were sent off – Chris Woods and Terry Butcher of Rangers and Frank McAvennie of Celtic. Woods and McAvennie had an altercation in the penalty area – McAvennie clipping Woods round the ear and Woods retaliating with an elbow to his assailant's face. Butcher pushed the striker away before Graham Roberts grabbed the

Celtic striker's throat and pushed him to the ground. Butcher was sent off later in the game.

The four players were later reported to the Procurator Fiscal and appeared in court on charges relating to their conduct in the game. The outcome – McAvennie was found not guilty, Roberts's case was not proven and Woods and Butcher were both convicted of a breach of the peace.

Francis is clear in his assessment. 'There was no doubt that this football match created legal precedents. There was a definite involvement from central government to put football in its place as far as its influence on the behaviour of fans. Many fans at the time felt that it all added to the football spectacle – nothing like a bit of aggro to get the crowd going.'

In *The Scotsman* newspaper Terry Butcher was quoted as saying, 'I have no doubt there was government interference and pressure applied from the highest level to bring convictions against us. We were convenient scapegoats, we were the role models who had to be slapped down and told how to behave so that the supporters would get the message.'

The charge against all four players was, 'while participating in a football match, you did conduct yourself in a disorderly manner and commit a breach of the peace'. At the trial, Assistant Chief Constable of Strathclyde, John Dickson, stated the four defendants through their actions had come dangerously close to provoking major public disorder. 'There was unbridled hatred on the faces of some of the fans when they were shouting obscenities and insults at each other.'

In passing sentence, Sheriff Archibald McKay said of Woods's actions, 'You jabbed McAvennie on the chin with your left forearm. It was an assault which constituted breach of the peace.' Butcher was guilty of a 'violent push which might reasonably have been expected to upset other Celtic players and their support … you must have been aware of your wider responsibilities and you failed to discharge them'.

Woods was fined £500, Butcher £250. Sixty-two supporters were arrested on the day of the game.

Following the match, *The Herald* sports journalist Jim Reynolds commented, 'I know there are those who stupidly believe that this kind of "red blooded" behaviour brings an extra thrill to the proceedings. It is downright hooliganism which, but for the admirable restraint shown by the fans, could have led to something much more serious.

'I wonder if these players, especially those who have come from England, fully understand the powder-keg situation they are in every time they take part in an Old Firm game. If not, then it is time for someone with a sense of responsibility to spell it out in full. Saturday will go down as the day the Old Firm clashes almost died of shame.

'For the second time in succession, this particular fixture left a nasty taste in the mouth and the fans showed themselves as being far more responsible than the richly rewarded stars they had paid to see.'

There was a seismic change in Scottish football – Mo Johnston, a Catholic, joined Celtic in 1984, signed for Nantes in 1987 and returned to Glasgow in 1989 to play for Rangers. Almost unheard of.

He became only the second player to cross the divide since the Second World War, and most particularly the first Catholic to play for Rangers since the First World War – the day he signed was described as 'one of Scotland's most historic days'.

The *Daily Record* reported, 'Scotland was stunned yesterday when Rangers broke their no-Catholic barrier in the most sensational way.' – and Johnston had turned down a return move to Celtic.

Under Graeme Souness, who as Rangers' player-manager signed Johnston, the end of the 1980s proved to be the start of a very successful period for the club that included nine successive league titles.

# Chapter 23

# European Club Competitions

ENGLISH CLUBS were banned from each of the three European club competitions – European Cup, European Cup Winners' Cup and the UEFA Cup – following the Heysel disaster in 1985. Against that background, the achievements of English clubs in Europe in the 1980s are that much more substantial.

The premier European competition in the 1980s was the European Cup – a competition open to the champions of each European league only. It was contested on a knockout basis.

English clubs dominated the European Cup in the first half of the decade. Nottingham Forest won the second of their successive European Cups in 1980, followed by Liverpool in 1981, Aston Villa in 1982 and Liverpool again in 1984.

After the 1-0 European Cup Final win against Hamburg in Madrid, Forest manager Brian Clough observed, 'I don't remember being so involved in a game before. It's the greatest moment of my career. We've achieved some things at Forest, but I think this was our personal best. We applied ourselves better than I have seen any side for many years. Our centre-forward didn't even have the strength to take his shinpads off.'

The following season, Liverpool made it to the final of the European Cup, playing Spanish club Real Madrid at the Parc des Princes in Paris. A couple of work colleagues from Ford at Dagenham travelled to the game – Greg Hunt and staunch Liverpool supporter Barry Keeling, whose encyclopaedic knowledge of his club and almost photographic recall of goals they'd scored I found astonishing.

On their return from Paris, I asked Greg about the trip – and the conversation went something like this:

'Enjoy your trip to Paris?'

'Yes, it was really good. We met Bill Shankly [ex-Liverpool manager] in the lobby of the hotel on the morning of the game.'

'No.'

'We did and he was very friendly and spent time talking with us. He always does with supporters.

'We said we were a bit concerned that Laurie Cunningham might be back and playing for Real in the match. He could be a real threat. Shanks was having none of it. "Nah, he's been out for three months, boys, it's a panic measure bringing him back for the game. Don't worry, boys, we'll win."

'We felt a whole lot better after that chat we had with Shanks.'

And, of course, Shanks was right – Liverpool won the game through an Alan Kennedy goal. And Cunningham? He was not fully fit, tightly marked and made little impression on the game.

Aston Villa's success is interesting – promoted to the First Division for the 1975/76 season under manager Ron Saunders, they progressed to become league champions in 1980/81, playing entertaining and thrilling football. Part way through the 1981/82 season Saunders left, succeeded by Tony Barton. Within three months of taking charge, Barton led the club to the European Cup, Villa defeating Bayern Munich 1-0 in Rotterdam.

Progress for Villa had been steady in the earlier rounds, despite being underdogs in each tie after their opening win of the competition.

The semi-final second leg against Anderlecht in Brussels was marred by serious crowd trouble on the terraces, which turned into a pitch invasion. The game held up for six minutes as police with dogs sought to restore order. The game ended 0-0, Villa winning the tie 1-0 on aggregate.

For the final, Villa's players were on £2,500-a-man win bonus, their opponents on four times that amount.

The pressure was all on the German team, Villa rank outsiders. The Villa players were relaxed before the game. 'Nottingham Forest manager Brian Clough, who was at the final as a co-commentator for ITV, remarked beforehand to Tony Barton that he could not believe how relaxed the team were. Villa's players were taking photos like they were tourists, while the Bayern players looked studious and nervous.' (*Ticket to the Moon*, Richard Sydenham, de Coubertin Books, 2018).

In the game's early stages, there were major problems for Villa. Goalkeeper Jimmy Rimmer had to come off with an injury after nine minutes, replaced by Nigel Spink, who had one first-team game to his credit in his five years at Villa Park. Spink played the proverbial blinder. Peter Withe's tap-in goal after 67 minutes was the only goal of the game. Against all the odds, Villa had won.

Tony Barton left within two seasons of the European Cup triumph and Villa – league champions in 1981, European Cup winners in 1982 – were relegated to Division Two in 1987.

The 1984 European Cup Final was held at the Stadio Olimpico, Rome, Liverpool defeating Roma 4-2 on penalties after the game finished 1-1 after extra time. One of the enduring images was Liverpool goalkeeper Bruce Grobbelaar's 'wobbly legs' routine as he faced the opposition's penalty-takers, followed by Francesco Graziani's crucial miss from the spot.

For Liverpool, Alan Kennedy took the crucial penalty in the shoot-out, although he wasn't expecting it. 'Joe Fagan asked me after extra time if I was okay and I said "Yeah" thinking it was a general enquiry. I'm wondering to Ronnie Moran who is down for the fifth penalty. He says. "It's you."'

Michael Robinson a Liverpool substitute on the night, recollected, 'Graeme [Souness] was a Trojan that night. Every player on the pitch was in awe of him. He was brave and magnificent, and led the team like a warrior.'

But there was trouble before and after the game for Liverpool supporters. Roma fans stabbed, slashed and were involved in violent confrontations with the away supporters. In Italy the following morning, there was embarrassment at the behaviour of the home fans. *La Republica* headlined, 'Manhunt against the English'. *Il Corriere dello Sport*, 'The aftermath of the match brought a night of vile, blind violence that disappointment cannot justify'. *Il Tiempo* reported, 'The usual group of fans with knives, bottles and sticks went on an odious manhunt.'

A year later – Heysel.

Of the remaining European Cup winners in the 1980s, perhaps the most impressive was AC Milan with successive wins in 1988/89 and 1989/90 – Marco van Basten, Ruud Gullit, Paolo Maldini, Franco Baresi, Frank Rijkaard, Carlo Ancelotti all stars of the Italian team managed by Arrigo Sacchi.

In the European Cup Winners' Cup, Barcelona triumphed twice in the decade, the only club to do so. Everton and Aberdeen were the British clubs to win the trophy. Everton defeated Rapid Vienna 3-1 in a one-sided game in the 1985 final in Rotterdam, while Aberdeen beat Real Madrid 2-1 after extra time in Gothenburg in 1983.

Arsenal made the final in 1980, losing 5-4 on penalties to Valencia after a 0-0 draw and extra time. This was the only time the competition was decided on penalties.

Anderlecht were the only club to win the UEFA Cup twice in the 1980s. Ipswich Town were winners in 1981, Tottenham Hotspur in 1984.

Ipswich defeated AZ Alkmaar, a 3-0 first-leg lead at Portman Road giving the Suffolk club a strong advantage. A see-saw game in the second leg at the Olympic Stadium in Amsterdam saw Town hold out for a 5-4 win on aggregate.

John Wark of Ipswich set a UEFA Cup scoring record that season with 14 goals.

Three years later, Tottenham defeated Anderlecht 4-3 on penalties after the tie had finished 2-2 on aggregate – both games ending 1-1. Spurs' hero was 21-year-old Tony Parkes, who made two saves in the penalty shoot-out to clinch the game.

The starting 11 for Spurs in the second leg of the final was made up of eight Englishmen, two Irishmen and a Scot.

# Chapter 24

# European Championships

EUROPE'S MAJOR tournament for national teams had historically not been one that England or the other home nations had enjoyed success in. The best any home nation had achieved prior to the 1980s was England's third place in 1968.

In 1980, the number of competing nations at the final stages of the tournament increased to eight. The competition was held in Italy. England took their place and would be the only home nation to qualify for the final stages of any European Championships in the 1980s. Hopes were high that Ron Greenwood's side would do well.

June 1980 – England's first game in the group stage against Belgium in Turin. The game broadcast live on television. Everyone left work that evening talking about the game, anticipation high, intending to watch it at home – and that included people who ordinarily had little interest in the game. This was the national team.

The game started well for England – 1-0 up after 26 minutes, a solo goal from Ray Wilkins. Minutes later, an equaliser for the Belgians. Cue fighting behind the England goal. Norman Fox wrote in *The Times*, 'The violence seemed to begin when the Italians cheered the Belgian goal.'

Italian police fired tear gas into the crowd. Smoke seen hanging over large parts of the terracing. Police went into the area occupied by England followers with their batons raised. Large empty spaces now visible on the terraces as people escaped the violence, tear gas and onrushing police. All on live television.

At the height of the trouble, with tear gas in the air, the game was stopped for five minutes, players affected by soreness in their eyes. The game played out to a 1-1 draw.

England's manager, Ron Greenwood, was furious. 'We are ashamed of people like this. We have done everything to create the right impression here, then they let you down … I wish they could all be put in a boat and dropped in the ocean.'

The Football Association was hit with an £8,000 fine from UEFA. FA chairman and Old Edwardian, Professor Sir Harold Thompson, commented, 'It is a lamentable disgrace that the work Ron Greenwood has done can be jeopardised by a few silly louts. They are not fans at all.' Watching the scenes on television, it was much more than a few.

There had been many instances of hooliganism abroad by followers of club teams – but not so much the national team. Thoughts of football evaporated. The television pictures left a sickening feeling in the stomach. Innocent people had been maimed or injured by supposed followers of the England football team.

Talk at work in the morning was solely of the scenes on the terraces. No one talked about the football. It didn't matter.

Looking back, it was a significant event – substantial numbers of people became disinterested, disengaged and dismayed by football, particularly those who only followed the national team on television in major tournaments. There was a real sense of shame about the violence perpetrated by the England followers.

I recollect men who served their country in the Second World War, and women who lived through the war at home, voicing their disgust at these pariahs who disgraced our country. They alienated themselves from civilised society. The problem was they were English – and everyone felt the shame by association.

It led to more debate at workplaces, in pubs and in the national media about what could be done? Some of the suggestions were clear and uncompromising – perhaps one of the more restrained was the recommendation to bring back National Service for boys in the 16–18 age bracket.

Abroad, hooliganism became known as the 'English disease'. John Motson said the events in Turin 'marked the start of a grim decade, hooliganism in foreign cities on a grim, frightening scale ... the bile and frustrations of a disenfranchised section of society were taken out not just on their own kind, but on unsuspecting and well-mannered European citizens ... watching or reporting England abroad became a game of hide-and-seek, trying to avoid the bars, restaurants, shops and hotels that were on the hooligans' hit list.' (*Motty*, John Motson, Virgin Books, 2009).

In the 1980 tournament, England failed to progress from the group stages. For many at home, there was now little interest. The eventual winners were West Germany, who defeated Belgium 2-1 in the final in Rome.

Four years on, the tournament was staged in France. Well before the qualifying stages were underway, there was real concern about England followers travelling the short distance to France and repeating the sort of mayhem seen in Italy. The concerns were reinforced by hooliganism and violent confrontations visited on European capitals by followers of the national team as England completed their qualifying games.

To the great relief of many on the continent, England failed to qualify for the final stages of the tournament. Interest in this country was very much from a distance as a result. The final, in Paris, saw the hosts defeat Spain 2-0.

The 1988 tournament took place in West Germany. The same fears and concerns about the England followers came to the fore. English clubs had been banned from Europe, but not the national team. This time England qualified. The Republic of Ireland, the Netherlands and the USSR were in their group. The games to be held in Stuttgart, Dusseldorf and Frankfurt.

Word of England's hooligans had spread to the United States. The *New York Times* of 10 June 1988 carried the headline, 'Soccer Alert: The British (Fans) are Coming' and commented, 'The residents of West Germany and battalions of police are girding for the least-welcome tourists from Britain: English soccer hooligans. The closest scrutiny and much of the crowd-control program will be directed at the English fans, the "bad boys" of the soccer world who are effectively on parole. Security preparations have been extraordinary. "The stadiums will have to look like bunkers, like fortresses surrounded by police," said Jacques Georges, the UEFA president.'

Pre-tournament fears about hooliganism proved well founded, with violence and lawless behaviour in each of the host cities. It was particularly acute at the second game against the Netherlands in Dusseldorf. The city saw its worst ever violence. Reporting on BBC Television, Archie Macpherson said, 'There wasn't a single street that we walked in that wasn't littered with glass. This is now an occupied city. There are police with riot shields, visors, truncheons, guns.' Headlines in the following day's newspapers were grim and unrelenting.

England lost all their group games and exited the tournament, which spelt relief for the organisers and the people of West Germany.

The final, between the Netherlands and the USSR, was contested at the Olympic Stadium, Munich. It was lit up by a fabulous volleyed goal from Marco van Basten, which clinched a 2-0 victory for the Dutch.

Some of the football played in the European Championships had been sparkling, but the shadow and spectre of hooliganism was an overriding image.

# Chapter 25

# Frankfurt

'YOU'RE GOING to Germany.'

'Don't be silly.'

'Yes, you are.'

'No, I'm not.'

'You are. It was on the radio on Saturday. You won a competition to go to Germany.'

This exchange took place in the playground of St Joseph's Primary School in Guildford one Monday morning in late May 1988. The participants were two eight-year-olds, my eldest son Ben and his friend Mark Maddock, who had been listening to LBC radio that weekend.

The radio had run a competition three weeks earlier, with the prize a trip to Frankfurt to watch England play the USSR in the European Championships. It included staying three nights in a luxury hotel for the winner and a friend. The competition was run in conjunction with Trebor Extra Strong Mints, the official England team sponsor.

The competition involved answering questions about previous European Championships and the winner drawn from all the correct entries. I don't recollect the precise questions – I do remember suggesting to my football-mad son that we might look in the *Rothmans Football Yearbook* for the answers.

Answers obtained, two competition entries made – one from me and one from Ben. Ben's in his own handwriting, his name supplemented with the words, 'Aged 8'. Another important part of the competition was that entries had to be submitted on postcards. All well and good. No doubt there were thousands of entries. How did ours stand out?

Bright, colourful postcards. Excess postcards purchased on holiday did have a use! Ben's postcard was a bright tourist map of Cornwall – the county surrounded by blue sea and a light cream colour, with bright red landmarks highlighted on it. It stood out and the age of the entrant was prominent. It might just work.

Whether or not the stand-out postcard had any bearing on the outcome, who knows? Suffice to say Mark Maddock was right – Ben was going to West Germany and with a friend!

The first I knew about the forthcoming continental football watching was a phone call at work that same Monday morning from Ben's mum Pauline. She passed on the key details – dates, flights and hotel – and the name of our main contact, Toby, representing the sponsors who would be looking after us in Frankfurt.

All well and good. I had two immediate concerns. The first – I'd only just started a new job with ICL and it was a particularly hectic time. As the personnel manager, I had the primary responsibility of ensuring the rules regarding vacations were applied and adhered to – and this included providing adequate notice for holiday requests.

One week into the job … I approached David Teague, my manager, with some concern about this immediate request. He couldn't have been more pleased or more accommodating – of course I could have the time off.

That was straightforward. The next concern was not.

I had spent my adult life avoiding any travel by aeroplane. I had a fear of flying, a deep-seated fear of flying. I had never set foot on an aeroplane. I felt sure the journey to Frankfurt had to be done by air. My preference of a car journey to a port, boarding a ferry and completing the journey to Frankfurt by road was fanciful at best.

How to address the fear? I knew I had to and ideally before the trip to Frankfurt. As circumstance would have it, there was a need to go to Edinburgh for work the next week – previously I'd been planning for the journey by car: late-night departure from Guildford, stay overnight with my parents in Sheffield and make an early start on the journey to Scotland.

Time to take the bull by the horns – flight booked, British Airways, Heathrow to Edinburgh return. I know I barely slept the night before the early-morning flight. Travel to Heathrow with trepidation – locate where I needed to be, not easy for a first visit to an airport. Check in at the British Airways desk – simple and straightforward. No security checks, of either bags or self, straight to the aircraft once the flight was called.

This was it. Nerves to the fore. I'd decided to tell the stewardess as I entered the cabin that this was my first flight and I had no idea what I was expected to do. She was very understanding and helpful – pointing to my seat, baggage in the overhead locker – and asking me to listen to the instructions about safety and the seatbelt that would be made. I listened and watched like a hawk, following the instructions to the letter.

I recollect the noise of the aircraft engines, the acceleration down the runway and the sensation of the plane leaving the ground. The first time it makes a great impression, and particularly on me given my concerns.

I knew the flight was scheduled to be an hour. Ten minutes from the end of that hour the stewardess walked down the cabin, looked at me and said, 'Because it's your first flight the captain's asked if you'd like to come up to the flight deck and sit with him as we fly into Edinburgh?' It was a request but not one in my nervous state I was likely to turn down. Seatbelt undone, I made my way out to the aisle to the accompaniment of loud, albeit well-intended instructions from my fellow passengers, 'Don't touch anything!' as I made my way down towards the cockpit.

Inside the cockpit, the captain very warm, amiable and welcoming. 'Take the seat next to me, strap yourself in and I'll talk you through our approach.' And he did. Fabulous views of the Firth of Forth and the approach to the runway. Touchdown, landed. He said it was a good landing. I had nothing to compare it with and took his word for it. More importantly, my nerves had gone. The captain and crew had been simply superb in dealing with their nervous and jittery first-time passenger.

Frankfurt here we come!

Ben's mum and his two younger brothers Sam and Tom came to Heathrow – all of them seeing it as a great adventure.

The flight – thankfully – was uneventful. It was a Pan Am flight and the stewardesses made a fuss of their eight-year-old first-time flyer.

Arriving at Frankfurt airport that evening, the most noteworthy interaction was at passport control – passport handed over, details checked, the immediate reaction from the West German official was a long – and for the recipient – very uncomfortable glare. No words proffered to the visitors. It seemed to last an age before what seemed a reluctant nod of the head and we proceeded on to foreign soil.

And the reason for the less-than-welcome greeting? I put it down to the actions of some of my fellow countrymen supporting England in the European Championships who had left a trail of destruction and mayhem as they followed their team to Stuttgart, on to Dusseldorf and now Frankfurt. Hooliganism at its worse. At home, media coverage of the hooliganism – on television and in the newspapers – had been extensive. Simply, England and their supporters were not welcome in West Germany.

We met Toby, the sponsor's representative, at the airport and made our way by taxi to the well-appointed Inter-Continental Hotel in central Frankfurt.

In the breakfast area the following morning there were several well-known faces evident – Mark Austin, then a television news reporter, sat close to us and other news journalists were in the area. Toby said that because of the extensive hooliganism, the number of news journalists exceeded the number of football journalists in Frankfurt.

Rumour had it that such was the apparent need for hard news stories that representatives of one of the tabloid newspapers had brought T-Shirts out to Frankfurt, with the red cross of St George on the front, and offered to pay local youths to wear them and throw stones, providing an apparent 'ideal photo opportunity'. There was no way of knowing the veracity or otherwise of that rumour, but such was the febrile and tense atmosphere surrounding England supporters it was not dismissed out of hand.

Interestingly, a year later England travelled to Stockholm for a World Cup qualifier against Sweden 'followed by a press corps who were expected to file stories of English hooligans on the rampage. They included Colin Ward, a former hooligan and serial chronicler of hooligan violence, who was hired by the *Today* newspaper to travel undercover with the fans. He returned convinced that the real story was not English hooligans looking for trouble but journalists looking for English hooligans and reinterpreting minor incidents as riots.' (*No Such Thing as Society*, Andy McSmith, Constable, 2011).

Back to Frankfurt for the England team and the game against the USSR – the third and final group game. It was academic in terms of any progress in the Championships. England had lost their opener to the Republic of Ireland in Stuttgart (1-0), their second game to the Netherlands in Dusseldorf (3-1) and could not progress to the knockout stages.

Toby had good news for us – they had arranged for us to go and watch England training in the Waldstadion (Eintracht Frankfurt's ground and venue for the game against the USSR). We would be going to the England hotel first and have transport from there to the ground.

The hotel was out of town, armed guards at the entrance and in the grounds. We joined a minibus carrying FA representatives and staff to the ground – the minibus followed the England team coach, a police escort speeding the convoy on its way. Glen Kirton (FA executive) and Fred Street (physio with England and Arsenal) were on the minibus, both very friendly and keen to know about the hooliganism that had followed England around West Germany. They had read newspapers and seen television news reports, but it became very evident they operated in their own bubble with the England team and were cocooned from the outside world. We had nothing material to tell them.

At the training session, Ben stood behind one goal. Once the ball went out of play he ran after it, returning it to the players. The England manager Bobby Robson shouted to him,

'Yes, my son' as he asked for the ball. Great paternal pride watching Ben as ball boy for the training session.

Robson looked very much 'hands-on' at the training session – players focused and responsive to his instructions from the sidelines.

During the session I was introduced to a young guy dressed in smart casual clothes on the side of the pitch. His name was Jon Smith, a football agent, his company 'First Artists'. With him was Adrian Heath, then with Everton but not in the England squad. Smith was very friendly and took time out to talk with Ben. He made a point of referencing Tony Cottee, then with West Ham United, who was being heavily linked with a transfer to Arsenal in the 1988 close season. Smith simply said Cottee would not be going to the Gunners and that Everton would be his destination. The Merseysiders had not featured in speculation in the media about Cottee's move from West Ham. And ... Cottee moved to Everton.

At the end of the training session, which lasted just over an hour, the England players walked off the pitch – Hoddle, Waddle, Hateley, Bryan Robson and the rest. I asked if they'd mind having a photo taken with Ben – all said it was no trouble. A lasting memento of the occasion.

Bobby Robson was last off the pitch with Peter Beardsley – he had his arm around the Liverpool player and looked as though he was talking earnestly with him. Beardsley was an unused substitute in the following day's game.

We made our way back to the England hotel. More activities were lined up – Ben would be interviewing John Barnes for LBC radio and prior to that we could attend the press conference the manager would be giving ahead of the game.

We saw several England players in the hotel lobby, and all were pleased to sign Ben's autograph book. Peter Reid made a point of talking with him about his football. I mentioned to Reid he'd upset me earlier in the season when he scored Everton's late equalising goal in the FA Cup third-round game at Hillsborough – 'only kick I had in the game,' he said. Some kick.

Toby took us to the large room holding the press conference – we stood at the back and were introduced to Bobby Charlton and commentator Tony Gubba, both working for the BBC. Bobby noticed Ben wearing a smart tracksuit with the sponsor's name, Trebor, on it. He pointed to the name and asked Ben what it spelt backwards – it took a short time before the answer was forthcoming.

And the press conference? Bobby Robson was seated behind a table on a raised platform at the front of the room. It started with Steve Curry of the *Daily Express* asking a question about the team and whether there were any injuries that might impact on the selection? Perfectly reasonable question, informative response from the England manager.

From that opening, the questions took a very different course – the poor showing by England, out of the tournament, the pressure on the manager. To them all, Bobby Robson responded clearly and with dignity, albeit the responses were quite short. And then the question that lit the blue touchpaper – the essence of which was, 'We've heard that there's dissension in the camp and that the captain is at odds with ...' You felt the atmosphere in the room change.

The England manager visibly drew breath and looked the questioner in the eye, responding clearly, unequivocally and with a sharp edge to his voice, 'There is no dissension in the camp and I'll get the captain [Bryan Robson] down here if you want, and he'll tell you, but if I were you I wouldn't be here when he arrives.' That stopped the line of questioning immediately. The press conference was over.

To my uneducated, non-journalistic ear, and as someone who had no experience of press conferences, it seemed like the primary line of questioning was looking for issues, looking for problems, and almost goading the manager into a reaction. I was not impressed. Earlier, arriving at the hotel, we'd seen a coach parked up with empty lager and beer cans visible inside and at the front of the vehicle. We were told this was the coach used to ferry the football journalists to and from the various grounds across the country.

After the press conference we were taken to meet Andrew Gidley, the LBC sports reporter who had arranged the interview with John Barnes. Andrew was very friendly and quickly engaged in discussion with Ben, making sure he felt comfortable talking to the England winger. He was. The reporter had prepared some questions. Ben read them and confirmed he was fine with the questions.

John Barnes arrived. Introductions completed, Andrew prepared his tape recording and microphone. And off we went – questions asked in a measured way, thoughtful and articulate responses from John Barnes. Examples included:

Ben: 'What is the spirit like in the camp?'

JB: 'Well, all things taken into consideration, it's very good. Because, as you'll know by now, we've not had a particularly good start. Well, we've had a disastrous start. You'll know we lost our first two games. So, taking that into consideration, the lads are relaxed and really looking forward to the game. Hopefully, we can win, and we can go home with some pride.'

Ben: 'How do you think the game will go?'

JB: 'Well, Russia need a point to make sure, virtually make sure of qualifying, so I think they're going to be playing it cagey. We have nothing to lose apart from our pride as everyone knows, so we're going to be going out to win. So, I think that says they'll probably be a bit defensive, but we'll be going all out to win.'

Interview completed, Ben read out the scripted conclusion: 'This is Ben Crooks reporting for LBC with the England team in Frankfurt'.

There was some minor editing prior to the interview being broadcast the following day as a preview to the game on LBC radio – a question I recollect being omitted focused on John Barnes's favourite sweet.

After the interview back to the hotel – it had been the proverbial day and a half. I sat and reflected, putting pen to paper to make sure I did not forget a quite amazing day – four full pages to record the day's events.

On the Saturday afternoon, prior to the interview being broadcast, the LBC sports programme host Mike Porter made this observation about Ben's trip to Frankfurt, 'If he was excited, his father was even more excited. He was to quote that old phrase over the moon when he realised he was going out there.' In fairness, I think 'over the moon' understates it.

We were taken by coach to the Waldstadion, joining a range of other guests and some well-known football names of the time who were accompanying the group. They included John Gregory (Aston Villa) and Roy Aitken (Glasgow Celtic). Both were friendly and easy to talk to.

It was a warm, sunny day, shirt sleeves in evidence in a stadium that was primarily open to the elements. We were seated centrally, high along one side of the ground. The bulk of the England supporters were positioned behind one goal to our right. The away support for the USSR was not particularly evident – odd pockets of the red flag with its hammer and sickle occasionally visible.

The year 1988 was before the fall of the Berlin Wall. Germany was still partitioned, East and West. The USSR consisted of its socialist republics – Russia, Georgia, Ukraine and the others. Chances were, it was not that easy for football supporters in the USSR to travel to the west to follow their national team.

The bulk of the crowd looked and sounded local – and they were in a positive, noisy mood. Before the game, several 'Mexican waves' were started in various parts of the stadium. Participation in the waves increased as it gained momentum, except when it arrived in the England supporters' section. They were not playing ball – or rather not making waves. They were singularly not interested in being part of a festival of football and joining in with the crowd. The rest of the crowd jeered and booed when the waves crashed and stopped with the England supporters.

And the game – Tony Adams equalised an early USSR goal but it proved a false dawn. Their opponents quickly took control and ran out comfortable 3-1 winners. An ignominious end to an ignominious tournament for the England team – all three games lost in their group and on their way home.

We had to leave the stadium and find our way back to the coach – easier said than done. Crowds dispersing and thronging outside the stadium. Other than remembering after we left the coach we had walked across railway tracks before seeing the stadium in front of us, I really had little recollection of how to find our way back. Railway tracks were not in evidence, lots of people's legs were. The only sentence

I could say in German was 'Ich bin ein junge.' Not helpful. A little bit of panic started to set in.

I saw uniforms. Ask a policeman – in fact it was a soldier and his colleagues gathered around their vehicle. I tried to explain – in English. He didn't understand. He talked back in German. I reciprocated the failure to understand. He talked to his colleagues – all in German. He called to another colleague some distance away. He came over and talked with us. In English. Relief. I explained about the railway tracks – he pointed and explained where they were and that coaches were parked some distance from them. Further relief. We found the coach.

Back at the hotel one further event – an evening dinner arranged by the sponsors. And some England players would be present – we saw Tony Adams and Mark Wright. Adams came over and Ben had a photo taken with him that subsequently found its way into the local Guildford newspaper.

The adventure over, we went to the airport for the Sunday morning flight back to London. A lot of England supporters were there. A small handful were puerile at best, making inane comments, when they saw two men wearing Texan hats in the queue for the flight.

On board and one more surprise – the England team were all seated at the front in the Pan Am 747. They had arranged the first flight out of West Germany for the team. We acknowledged John Barnes and Fred Street as we walked along the aisle. Other passengers milled round the team until the captain announced we were ready for take-off.

Back at Heathrow and one final, brief discussion with Fred Street as we both picked up our luggage from the carousel.

And looking back – that was an incredible experience.

# Chapter 26

# World Cup

THERE WERE two World Cups during the 1980s – the 1982 tournament in Spain and the 1986 competition in Mexico. Both had more than their fair share of controversy.

England, Scotland and Northern Ireland qualified in 1982, amongst an expanded number of teams – 24.

England's mascot for the tournament, a bulldog, caused some furore, given the reputation of some of the country's followers. It was juxtaposed against the tournament mascot – 'Naranjito' – a small orange with a big grin dressed in the host nation's kit. The comparison was stark.

England and Northern Ireland progressed from the first group stage; Scotland went out. Northern Ireland achieved one of the greatest wins in their history, defeating hosts Spain 1-0 in Valencia, Gerry Armstrong's celebrated goal doing the business.

At the second group stage, both England and Northern Ireland were knocked out of the tournament, the winners of the four sections qualifying for the semi-final stage.

And one of those semi-finals, between France and West Germany in Seville, resonates to this day. A hard-fought game between the two teams ended 1-1 in normal time. Then the cataclysmic moment – French forward Patrick Battiston had the ball played through to him as he approached the West German penalty area at speed. Coming in the opposite direction towards him at possibly greater speed was the German goalkeeper Harald Schumacher.

Instant impact. Just outside the penalty area. The ball untouched. It happened in a flash – unexpected and without warning. The West German had taken out the Frenchman. Battiston was prostrate on the ground and looked in a bad way. If Battiston had reached the ball, every likelihood he'd have scored. Schumacher extinguished that possibility. He had no interest in the ball, just the man. A red card surely.

The incident is distinct, clear and vivid in the memory. At the time, watching on television, it caused a jolt just sitting on the sofa.

The delay to restart the game took an age, Battiston requiring medical attention and treatment. He was stretchered off. The German goalkeeper not injured, everyone thought, 'Here comes the red card.' Except no. What? How, could that not be a red card? I'm certain many millions of television viewers felt the same way, even those in West Germany. It had to be a red card. But no, there was no card, of any colour. It was not a foul, according to the referee. Are you mad? The referee had inexplicably bottled it.

Schumacher's thoughts are reflected in his autobiography. 'It's obviously risky coming off the line ... there's no time to stop and think about it. I come hurtling out from the goal ... Battiston comes running towards me ... Patrick does not make contact with the ball ... I couldn't stop and couldn't avoid him. I came crashing down on Battiston with my knees bent ... and caught him on the head with my hip bone and backside. He fell to the ground. So did I. I'd also been hit on the side, but the pain quickly went. The ball missed the net ...

Everything was OK. I rolled over, then turned around. Patrick was still on the ground. I walked past him and went and stood on the line. I didn't think it wise to go over to Battiston to express my concern.' (*Blowing the Whistle*, Toni Schumacher, Star Books, 1988).

The incident rerun on television many times whilst Battiston received attention and treatment. Battiston was unconscious with two missing teeth, three cracked ribs and damaged vertebrae.

Schumacher had got away with it. To no one's surprise, the incident was a critical moment in the game, which ended 3-3 after extra time. Penalty shoot-out. Two saves by Schumacher and his team were through to the World Cup Final against Italy.

Schumacher was the hero of the moment for the German team. After the game, he did not contact Patrick Battiston or indeed ask about his condition or go to the hospital, for which he later chastised himself. He goes on, 'I was very alarmed by my mother's reaction. "It looked dreadful," she told me on the phone … I had been branded a bastard in the eyes of the whole world, without my knowing it. Everyone who had seen the match on television – in France, Germany, everywhere – journalists, specialists, experts, people all over the world hated me.'

The title of the next chapter of his autobiography underlined his new-found reputation, 'The Monster of Seville'.

The incident and outcome had unforeseen consequences. At that time, I worked for Ford at Dagenham, for its European Power Train Operations – a key part of that role to co-ordinate the company's various manufacturing plants across the continent. The morning after the semi-final, calls made to the plants in Duren (near Cologne), West Germany and Bordeaux, France. The reaction from the two locations understandably differed – 'We were lucky and got away with it,' the German line, whilst the French perspective, 'We were robbed by the referee.' Fortunately, the company's international language was English and no translation required.

But the feelings ran much deeper – for that whole day, the guys I dealt with in Bordeaux refused to talk with their West German colleagues in Duren. It seemed an overreaction to me – but it was not my team. My nation had not been robbed on the football field whilst the Germans had progressed blithely on. Best to leave them for the day. In time, relations healed but there was no doubting who the French were rooting for in the World Cup Final. And I think their view was shared by most people, certainly by everyone at work, and amongst friends and family.

The final took place the following Sunday. We had seen a friend in London and made it back just in time for the start of the game. Early on, the Italians played the better football, maybe riding that tide of emotion willing them to win. They took the lead and then came the second goal – or more particularly its celebration by Marco Tardelli. The celebration is a thing of beauty, raw, unbridled emotion, he's in his own world, he's in *everyone's* world, arms spontaneously jerking backwards and forwards in tandem as he ran away from goal with pure joy etched on his face.

That goal provided the platform for the Italians, the game played out with little danger of a comeback by the West Germans. A well-deserved 3-1 win for Italy.

For the 1986 World Cup tournament in Mexico, England, Northern Ireland and Scotland had qualified. England were the only one of the home nations to progress to the knockout stage. A 3-0 win against Paraguay in the Round of 16 led to a quarter-final tie against Argentina.

And this game is best remembered by England supporters for the so-called 'hand of God' goal scored by Diego Maradona for Argentina. Watching on television, it was not obvious there was a handball in the 'headed' goal by the Argentinian. BBC commentator Barry Davies had not spotted it – but goalkeeper Peter Shilton was adamant, vociferous and furious that the 'goal' had been scored by Maradona's hand. The television replay was clear – it was a blatant handball and the goal should have been disallowed. It wasn't.

Maradona called it the 'hand of God' – the game four years after the Falklands War during which the British defeated the Argentinians in the latter's quest to reclaim the 'Malvinas'.

More than 30 years later, Shilton was still having none of it. 'He cheated … he didn't apologise or show any remorse … I was brought up to respect the game. I've seen other players cheat, admit to it and apologise … But he won't apologise, and I won't shake hands with him or acknowledge him … I don't respect him as a sportsman and I never will. Same as Terry Butcher won't.' (*The Guardian*, 15 January 2020).

England manager Bobby Robson said, 'I blame the referee, I don't blame players. Players will try some things, saying they're legitimate, a little nudge or whatever, but his was a blatant handball. I don't think for one moment Maradona thought he would ever get away with it.'

Maradona's second and winning goal was something else – he dribbled brilliantly past five England players before ghosting away from the England goalkeeper and slotting it past him. On BBC Radio, Bryon Butler's commentary captures the moment. 'Maradona, turns like a little eel, he comes away from trouble, little squat man, comes inside Butcher and leaves him for dead and puts the ball away … and that is why Maradona is the greatest player in the world … he buried the English defence, he picked up that ball 40 yards out, first he left one man for dead, then he went past Sansom. It's a goal of great quality by a player of the greatest quality.'

That was the other side of Diego Maradona – a brilliant footballer.

Argentina went on to win the World Cup, defeating West Germany 3-2 at the Azteca Stadium in Mexico City.

Two legacies came out of this World Cup tournament – it saw the creation of the 'Mexican wave', and it was the last World Cup to have sponsorship from tobacco companies.

# Chapter 27

# Television

TOWARDS THE end of the 1970s, ITV achieved what the London *Evening News* headlined, 'Snatch of the Day' – £5 million for a four-year deal to televise football highlights on Saturday night, beating the BBC to land the deal. Only three television channels were on air at the time – BBC1, BBC2 and ITV.

Although the deal was blocked after the BBC complained of a monopoly, ITV had the opportunity they'd wanted for a long time – an agreement with the BBC to alternate coverage of football highlights, one season on Saturday nights, the next season on Sunday afternoons. But viewing figures were down.

As an indicator, the 1982 World Cup viewing figures were poor compared to the tournament held four years earlier in Argentina. BBC and ITV confirmed 13 million viewers had watched the 1982 World Cup Final between Italy and West Germany compared to 23 million for the 1978 World Cup Final between Argentina and Holland.

By 1983, the BBC and ITV were looking for something different to a highlights package of league games. They could see the potential benefits of live televised league football and made a joint bid of £5.2 million to alternate live coverage on a Saturday evening or Sunday afternoon. Many in the game were against live coverage, fearing it would result in a substantial decline in attendances.

Running alongside televised football was the key issue of shirt sponsorship, or rather the appearance, or not, of sponsored shirts on television. TV companies refused to allow sponsored shirts to appear on television, resulting in teams having to revert to shirts without sponsors' names for televised games.

This reluctance to allow sponsors' names on shirts made the clubs less keen on a joint rights' bid from the BBC and ITV; they turned their attention to a company, Telejector Video Communications Systems Ltd.

The company offered £8 million to broadcast coverage to 5,000 installed screens in pubs, clubs, hospitals and schools. *The Guardian* reported the league was interested in the bid, both financially and because it would mean a television audience of about a million, which would not detract so much from live attendances at games.

Telejector eventually pulled out of the bidding for televised rights. The BBC and ITV's joint bid offered no additional money but importantly from the clubs' perspective they were prepared to televise games with sponsors' names on the shirts – albeit with the names reduced in size by a half. The deal, signed in July 1983, allowed live televised coverage for the first time – ten football league games.

The two-year television deal resulted in £25,000 for each club in the Football League regardless of whether they appeared on television, as well as a payment for those that appeared in live games. The big clubs were not convinced the monies adequately rewarded them.

That first landmark game was at White Hart Lane on 2 October 1983 between Tottenham Hotspur and Nottingham Forest, broadcast on ITV. The commentator was Brian Moore with Jimmy Greaves the pundit. I recollect watching the game and whilst I'd seen cup finals and international games broadcast live, there was something quite different about this occasion. The game was an interesting one, with goals and incidents, but afterwards Brian Clough, Forest's manager, was not overly enthusiastic about the live coverage.

The Tottenham chairman Irving Scholar had expressed some concern before the game about the impact live coverage could have on the attendance. At 30,596 it was the largest attendance of the weekend, and well above the club's average of 28,701. Spurs won the game 2-1. Television host Jim Rosenthal proffered the view that 'as an advertisement for live football both teams have done us proud'.

Wednesday's first live televised game, on ITV, was an FA Cup sixth-round tie at Hillsborough against Southampton in March 1984 – a Sunday, 2.35pm kick-off. Wednesday, then a Second Division club, and Saints an established First Division outfit. I went to the game. It had a novelty about it. Thoughts included how the game was coming across on television – thoughts amplified when it ended 0-0. For the neutral, it was hardly a thrilling match.

The attendance, at 43,030, was substantial and nearly double the season's average league attendance of 22,770.

Time for the next set of negotiations for a television deal – £19 million offered over four years, a 46 per cent increase on the last deal. The Football League rejected it in February 1985. The TV companies were in no mood to negotiate further. Things went from bad to worse for football as the season ended – riots at Kenilworth Road, Luton, the Bradford fire and Heysel. Television screens were blank from the start of 1985/86 through to January 1986. The football authorities were on the backfoot – no television income, sponsors at risk.

The impasse had to be addressed. The Football League agreed a deal worth £6.2 million over two years, the rate significantly down on that previously offered. It provided for 14 live televised league games per season, one leg of a League Cup semi-final and the final. But no guarantee of recorded highlights of games.

One key part of the deal for clubs was the split of money across the Football League. The big clubs exerted their influence in the same way they had on monies from sponsorship of the Football League. The split for the clubs – as with the sponsorship deal – was 50 per cent for First Division clubs, 25 per cent for Second Division clubs and 25 per cent for Third and Fourth Division clubs. No longer equal shares for all. It meant £61,000 for each First Division club, £29,750 in the Second Division and £14,255 in the Third and Fourth Divisions.

For the next deal, much manoeuvring by the top clubs and television companies – this time including British Satellite Broadcasting (BSB). Ultimately, it was Greg Dyke at ITV who trumped all competitors with a four-year deal worth £11 million a season for 21 live matches (18 Football League, two League Cup semi-finals and the final). Crucially, it contained an increase in the share for First Division clubs – 75 per cent compared to the previous 50 per cent.

Live games were shown on Sunday afternoons fronted by presenter Elton Welsby.

To contextualise the small number of live games in the 1980s, the number of Manchester United home league games broadcast live were: 1983/84 – 1; 1984/85 – 1; 1985/86 – 1; 1986/87 – 2; 1987/88 – 1; 1988/89 – 3; 1989/90 – 2.

A family-related matter regarding television occurred in April 1984. My sister Jill, then aged 12, delivered the local evening newspaper, the *Sheffield Star*. She had been awarded the national title of 'Newspaper Girl of the Year' and as a result invited to appear on BBC's Breakfast Time television programme one Friday morning with presenters Nick Ross and Selina Scott. It meant her getting down to London by train on the Thursday night from Sheffield.

No doubt given her age both our parents were a little anxious as she travelled alone down to the capital. She was due to be met by a driver working for the BBC and taken to her hotel. For parental reassurance, I confirmed I'd meet my young sister when the train arrived at 9.45pm that night.

It was a good job I did. Train arrived at St Pancras. Passengers disembarked – including Jill. No sign of any driver from the BBC. We waited a good ten minutes. An anxious-looking man came up to us.

'Is this Jill?'

'Yes.'

'I'm sorry, I've been delayed by traffic.'

I looked in his direction, said nothing, raised my eyebrows, which was meant to say everything.

A young girl of 12 would have been alone on her own at night at a mainline London train station if I'd not been there. Wholly unacceptable.

I called Dad and confirmed Jill had arrived and was now with the driver on the way to the hotel. He was reassured. No point in going into more detail.

Come the Friday morning, I was at work at Ford's Truck Operations in Basildon. I took time out to go to the security office, where there was a television. At the appointed time there was Jill, together with a young lad from Wolverhampton, who had been awarded 'Newspaper Boy of the Year'.

Selina Scott was the presenter for this item, asking her young guests who they were, where they were from and some other details. I was impressed by my young sister's clear and straightforward responses.

The presenter moved on to ask what hobbies and interests her guests had.

'Football'

'You like football, Jill?'

'Yes.'

'Any particular team?'

'Sheffield Wednesday.'

'Who are the players in the team?'

Short pause, players' names proffered and then, 'Heardy'.

'And what's he like?'

'Rubbish.'

Direct and to the point. This response galvanised Selina to quickly move on and change the subject.

For most of the viewers, I suspect they would not have understood the detail on the player.

Watching in the security office, I almost convulsed.

Jill's observation about 'Heardy' related to the Wednesday midfielder Pat Heard. I doubt she'd ever seen him play. She only went to the occasional game. No doubt her opinion had been informed by her two older brothers, who were clear and forthright on their views of individual Wednesday players.

Selina was no doubt right to move the conversation on before any other players and their reputations were put at risk.

When asked days later about her interview with Selina Scott, my sister was very matter of fact. 'I answered her questions.' She had clearly no concerns or compunctions about her player assessment!

On the other side, ITV, a new Saturday football magazine-style programme, *Saint and Greavsie,* was launched in the 1980s, hosted by ex-international footballers Ian St John

(Liverpool and Scotland) and Jimmy Greaves (Tottenham Hotspur and England). The more informal chat-show style appealed to a wide audience. On the programme, Greaves seemed to adopt 'The Accies' (Hamilton Academical) and brought the then lowly Scottish club to the attention of a wider national audience.

Norman Giller, the football journalist and television scriptwriter, recollects 'kick-starting' Greaves's television career in the 1980s prior to his becoming half of *Saint and Greavsie*. 'I took him along to TV-am's Egg-Cup Towers to try to sell Jimmy to new managing director Greg Dyke as a Voice of Football for the crisis-hit company.

'Off the top of his head, Dyke – who had turned to Roland Rat to save the sinking ship – said to Greavsie, "What d'you know about television?"

'"Well, I watch it," Jim said.

'"That's good enough," said Dyke. "You can be our television critic."' (*Headlines Deadlines All My Life*, Norman Giller, NGB, 2015).

This was the foundation of Greaves's television football punditry and his teaming up with Ian St John. Giller said, 'Jimmy is prouder of all that he achieved in television than anything in football. Playing the game came naturally to him, but he had to really work at conquering the TV medium.'

# Chapter 28

# Radio and Newspapers

RADIO COVERAGE of the game increased during the 1980s – national and local coverage, including live commentary, on BBC Radio and an increasing number of commercial stations.

Being a radio reporter had its challenges. Frank Gilfeather recollects an incident with Alex Ferguson, manager of Aberdeen. 'How well I recall him roaring down the telephone at me one Monday morning after he had discovered that, on Radio Clyde the previous Saturday, Jim Leighton, his international goalkeeper, had been dropped and was not, as Ferguson had claimed, unavailable because of injury. A club director had offered me this intelligence moments before I entered the football ground … The rage emanating from the telephone was audible enough to attract the attention of everyone in that Grampian TV room that morning … I was told I was banned, not from reporting Aberdeen's home games, but from access to him for interviews.' (*Henrik, Hairdryers and The Hand of God*, Edited by Brian Marjoribanks, BackPage Press, 2012).

The first after-match supporters' phone-in programme was introduced on BBC Radio Sheffield in 1986. It was devised by presenter Robert Jackson and originally called *Grumble*. 'We invented a phone-in at around about 5.05pm on a Saturday night, 40 seconds for the person to have a grumble about anything to do with local sport. If they couldn't say it in 40 seconds, we just switched them off and went to the next caller.' The programme's title changed to *Praise and Grumble* after one caller said he wanted to praise his team – Sheffield Wednesday – after they won 5-0.

National newspapers maintained a clear focus on football – reporters of the time included Hugh McIlvanney (*Sunday Times*), Brian James (*Daily Mail*), John Sadler, Peter Batt (*The Sun*), Ken Montgomery, Harry Harris, Peter Cooper (*Daily Mirror*), David Lacey (*The Guardian*), David Miller, Steve Curry, Norman Giller (*Daily Express*), Ken Jones (*Sunday Mirror*), Mike Langley (*Sunday People*), Alan Biggs (*Today*).

Some of the tabloid newspapers started to take a more opinionated and forthright view of the England national team in the 1980s. One of those, *The Sun*, made its view on the England manager Ron Greenwood clear before the 1982 World Cup Finals in Spain. 'For God's sake Go, Ron' screamed the back-page headline.

Greenwood later acknowledged, 'This *Sun* newspaper article. I mean, they do get to you, don't they, articles?' (*Kicking and Screaming*, BBC Television). Evidently, having won a game in Hungary, Greenwood decided on the plane journey home that was it, he'd retire and let a new man come in for the World Cup. Having learnt of the manager's decision on the flight, it was the players who reacted strongly against it. '"Don't be stupid," they said, and I had great respect for them, Keegan and Brooking and Phil Neal and all of them, and they were genuine in what they said. "Don't retire, let's see it all out together." They changed my mind for me.' (Ron Greenwood, *Kicking and Screaming*, BBC Television).

Reporters could see games differently – for example, West Ham United v Sheffield Wednesday, December 1980. David Miller in the *Daily Express*, 'The irresistible Terry Curran made up for most of the things one dislikes about Sheffield Wednesday. But it was Wednesday's initial ten-man defence, their wretched offside tactics and cynical fouling that spoiled the image.' The same game and the *News of the World* reported, 'Sheffield Wednesday left West Ham with a host of admirers wondering why they have such an uninspiring away record. They turned in an impressive display. Second Division leaders West Ham were given a fright by Wednesday's eye-catching efforts.'

Some assessments could also be cutting – and inaccurate. 'John Sheridan, the man who never was, returns to Forest with Wednesday, the team that never will be,' wrote David Lacey in his preview of the game in *The Guardian* in November 1989.

Local newspapers had their own focus on football; their reporters dedicated to clubs in their areas and responsible for the daily filing of news about them.

In Sheffield, for *The Star* newspaper, Paul Thompson reported on Sheffield Wednesday and Tony Pritchett on Sheffield United – Pritchett had initially worked as *The Star*'s Wednesday reporter, an assignment that meant some United supporters never fully accepted him with the Blades.

The local Saturday night sports paper, focusing on the afternoon's football results and reports on the local teams, was an institution in major towns and cities. They included the *Green 'Un* in Sheffield, the *Pink 'Un* in Manchester, *Buff* in Newcastle and the *Sports Pink* in Burnley. For football reporters, the adrenalin flowed as they gave contemporaneous reports over the phone back to their office.

For the readers, there were immediate first-hand reports of the game, save for goals scored in the last five minutes that were simply referenced as 'Goal', with the goalscorer's name in the 'Stop Press' column of the newspaper. No time for details as the paper went to production shortly after 5pm for its Saturday evening distribution.

A different issue faced a female reporter of Crystal Palace. In the club programme in January 1982, Wendy Gee of the *Croydon Borough News* had a full page 'Press Report' article – her focus on the treatment of women sports journalists in general and her own experiences in particular. She reflected, 'Many a time, hard-talking managers have come into the press room set to give their team (or the opposition) a verbal roasting. But more often than not, my presence turns a possible slanging match into a discussion fit to grace a royal garden party. It's an attitude I find a little hard to swallow.'

She highlights more concerns. 'It was hardly confidence boosting when, at the end of my first ever match as a reporter, the host manager volunteered, "By the way love, we were the ones playing in red." As for some of the chairmen. 'Addressing a male reporter next to me, he said, "Oh I see you've brought your secretary with you."'

And as for fellow reporters – 'For some weeks, two of them insisted on letting me go first up the stairs and into the stand. At first I was chuffed by their kindness – then I realised it was all part of a contest to guess the colour of my undies!'

# Chapter 29

# Programmes and Fanzines

CLUB PROGRAMMES over the course of the decade became slicker and more professionally produced than in the 1970s, with an increase in written material. Colour photographs became standard for programmes produced by top-flight clubs.

A small number of clubs, such as Sheffield Wednesday, Sheffield United, Coventry City, Bristol City, Bristol Rovers and Southend United, included a stapled football magazine insert in their programme in the early seasons of the decade. It was 'Programme Plus', primarily focused on football-related articles but not home-club specific. Feedback from supporters was generally negative for that reason and the inserts disappeared after a couple of seasons.

West Ham United maintained their small, pocket-sized programme until the 1982/83 season. It was a feature of the programme world for over two decades until the dimensions of the Hammers' programme changed to normal size. The switch heralded a change of publisher and printer from Helliar and Sons to Maybank Press Ltd, printers of England's home programmes.

Interesting special edition of the Hammers' programme for the so-called 'ghost match' against Castilla Club de Futbol in the European Cup Winners' Cup in October 1980, when Upton Park was closed to spectators after trouble in Madrid in the first leg. It cost 50p. For league games, the programme retailed at 30p. The special edition had no additional pages or features. It noted, 'It has been issued as a limited edition in its present form, and as such is likely to come into the category of a "collector's item".' And a two-thirds increase in price to boot!

Swearing was becoming a problem at Upton Park and the club used their programme for a half-page address to supporters with the headline, 'SWEARING OFFENDS', observing, 'We wish to encourage the support of women and children. Therefore, language being used is such that you should ask yourself, "Would you swear like that in front of your wife, children, mother and father, teacher etc." We are sure the answer would be no.'

For the early part of the decade, Derby County, like a handful of other clubs, produced a newspaper entitled *Britain's First Newspaper Programme*. By the middle of the decade, they had returned to a more traditional style of programme production, and perhaps reflecting the times, the award-winning *Ram Magazine* sported a young female model on its front cover in November 1986. The model was covered only by a Derby County banner made of a diaphanous material that covered her from the chest down to her upper thighs. Inside the programme, it helpfully explained, 'Belper model Karen Hubbard displays the Derby County banner.'

It's interesting to consider the price progression of programmes for clubs in different divisions:

|                     | 1980/81 | 1984/85 | 1989/90 |
|---------------------|---------|---------|---------|
| Sheffield Wednesday | 30p     | 50p     | £1      |
| Sheffield United    | 25p     | 50p     | 80p     |

| Southend | 30p | 40p | 80p |
|---|---|---|---|
| Aldershot | 25p | 40p | 80p |
| Arsenal | 30p | 50p | £1 |
| Chelsea | 35p | 60p | £1 |
| West Ham United | 30p | 50p | £1/£1.25# |

# the higher price quoted on the cover as the 'Off Stadium Price'

Managers' notes in programmes were commonplace, although perhaps not many as honest as this one from Terry Cooper, manager of Bristol Rovers, in the programme for the game against Sheffield Wednesday in October 1980. 'The defeat by Cambridge on our homecoming was a real blow. It was not just the result that was bad. Our performance looked as if I had gone out on the streets ten minutes before the kick-off and asked 11 lads to come and play for us. I don't know what went wrong.'

Chairman of Chelsea, Ken Bates, always made his point in his column in the programme. Before the game against West Ham United in December 1987, he noted that ex-player Micky Droy had described Chelsea in a tabloid paper as '"Pathetic. A sick joke." This is the last display of sour grapes from a man that Chelsea supported loyally through a series of injuries which saw him unfit for 15 weeks in season 1982/83 and 16 weeks in 1983/84. The following year, he refused a transfer to Portsmouth because he felt that a £25,000 tax-free leaving present wasn't enough!!'

Southend United's manager Dave Smith made several offbeat observations in his column. In January 1982, he wrote, 'I believe we must analyse all aspects of our game. And I am reminded of a poem by Kipling in which he says, "I keep six honest servants and they taught me all I knew. Their names are what, why, and when and how, and where and who."

In April 1982, he observed, 'I love quotes and there is one which goes, "No passion so effectively robs the mind of all its powers of acting and reasoning as fear."'

In an unusual move in December 1985, Essex Police took out a full page in the Southend United programme, appealing for information regarding the murder of Jason Swift.

Many club programmes of the decade featured interviews with players, their likes and dislikes. Perhaps one of the more unusual ones featured Rob Johnson of Luton Town – a 'pigeon fancier'. In the programme for the game against Queens Park Rangers in September 1985, he said, 'I was about 12 when I got interested at school. Now I keep about 35 birds. I like to look after them. It is a great relaxation and something quite different from anything else.'

A souvenir programme – price 50p – was produced for the Aldershot v Manchester United game in August 1982, which was held in aid of the South Atlantic Fund set up for the casualties and families of victims of the Falklands War. Aldershot was the home of the British Army and Manchester United arguably the biggest attraction of any football club in the country at that time.

The inside cover of the programme headed, 'The Price of Freedom', had a full-page article by the Aldershot chairman, R. J. Driver. It focused on the free society we live in and its values. 'The one certain thing is that we are not only grateful to our task force for defending our right to be free; we are also proud of the way that they did it, and many who are not British share our views and benefits, for it was an act in defence of freedom throughout the world. Now, however, and not for the first time, we have to pay the price of that freedom, and none will pay so dearly as those who lost their loved ones or had them returned permanently disabled.

Money will not cure their pain, but it will help them live a more normal life.'

A consistent theme of programmes in the 1980s was the 'Miss Football Club'. In 1981, the competition for Miss Coventry City featured in the club programme with the opportunity to win cash prizes and 'the honour of representing the football club in the National Miss Football Queen competition ... so come on girls, don't be shy.'

The competition to be Miss SWFC 1987 was prominently featured on an inside page of the programme for the game against Manchester United in October 1987. Three young ladies were shown posing 'hoping to win the title of Miss Sheffield Wednesday'.

Adverts were a key feature of many programmes, supporting the costs of their production. New cars were prominent in advertising – the Austin Ambassador at Henlys in the Southend United programme in 1981/82, the Ford Sierra at Perrys in 1982/83 and the Vauxhall Cavalier in a Luton Town programme in October 1984. In the same programme, we learnt that the club's players 'Drink Unigate Milk'.

The Everton programme carried an advert for Newcastle Bitter with the slogan, 'It's got a better head on it than Tommy Lawton.'

The emergence of fanzines from the mid-1980s reflected the growing disenchantment of some supporters with their football club's 'official news' through the club's programme, and the club's perspective reflected in local newspapers. The 'party line' contained little controversy and little debate.

By the end of 1986/87, there were a handful of fanzines in existence. 'Of the club-based ones, most were ostensibly supporters' club magazines, albeit taking the first tentative steps away from the safe, staid, sterile type of offering normally associated with such sources into an altogether harder-hitting, more critical and more importantly more humorous realm. Honest views and opinions of the type heard on the terraces were actually being heard for the first time.' (*About Fanzines*, Quentin Percival Rogers, Fanzine Publishing Limited, 1989).

Many fanzines were creatively titled: *Brian Moore's Head Looks Remarkably Like The London Planetarium* (Gillingham), *There's Only one F in Fulham* (Fulham), *King of the Kippax* (Manchester City), *Fly Me to the Moon* (Middlesbrough), *Tired and Weary* (Birmingham City), *The Almighty Brian* (Nottingham Forest), *When Skies are Grey* (Everton), *Just Another Wednesday* (Sheffield Wednesday), *Flashing Blade* (Sheffield United), *The Oatcake* (Stoke City), *The Crooked Spireite* (Chesterfield) and *Fortune's Always Hiding* (West Ham United).

At the beginning most fanzines were basic in their appearance, focusing on content rather than costly production. That content was invariably interesting, topical, humorous, irreverent, incisive and to the point. Sold outside the grounds, the fanzines usually cost less than the club's official programme.

As the 1980s came to a close, fanzines were on an upward curve with many of the top-flight clubs having two or more fanzines commenting on their fortunes.

# Chapter 30

# It Happened in the 1980s

April 1980 saw two English clubs make it to the final of Europe's two premier cup competitions for the first time – Nottingham Forest to the European Cup Final, Arsenal to the European Cup Winners' Cup Final.

In Italy in May 1980, AC Milan were relegated to the Second Division as a result of their part in the Italian bribery scandal, Paolo Rossi suspended for three years and Bruno Giodano for 18 months. Both players would have been in the Italy squad for the European Championships in June 1980.

Cricketer Ian Botham made 11 first-team appearances for Scunthorpe United in the 1980s.

On 25 April 1981, freak weather rendered several Stockport County players unable to reach Gigg Lane, Bury, where their club had a Fourth Division game. County played the entire first half with nine players and reached the break level at 0-0. With a full team in the second half, the visitors won 1-0.

In August 1981, New Zealand defeated Fiji with a record win in a World Cup qualifying game in Auckland – 13-0.

A record crowd watched the FA Charity Shield game at the start of the 1981/82 season between Aston Villa and Tottenham Hotspur, 92,500 producing receipts of £431,000 at Wembley.

At the conclusion of the Norway v England World Cup qualifying game in Oslo in September 1981 – a game won 2-1 by the Norwegians – the local commentator Bjorge Lillelien famously declared in ecstatic tones, 'Lord Nelson, Lord Beaverbrook, Sir Winston Churchill, Sir Anthony Eden, Clement Attlee, Henry Cooper, Lady Diana, Maggie Thatcher, can you hear me ? Maggie Thatcher, your boys took a hell of a beating. Your boys took a hell of a beating.'

In January 1982, John Hewitt scored the fastest recorded goal in Scottish Cup history – 9.6 seconds for Aberdeen at Motherwell.

In May 1982, 21-year-old Diego Maradona joined Barcelona from Boca Juniors for a world-record fee of £4,235,000.

Arnaldo Coelho, a Brazilian businessman, became the first non-European to referee a World Cup Final when he took charge of the game between Italy and West Germany in Madrid on 11 July 1982.

Ipswich Town made a poor start to the 1982/83 season. Chairman Patrick Cobbold was asked what would constitute a crisis at the club? His response: 'When we run out of dry white wine.'

In an attempt to speed up play, the International Football Association Board changed the laws of the game to require a goalkeeper to release the ball in his possession into play after taking four steps – the change effective for the 1983/84 season.

A 'Charity Soccer Match for the Harrods Bomb Blast Victims' took place at Craven Cottage, Fulham on Sunday, 4 March 1984 between a Malcolm Macdonald XI – including Bobby Moore, George Best and Jimmy Greaves – and a Denis Waterman XI – including Martin Peters, Peter Bonetti and Roger Hunt. Admission £2 adults, £1 OAPs/children. The Harrods bomb blast had taken place outside the department store on 17 December 1983, killing 6 people and injuring 90.

In May 1984 Dave Bassett, then Wimbledon manager, agreed to join Crystal Palace. His tenure at Selhurst Park? Four days. 'Four days was all it took for me to realise that I had made the biggest mistake of my life so far.' He returned to Plough Lane and continued as manager of Wimbledon.

The Home Internationals – the British International Championship – came to an end on 26 May 1984 after 100 years. The final game was a 1-1 draw at Hampden Park between Scotland and England. Northern Ireland won the championship on goal difference.

In February 1985, the scheduled Second Division game between Sheffield United and Oldham Athletic had to be postponed because of the discovery of a Second World War bomb close to United's Bramall Lane ground.

The start of the 1985/86 season saw team captains wear distinguishing armbands for the first time.

The 1986/87 season heralded the introduction of two substitutes in FA Cup games. The Football League followed suit with two substitutes allowed in its competition the following season.

Lawrie McMenemy, then Sunderland manager, left the club in April 1987. *The Sun* exclusively revealed his departure, John

Roberts stating, 'The omens weren't the best when Lawrie McMenemy moved in at Sunderland. He found a copy of a previous manager's last will and testament in his desk drawer.'

In March 1988, FIFA decided to make the wearing of shin pads compulsory in all its competitions.

# Afterword

THE FIRST Sheffield derby of the 1980s – Easter Saturday 1980 at Bramall Lane. Both Sheffield clubs in the Third Division for the first time together that season.

Interestingly, United had played the previous day – Good Friday – in a Third Division game at Roots Hall, Southend. In those times, it was not unusual for games to be played on consecutive days over a holiday period, albeit Wednesday had enjoyed the benefit of a week's rest since their previous game.

Living in Leigh-on-Sea, Essex, I went to that game at Southend. Primary recollections are of a windy day, not much good football on offer, United's star name, the Argentinian Alex Sabella, not playing and a Shrimpers win, 2-0. Hardly the preparation the Blades needed as they hosted Wednesday 24 hours later.

And another recollection – at the end of the game, when the crowd was dispersing and spectators disgorging into the large car park behind the main stand, there was a loud roar and threatening noise from a group of youths running into the car park – maybe 30 strong – from the away end. Momentarily, there was alarm amongst departing spectators until it became clear the away supporters' charge was impeded by lines of closely parked cars. No danger, they were ignored.

Context for the Sheffield derby is everything. United relegated to the Third Division for the first time in their history at the end of the previous season, for Wednesday, it was their fifth season in the third tier. United had started the season well – top of the division on the morning of the Hillsborough game on Boxing Day. Wednesday in the top half of the table but not threatening the promotion places.

Come the Easter Saturday derby, Wednesday were third in the division and very much in the mix for promotion – three clubs promoted automatically and at the time it was two points for a win and one for a draw. United had fallen away in the promotion race as the season progressed.

Huge interest in the game, as always for a derby, added to by United's need for revenge for their reverse earlier in the season at Hillsborough and by Wednesday's desire to keep their promotion push on track. The game all-ticket – the first time for a league derby at Bramall Lane.

On-sale dates for tickets advertised in the local press – *The Star* and *Morning Telegraph* and in the club's respective programmes. Season ticket holders had priority and then the general public. Purchase by post or in person at the clubs' ticket offices. Living in Essex a problem – applying for tickets by post risked a real chance of them selling out. Dad came to the rescue – he queued for tickets at Hillsborough. Two tickets for the John Street terrace in front of the John Street Main Stand, opposite the South Stand opened in 1975 that replaced the cricket field. Cost of the ticket £1.50 and the ticket stated, 'v Sheffield Wednesday, Special League Match'. Too right.

A drive to Sheffield and my parents' home in Gleadless on the morning of the game, adrenalin flowing and expectation rising for the derby. It always does. Parking straightforward – in Heeley, a mile from the ground. Police presence clear and obvious as we approached the ground. Through the turnstiles – no checks by stewards or police – taking our place on the terrace, a sunny day. Wednesday's section of the terrace covered the length of the pitch from the halfway line to the Bramall Lane Stand. Wednesday supporters occupied that stand and the terrace behind the goal. The terracing behind red metal fences. In the rest of the ground, the home supporters.

Tightly packed terracing, singing, noise, passion, colours, tribal. Us. Them. This is the derby – our team, our club, our history, our supporters and all on the line over the next 90 minutes against them. It had always been so, from playing in the streets as a little lad at school. This is the one that mattered. And they felt precisely the same way about us.

From our perspective, the first half did not go well. In the last minute of the half, United's MacPhail had followed up a Butlin header that hit Bolder's post and came back to him for the opening goal. Utter silence and bewilderment amongst Wednesdayites. A pin could have dropped, but we wouldn't have heard it. Three sides of the ground with their red and white favours were going berserk. They were chanting, cheering, baying at the blue and white followers. Not pleasant but entirely expected. Depressing end to the first half – 1-0 down.

Half-time entertainment included the Sheffield comedian Bobby Knutt (garage owner Ron Sykes in *Coronation Street* and married to the golden girl of British athletics in the 1970s, Donna Murray). He came on to the pitch and his focus was initially on United's Shoreham Street Kop and that half of the adjacent John Street terracing with Unitedites. Standing in front of them – back to us – he did something that caused the red and white supporters to cheer.

Then he came over to the Wednesdayites on the John Street terrace and the Bramall Lane End, turned around and lifted his jacket to reveal a blue and white striped Wednesday shirt. Massive cheer from the Wednesdayites. Bobby Knutt was one of us!

Except, we had not appreciated that he had opened the front of his jacket to reveal to the home supporters a red and white striped shirt!

A half and half shirt – Knutt knew how to get the crowd on his side. From his pitch performance, you would not have known that Bobby Knutt was a keen Blade.

Momentarily, the half-time antics had taken our mind off the game, but Wednesday had it all to do in the second half. Being behind to your greatest rivals is the worst feeling. The Blades supporters milking it. And it fell to Wednesday winger and cult hero Terry Curran to turn the tide – and how. He scored a brilliant individual goal to equalise at the Bramall Lane End.

Curran was hemmed in by three United defenders close to the corner flag by the Bramall Lane End and South Stand. Commentating on *Match of the Day* that night, Barry Davies observed, 'Curran, this time it's Cutbush at his back … and Sabella. He's got away from them. Oh, and he does so well. He had three men around him and he just came round in a wide arc, and no wonder he falls to his knees in front of the Wednesday supporters. But the United supporters must be wondering how on earth he was allowed to go away? He came away in an arc and when he was in space, he hit a right-foot shot that was beating the goalkeeper from the moment it was struck.'

Utter joy for Wednesdayites.

Any goal for us – particularly in the derby – is celebrated, but this one was a really special goal, the best individual goal I'd seen by a Wednesday player. Delirium. The John Street terrace ablaze with blue and white favours, joy unconfined.

No thought given to footholds on the terracing, the sheer exuberance of the moment took over – supporters propelled forward and sideways. No one cared – we'd scored.

United defender Tony Kenworthy remembers the goal. 'He let rip with a 20-yard shot that tore into the roof of the net. It was a fine shot and a hell of a goal.' (*Blade Heart: The Tony Kenworthy Autobiography*, Tony Kenworthy with John Brindley, Vertical Editions, 2013).

The game finished a 1-1 draw. Given how the game had played out, the blue and white supporters satisfied.

Wednesday hero Curran observed later, 'I ensured the TV men had plenty to get their teeth stuck into afterwards by having a running battle with United's Tony Kenworthy … [He] was kicking me as far in the air as possible and generally ensuring I was too knackered to cause any damage. I respected Tony as a very good player and he quickly let me know he was there by getting in a couple of crunching tackles … Later in the first half, I got my revenge with a "mistimed" challenge on Kenworthy before mockingly slapping him around the chops.' (*Regrets of a Football Maverick*, Terry Curran with John Brindley, Vertical Editions, 2012).

*Match of the Day* focused on separate interviews with Curran and Kenworthy after the game. The dialogue is interesting:

Tony Kenworthy: 'The derby games get a bit heated. He stood on my foot and I felt it a little bit and I obviously went down.'

Barry Davies: 'The incident that led up to that, he seemed to be chiding you. He said he was doing it in quite a friendly way, but you obviously didn't take it that way.'

Tony Kenworthy: 'The first time I let it go, not the second time, he slapped me across the face and, no, I didn't like it.'

Curran's interview with Barry Davies showed him smiling and making the point that defenders 'like to dish it out' but they were not so keen when the attacker had a go back. Wednesdayites liked that interview.

In his summary at the end of *Match of the Day*, presenter Jimmy Hill praised the referee Joe Worrall for his handling of a difficult game, although he was not impressed with United's shirts – he could not readily distinguish the numbers on the back!

The game over, segregation in place, egress from the Bramall Lane ground took place for all supporters simultaneously – no holding back any spectators. A heavy police presence in place outside the ground, we saw no trouble as we returned to our car.

# Appendix 1
## Football League Tables 1979/80 – 1989/90

## 1979/80
### First Division

| | | Pld | W | D | L | F | A | W | D | L | F | A | GD | Pts | Ave Gate |
|---|---|---|---|---|---|---|---|---|---|---|---|---|---|---|---|
| 1 | Liverpool | 42 | 15 | 6 | 0 | 46 | 8 | 10 | 4 | 7 | 35 | 22 | 51 | 60 | 44,586 |
| 2 | Manchester United | 42 | 17 | 3 | 1 | 43 | 8 | 7 | 7 | 7 | 22 | 27 | 30 | 58 | 51,608 |
| 3 | Ipswich Town | 42 | 14 | 4 | 3 | 43 | 13 | 8 | 5 | 8 | 25 | 26 | 29 | 53 | 21,620 |
| 4 | Arsenal | 42 | 8 | 10 | 3 | 24 | 12 | 10 | 6 | 5 | 28 | 24 | 16 | 52 | 33,596 |
| 5 | Nottingham Forest | 42 | 16 | 4 | 1 | 44 | 11 | 4 | 4 | 13 | 19 | 32 | 20 | 48 | 26,350 |
| 6 | Wolverhampton Wanderers | 42 | 9 | 6 | 6 | 29 | 20 | 10 | 3 | 8 | 29 | 27 | 11 | 47 | 25,731 |
| 7 | Aston Villa | 42 | 11 | 5 | 5 | 29 | 22 | 5 | 9 | 7 | 22 | 28 | 1 | 46 | 27,978 |
| 8 | Southampton | 42 | 14 | 2 | 5 | 53 | 24 | 4 | 7 | 10 | 12 | 29 | 12 | 45 | 21,335 |
| 9 | Middlesbrough | 42 | 11 | 7 | 3 | 31 | 14 | 5 | 5 | 11 | 19 | 30 | 6 | 44 | 18,739 |
| 10 | West Bromwich Albion | 42 | 9 | 8 | 4 | 37 | 23 | 2 | 11 | 8 | 17 | 27 | 4 | 41 | 22,418 |
| 11 | Leeds United | 42 | 10 | 7 | 4 | 30 | 17 | 3 | 7 | 11 | 16 | 33 | -4 | 40 | 22,788 |
| 12 | Norwich City | 42 | 10 | 8 | 3 | 38 | 30 | 3 | 6 | 12 | 20 | 36 | -8 | 40 | 17,225 |
| 13 | Crystal Palace | 42 | 9 | 9 | 3 | 26 | 13 | 3 | 7 | 11 | 15 | 37 | -9 | 40 | 29,794 |
| 14 | Tottenham Hotspur | 42 | 11 | 5 | 5 | 30 | 22 | 4 | 5 | 12 | 22 | 40 | -10 | 40 | 32,018 |
| 15 | Coventry City | 42 | 12 | 2 | 7 | 34 | 24 | 4 | 5 | 12 | 22 | 42 | -10 | 39 | 19,315 |
| 16 | Brighton & Hove Albion | 42 | 8 | 8 | 5 | 25 | 20 | 3 | 7 | 11 | 22 | 37 | -10 | 37 | 24,745 |
| 17 | Manchester City | 42 | 8 | 8 | 5 | 28 | 25 | 4 | 5 | 12 | 15 | 41 | -23 | 37 | 35,272 |
| 18 | Stoke City | 42 | 9 | 4 | 8 | 27 | 26 | 4 | 6 | 11 | 17 | 32 | -14 | 36 | 20,176 |
| 19 | Everton | 42 | 7 | 7 | 7 | 28 | 25 | 2 | 10 | 9 | 15 | 26 | -8 | 35 | 28,711 |
| 20 | Bristol City | 42 | 6 | 6 | 9 | 22 | 30 | 3 | 7 | 11 | 15 | 36 | -29 | 31 | 18,932 |
| 21 | Derby County | 42 | 9 | 4 | 8 | 36 | 29 | 2 | 4 | 15 | 11 | 38 | -20 | 30 | 19,904 |
| 22 | Bolton Wanderers | 42 | 5 | 11 | 5 | 19 | 21 | 0 | 4 | 17 | 19 | 52 | -35 | 25 | 16,353 |

### Second Division

| | | Pld | W | D | L | F | A | W | D | L | F | A | GD | Pts | Ave Gate |
|---|---|---|---|---|---|---|---|---|---|---|---|---|---|---|---|
| 1 | Leicester City | 42 | 12 | 5 | 4 | 32 | 19 | 9 | 8 | 4 | 26 | 19 | 20 | 55 | 18,636 |
| 2 | Sunderland | 42 | 16 | 5 | 0 | 47 | 13 | 5 | 7 | 9 | 22 | 29 | 27 | 54 | 27,119 |
| 3 | Birmingham City | 42 | 14 | 5 | 2 | 37 | 16 | 7 | 6 | 8 | 21 | 22 | 20 | 53 | 20,427 |
| 4 | Chelsea | 42 | 14 | 3 | 4 | 34 | 16 | 9 | 4 | 8 | 32 | 36 | 14 | 53 | 23,266 |
| 5 | Queens Park Rangers | 42 | 10 | 9 | 2 | 46 | 25 | 8 | 4 | 9 | 29 | 28 | 22 | 49 | 14,087 |
| 6 | Luton Town | 42 | 9 | 10 | 2 | 36 | 17 | 7 | 7 | 7 | 30 | 28 | 21 | 49 | 11,676 |
| 7 | West Ham United | 42 | 13 | 2 | 6 | 37 | 21 | 7 | 5 | 9 | 17 | 22 | 11 | 47 | 22,872 |
| 8 | Cambridge United | 42 | 11 | 6 | 4 | 40 | 23 | 3 | 10 | 8 | 21 | 30 | 8 | 44 | 6,127 |
| 9 | Newcastle United | 42 | 13 | 6 | 2 | 35 | 19 | 2 | 8 | 11 | 18 | 30 | 4 | 44 | 23,345 |
| 10 | Preston North End | 42 | 8 | 10 | 3 | 30 | 23 | 4 | 9 | 8 | 26 | 29 | 4 | 43 | 9,751 |
| 11 | Oldham Athletic | 42 | 12 | 5 | 4 | 30 | 21 | 4 | 6 | 11 | 19 | 32 | -4 | 43 | 7,918 |
| 12 | Swansea City | 42 | 13 | 1 | 7 | 31 | 20 | 4 | 8 | 9 | 17 | 33 | -5 | 43 | 14,391 |
| 13 | Shrewsbury Town | 42 | 12 | 3 | 6 | 41 | 23 | 6 | 2 | 13 | 19 | 30 | 7 | 41 | 8,782 |
| 14 | Orient | 42 | 7 | 9 | 5 | 29 | 31 | 5 | 8 | 8 | 19 | 23 | -6 | 41 | 7,245 |
| 15 | Cardiff City | 42 | 11 | 4 | 6 | 21 | 16 | 5 | 4 | 12 | 20 | 32 | -7 | 40 | 9,926 |
| 16 | Wrexham | 42 | 13 | 2 | 6 | 26 | 15 | 3 | 4 | 14 | 16 | 38 | -9 | 38 | 10,090 |
| 17 | Notts County | 42 | 4 | 11 | 6 | 24 | 22 | 7 | 4 | 10 | 27 | 30 | -1 | 37 | 8,818 |
| 18 | Watford | 42 | 9 | 6 | 6 | 27 | 18 | 3 | 7 | 11 | 12 | 28 | -7 | 37 | 15,462 |
| 19 | Bristol Rovers | 42 | 9 | 8 | 4 | 33 | 23 | 2 | 5 | 14 | 17 | 41 | -14 | 35 | 7,399 |
| 20 | Fulham | 42 | 6 | 4 | 11 | 19 | 28 | 5 | 3 | 13 | 23 | 46 | -32 | 29 | 8,419 |
| 21 | Burnley | 42 | 5 | 9 | 7 | 19 | 23 | 1 | 6 | 14 | 20 | 50 | -34 | 27 | 8,118 |
| 22 | Charlton Athletic | 42 | 6 | 6 | 9 | 25 | 31 | 0 | 4 | 17 | 14 | 47 | -39 | 22 | 7,175 |

## Third Division

| | | Pld | W | D | L | F | A | W | D | L | F | A | GD | Pts | Ave Gate |
|---|---|---|---|---|---|---|---|---|---|---|---|---|---|---|---|
| 1 | Grimsby Town | 46 | 18 | 2 | 3 | 46 | 16 | 8 | 8 | 7 | 27 | 26 | 31 | 62 | 10,618 |
| 2 | Blackburn Rovers | 46 | 13 | 5 | 5 | 34 | 17 | 12 | 4 | 7 | 24 | 19 | 22 | 59 | 10,311 |
| 3 | Sheffield Wednesday | 46 | 12 | 6 | 5 | 44 | 20 | 9 | 10 | 4 | 37 | 27 | 34 | 58 | 18,288 |
| 4 | Chesterfield | 46 | 16 | 5 | 2 | 46 | 16 | 7 | 6 | 10 | 25 | 30 | 25 | 57 | 7,760 |
| 5 | Colchester United | 46 | 10 | 10 | 3 | 39 | 20 | 10 | 2 | 11 | 25 | 36 | 8 | 52 | 3,816 |
| 6 | Carlisle United | 46 | 13 | 6 | 4 | 45 | 26 | 5 | 6 | 12 | 21 | 30 | 10 | 48 | 4,406 |
| 7 | Reading | 46 | 14 | 6 | 3 | 43 | 19 | 2 | 10 | 11 | 23 | 46 | 1 | 48 | 6,843 |
| 8 | Exeter City | 46 | 14 | 5 | 4 | 38 | 22 | 5 | 5 | 13 | 22 | 46 | -8 | 48 | 4,574 |
| 9 | Chester | 46 | 14 | 6 | 3 | 29 | 18 | 3 | 7 | 13 | 20 | 39 | -8 | 47 | 3,726 |
| 10 | Swindon Town | 46 | 15 | 4 | 4 | 50 | 20 | 4 | 4 | 15 | 21 | 43 | 8 | 46 | 8,902 |
| 11 | Barnsley | 46 | 10 | 7 | 6 | 29 | 20 | 6 | 7 | 10 | 24 | 36 | -3 | 46 | 11,890 |
| 12 | Sheffield United | 46 | 13 | 5 | 5 | 35 | 21 | 5 | 5 | 13 | 25 | 45 | -6 | 46 | 16,584 |
| 13 | Rotherham United | 46 | 13 | 4 | 6 | 38 | 24 | 5 | 6 | 12 | 20 | 42 | -8 | 46 | 5,992 |
| 14 | Millwall | 46 | 14 | 6 | 3 | 49 | 23 | 2 | 7 | 14 | 16 | 36 | 6 | 45 | 5,918 |
| 15 | Plymouth Argyle | 46 | 13 | 7 | 3 | 39 | 17 | 3 | 5 | 15 | 20 | 38 | 4 | 44 | 5,776 |
| 16 | Gillingham | 46 | 8 | 9 | 6 | 26 | 18 | 6 | 5 | 12 | 23 | 33 | -2 | 42 | 6,131 |
| 17 | Oxford United | 46 | 10 | 4 | 9 | 34 | 24 | 4 | 9 | 10 | 23 | 38 | -5 | 41 | 4,832 |
| 18 | Blackpool | 46 | 10 | 7 | 6 | 39 | 34 | 5 | 4 | 14 | 23 | 40 | -12 | 41 | 5,818 |
| 19 | Brentford | 46 | 10 | 6 | 7 | 33 | 26 | 5 | 5 | 13 | 26 | 47 | -14 | 41 | 7,818 |
| 20 | Hull City | 46 | 11 | 7 | 5 | 29 | 21 | 1 | 9 | 13 | 22 | 48 | -18 | 40 | 5,986 |
| 21 | Bury | 46 | 10 | 4 | 9 | 30 | 23 | 6 | 3 | 14 | 15 | 36 | -14 | 39 | 4,239 |
| 22 | Southend United | 46 | 11 | 6 | 6 | 33 | 23 | 3 | 4 | 16 | 14 | 35 | -11 | 38 | 4,758 |
| 23 | Mansfield Town | 46 | 9 | 9 | 5 | 31 | 24 | 1 | 7 | 15 | 16 | 34 | -11 | 36 | 5,467 |
| 24 | Wimbledon | 46 | 6 | 8 | 9 | 34 | 38 | 4 | 6 | 13 | 18 | 43 | -29 | 34 | 3,426 |

## Fourth Division

| | | Pld | W | D | L | F | A | W | D | L | F | A | GD | Pts | Ave Gate |
|---|---|---|---|---|---|---|---|---|---|---|---|---|---|---|---|
| 1 | Huddersfield Town | 46 | 16 | 5 | 2 | 61 | 18 | 11 | 7 | 5 | 40 | 30 | 53 | 66 | 8,714 |
| 2 | Walsall | 46 | 12 | 9 | 2 | 43 | 23 | 11 | 9 | 3 | 32 | 24 | 28 | 64 | 5,549 |
| 3 | Newport County | 46 | 16 | 5 | 2 | 47 | 22 | 11 | 2 | 10 | 36 | 28 | 33 | 61 | 5,139 |
| 4 | Portsmouth | 46 | 15 | 5 | 3 | 62 | 23 | 9 | 7 | 7 | 29 | 26 | 42 | 60 | 15,850 |
| 5 | Bradford City | 46 | 14 | 6 | 3 | 44 | 14 | 10 | 6 | 7 | 33 | 36 | 27 | 60 | 5,744 |
| 6 | Wigan Athletic | 46 | 13 | 5 | 5 | 42 | 26 | 8 | 8 | 7 | 34 | 35 | 15 | 55 | 5,905 |
| 7 | Lincoln City | 46 | 14 | 8 | 1 | 43 | 12 | 4 | 9 | 10 | 21 | 30 | 22 | 53 | 3,713 |
| 8 | Peterborough United | 46 | 14 | 3 | 6 | 39 | 22 | 7 | 7 | 9 | 19 | 25 | 11 | 52 | 4,135 |
| 9 | Torquay United | 46 | 13 | 7 | 3 | 47 | 25 | 2 | 10 | 11 | 23 | 44 | 1 | 47 | 3,184 |
| 10 | Aldershot | 46 | 10 | 7 | 6 | 35 | 23 | 6 | 6 | 11 | 27 | 30 | 9 | 45 | 3,859 |
| 11 | AFC Bournemouth | 46 | 8 | 9 | 6 | 32 | 25 | 5 | 9 | 9 | 20 | 26 | 1 | 44 | 3,924 |
| 12 | Doncaster Rovers | 46 | 11 | 6 | 6 | 37 | 27 | 4 | 8 | 11 | 25 | 36 | -1 | 44 | 4,321 |
| 13 | Northampton Town | 46 | 14 | 5 | 4 | 33 | 16 | 2 | 7 | 14 | 18 | 50 | -15 | 44 | 3,024 |
| 14 | Scunthorpe United | 46 | 11 | 9 | 3 | 37 | 23 | 3 | 6 | 14 | 21 | 52 | -17 | 43 | 2,266 |
| 15 | Tranmere Rovers | 46 | 10 | 4 | 9 | 32 | 24 | 4 | 9 | 10 | 18 | 32 | -6 | 41 | 2,246 |
| 16 | Stockport County | 46 | 9 | 7 | 7 | 30 | 31 | 5 | 5 | 13 | 18 | 41 | -24 | 40 | 2,911 |
| 17 | York City | 46 | 9 | 6 | 8 | 35 | 34 | 5 | 5 | 13 | 30 | 48 | -17 | 39 | 2,716 |
| 18 | Halifax Town | 46 | 11 | 9 | 3 | 29 | 20 | 2 | 4 | 17 | 17 | 52 | -26 | 39 | 2,582 |
| 19 | Hartlepool United | 46 | 10 | 7 | 6 | 36 | 28 | 4 | 3 | 16 | 23 | 36 | -5 | 38 | 2,915 |
| 20 | Port Vale | 46 | 8 | 6 | 9 | 34 | 24 | 4 | 6 | 13 | 22 | 46 | -14 | 36 | 3,462 |
| 21 | Hereford United | 46 | 8 | 7 | 8 | 22 | 21 | 3 | 7 | 13 | 16 | 31 | -14 | 36 | 3,355 |
| 22 | Darlington | 46 | 7 | 11 | 5 | 33 | 26 | 2 | 6 | 15 | 17 | 48 | -24 | 35 | 1,972 |
| 23 | Crewe Alexandra | 46 | 10 | 6 | 7 | 25 | 27 | 1 | 7 | 15 | 10 | 41 | -33 | 35 | 2,745 |
| 24 | Rochdale | 46 | 6 | 7 | 10 | 20 | 28 | 1 | 6 | 16 | 13 | 51 | -46 | 27 | 1,926 |

Hereford United, Darlington, Crewe Alexandra and Rochdale re-elected to the Football League

# 1980/81

## First Division

| | | Pld | W | D | L | F | A | W | D | L | F | A | GD | Pts | Ave Gate |
|---|---|---|---|---|---|---|---|---|---|---|---|---|---|---|---|
| 1 | Aston Villa | 42 | 16 | 3 | 2 | 40 | 13 | 10 | 5 | 6 | 32 | 27 | 32 | 60 | 33,641 |
| 2 | Ipswich Town | 42 | 15 | 4 | 2 | 45 | 14 | 8 | 6 | 7 | 32 | 29 | 34 | 56 | 24,619 |
| 3 | Arsenal | 42 | 13 | 8 | 0 | 36 | 17 | 6 | 7 | 8 | 25 | 28 | 16 | 53 | 32,480 |
| 4 | West Bromwich Albion | 42 | 15 | 4 | 2 | 40 | 15 | 5 | 8 | 8 | 20 | 27 | 18 | 52 | 20,331 |
| 5 | Liverpool | 42 | 13 | 5 | 3 | 38 | 15 | 4 | 12 | 5 | 24 | 27 | 20 | 51 | 37,547 |
| 6 | Southampton | 42 | 15 | 4 | 2 | 47 | 22 | 5 | 6 | 10 | 29 | 34 | 20 | 50 | 21,481 |
| 7 | Nottingham Forest | 42 | 15 | 3 | 3 | 44 | 20 | 4 | 9 | 8 | 18 | 24 | 18 | 50 | 24,483 |
| 8 | Manchester United | 42 | 9 | 11 | 1 | 30 | 14 | 6 | 7 | 8 | 21 | 22 | 15 | 48 | 45,071 |
| 9 | Leeds United | 42 | 10 | 5 | 6 | 19 | 19 | 7 | 5 | 9 | 20 | 28 | -8 | 44 | 21,377 |
| 10 | Tottenham Hotspur | 42 | 9 | 9 | 3 | 44 | 31 | 5 | 6 | 10 | 26 | 37 | 2 | 43 | 30,724 |
| 11 | Stoke City | 42 | 8 | 9 | 4 | 31 | 23 | 4 | 9 | 8 | 20 | 37 | -9 | 42 | 15,580 |
| 12 | Manchester City | 42 | 10 | 7 | 4 | 35 | 25 | 4 | 4 | 13 | 21 | 34 | -3 | 39 | 33,587 |
| 13 | Birmingham City | 42 | 11 | 5 | 5 | 32 | 23 | 2 | 7 | 12 | 18 | 38 | -11 | 38 | 19,248 |
| 14 | Middlesbrough | 42 | 14 | 4 | 3 | 38 | 16 | 2 | 1 | 18 | 15 | 45 | -8 | 37 | 16,432 |
| 15 | Everton | 42 | 8 | 6 | 7 | 32 | 25 | 5 | 4 | 12 | 23 | 33 | -3 | 36 | 26,105 |
| 16 | Coventry City | 42 | 9 | 6 | 6 | 31 | 30 | 4 | 4 | 13 | 17 | 38 | -20 | 36 | 16,904 |
| 17 | Sunderland | 42 | 10 | 4 | 7 | 32 | 19 | 4 | 3 | 14 | 20 | 34 | -1 | 35 | 26,477 |
| 18 | Wolverhampton Wanderers | 42 | 11 | 2 | 8 | 26 | 20 | 2 | 7 | 12 | 17 | 35 | -12 | 35 | 21,551 |
| 19 | Brighton & Hove Albion | 42 | 10 | 3 | 8 | 30 | 26 | 4 | 4 | 13 | 24 | 41 | -13 | 35 | 18,984 |
| 20 | Norwich City | 42 | 9 | 7 | 5 | 34 | 25 | 4 | 0 | 17 | 15 | 48 | -24 | 33 | 17,140 |
| 21 | Leicester City | 42 | 7 | 5 | 9 | 20 | 23 | 6 | 1 | 14 | 20 | 44 | -27 | 32 | 19,476 |
| 22 | Crystal Palace | 42 | 6 | 4 | 11 | 32 | 37 | 0 | 3 | 18 | 15 | 46 | -36 | 19 | 19,280 |

## Second Division

| | | Pld | W | D | L | F | A | W | D | L | F | A | GD | Pts | Ave Gate |
|---|---|---|---|---|---|---|---|---|---|---|---|---|---|---|---|
| 1 | West Ham United | 42 | 19 | 1 | 1 | 53 | 12 | 9 | 9 | 3 | 26 | 17 | 50 | 66 | 27,140 |
| 2 | Notts County | 42 | 10 | 8 | 3 | 26 | 15 | 8 | 9 | 4 | 23 | 23 | 11 | 53 | 9,551 |
| 3 | Swansea City | 42 | 12 | 5 | 4 | 39 | 19 | 6 | 9 | 6 | 25 | 25 | 20 | 50 | 13,143 |
| 4 | Blackburn Rovers | 42 | 12 | 8 | 1 | 28 | 7 | 4 | 10 | 7 | 14 | 22 | 13 | 50 | 11,684 |
| 5 | Luton Town | 42 | 10 | 6 | 5 | 35 | 23 | 8 | 6 | 7 | 26 | 23 | 15 | 48 | 10,291 |
| 6 | Derby County | 42 | 9 | 8 | 4 | 34 | 26 | 6 | 7 | 8 | 23 | 26 | 5 | 45 | 16,682 |
| 7 | Grimsby Town | 42 | 10 | 8 | 3 | 21 | 10 | 5 | 7 | 9 | 23 | 32 | 2 | 45 | 10,961 |
| 8 | Queens Park Rangers | 42 | 11 | 7 | 3 | 36 | 12 | 4 | 6 | 11 | 20 | 34 | 10 | 43 | 10,936 |
| 9 | Watford | 42 | 13 | 5 | 3 | 34 | 18 | 3 | 6 | 12 | 16 | 27 | 5 | 43 | 13,108 |
| 10 | Sheffield Wednesday | 42 | 14 | 4 | 3 | 38 | 14 | 3 | 4 | 14 | 15 | 37 | 2 | 42 | 18,624 |
| 11 | Newcastle United | 42 | 11 | 7 | 3 | 22 | 13 | 3 | 7 | 11 | 8 | 32 | -15 | 42 | 16,001 |
| 12 | Chelsea | 42 | 8 | 6 | 7 | 27 | 15 | 6 | 6 | 9 | 19 | 26 | 5 | 40 | 17,897 |
| 13 | Cambridge United | 42 | 13 | 1 | 7 | 36 | 23 | 4 | 5 | 12 | 17 | 42 | -12 | 40 | 5,796 |
| 14 | Shrewsbury Town | 42 | 9 | 7 | 5 | 33 | 22 | 2 | 10 | 9 | 13 | 25 | -1 | 39 | 5,616 |
| 15 | Oldham Athletic | 42 | 7 | 9 | 5 | 19 | 16 | 5 | 6 | 10 | 20 | 32 | -9 | 39 | 6,510 |
| 16 | Wrexham | 42 | 5 | 8 | 8 | 22 | 24 | 7 | 6 | 8 | 21 | 21 | -2 | 38 | 6,495 |
| 17 | Orient | 42 | 9 | 8 | 4 | 34 | 20 | 4 | 4 | 13 | 18 | 36 | -4 | 38 | 6,076 |
| 18 | Bolton Wanderers | 42 | 10 | 5 | 6 | 40 | 27 | 4 | 5 | 12 | 21 | 39 | -5 | 38 | 9,847 |
| 19 | Cardiff City | 42 | 7 | 7 | 7 | 23 | 24 | 5 | 5 | 11 | 21 | 36 | -16 | 36 | 6,767 |
| 20 | Preston North End | 42 | 8 | 7 | 6 | 28 | 26 | 3 | 7 | 11 | 13 | 36 | -21 | 36 | 7,631 |
| 21 | Bristol City | 42 | 6 | 10 | 5 | 19 | 15 | 1 | 6 | 14 | 10 | 36 | -22 | 30 | 9,765 |
| 22 | Bristol Rovers | 42 | 4 | 9 | 8 | 21 | 24 | 1 | 4 | 16 | 13 | 41 | -31 | 23 | 5,929 |

## Third Division

| | | Pld | W | D | L | F | A | W | D | L | F | A | GD | Pts | Ave Gate |
|---|---|---|---|---|---|---|---|---|---|---|---|---|---|---|---|
| 1 | Rotherham United | 46 | 17 | 6 | 0 | 43 | 8 | 7 | 7 | 9 | 19 | 24 | 30 | 61 | 7,985 |
| 2 | Barnsley | 46 | 15 | 5 | 3 | 46 | 19 | 6 | 12 | 5 | 26 | 26 | 27 | 59 | 12,800 |
| 3 | Charlton Athletic | 46 | 14 | 6 | 3 | 36 | 17 | 11 | 3 | 9 | 27 | 27 | 19 | 59 | 7,206 |
| 4 | Huddersfield Town | 46 | 14 | 6 | 3 | 40 | 11 | 7 | 8 | 8 | 31 | 29 | 31 | 56 | 11,548 |
| 5 | Chesterfield | 46 | 17 | 4 | 2 | 42 | 16 | 6 | 6 | 11 | 30 | 32 | 24 | 56 | 7,331 |
| 6 | Portsmouth | 46 | 14 | 5 | 4 | 35 | 18 | 8 | 4 | 11 | 20 | 28 | 8 | 53 | 13,514 |
| 7 | Plymouth Argyle | 46 | 14 | 5 | 4 | 35 | 18 | 5 | 9 | 9 | 21 | 26 | 12 | 52 | 6,766 |
| 8 | Burnley | 46 | 13 | 5 | 5 | 37 | 21 | 5 | 9 | 9 | 23 | 27 | 12 | 50 | 6,469 |
| 9 | Brentford | 46 | 7 | 9 | 7 | 30 | 25 | 7 | 10 | 6 | 22 | 24 | 3 | 47 | 6,752 |
| 10 | Reading | 46 | 13 | 5 | 5 | 39 | 22 | 5 | 5 | 13 | 23 | 40 | 0 | 46 | 5,439 |
| 11 | Exeter City | 46 | 9 | 9 | 5 | 36 | 30 | 7 | 4 | 12 | 26 | 36 | -4 | 45 | 4,559 |
| 12 | Newport County | 46 | 11 | 6 | 6 | 38 | 22 | 4 | 7 | 12 | 26 | 39 | 3 | 43 | 5,683 |
| 13 | Fulham | 46 | 8 | 7 | 8 | 28 | 29 | 7 | 6 | 10 | 29 | 35 | -7 | 43 | 5,060 |
| 14 | Oxford United | 46 | 7 | 8 | 8 | 20 | 24 | 6 | 9 | 8 | 19 | 23 | -8 | 43 | 4,132 |
| 15 | Gillingham | 46 | 9 | 8 | 6 | 23 | 19 | 3 | 10 | 10 | 25 | 39 | -10 | 42 | 4,676 |
| 16 | Millwall | 45 | 10 | 9 | 4 | 30 | 21 | 4 | 5 | 14 | 13 | 39 | -17 | 42 | 4,494 |
| 17 | Swindon Town | 46 | 10 | 6 | 7 | 35 | 27 | 3 | 9 | 11 | 16 | 29 | -5 | 41 | 6,933 |
| 18 | Chester | 46 | 11 | 5 | 7 | 25 | 17 | 4 | 6 | 13 | 13 | 31 | -10 | 41 | 2,892 |
| 19 | Carlisle United | 46 | 8 | 9 | 6 | 32 | 29 | 6 | 4 | 13 | 24 | 41 | -14 | 41 | 4,064 |
| 20 | Walsall | 46 | 8 | 9 | 6 | 43 | 43 | 5 | 6 | 12 | 16 | 31 | -15 | 41 | 4,265 |
| 21 | Sheffield United | 46 | 12 | 6 | 5 | 38 | 20 | 2 | 6 | 15 | 27 | 43 | 2 | 40 | 12,772 |
| 22 | Colchester United | 46 | 12 | 7 | 4 | 35 | 22 | 2 | 4 | 17 | 10 | 43 | -20 | 39 | 2,645 |
| 23 | Blackpool | 46 | 5 | 9 | 9 | 19 | 28 | 4 | 5 | 14 | 26 | 47 | -30 | 32 | 5,863 |
| 24 | Hull City | 46 | 7 | 8 | 8 | 23 | 22 | 1 | 8 | 14 | 17 | 49 | -31 | 32 | 4,319 |

## Fourth Division

| | | Pld | W | D | L | F | A | W | D | L | F | A | GD | Pts | Ave Gate |
|---|---|---|---|---|---|---|---|---|---|---|---|---|---|---|---|
| 1 | Southend United | 46 | 19 | 4 | 0 | 47 | 6 | 11 | 3 | 9 | 32 | 25 | 48 | 67 | 6,095 |
| 2 | Lincoln City | 46 | 15 | 7 | 1 | 44 | 11 | 10 | 8 | 5 | 22 | 14 | 41 | 65 | 4,715 |
| 3 | Doncaster Rovers | 46 | 15 | 4 | 4 | 36 | 20 | 7 | 8 | 8 | 23 | 29 | 10 | 56 | 5,412 |
| 4 | Wimbledon | 46 | 15 | 4 | 4 | 42 | 17 | 8 | 5 | 10 | 22 | 29 | 18 | 55 | 2,484 |
| 5 | Peterborough United | 46 | 11 | 8 | 4 | 37 | 21 | 6 | 10 | 7 | 31 | 33 | 14 | 52 | 4,137 |
| 6 | Aldershot | 46 | 12 | 9 | 2 | 28 | 11 | 6 | 5 | 12 | 15 | 30 | 2 | 50 | 2,989 |
| 7 | Mansfield Town | 46 | 13 | 5 | 5 | 36 | 15 | 7 | 4 | 12 | 22 | 29 | 14 | 49 | 3,400 |
| 8 | Darlington | 46 | 13 | 6 | 4 | 43 | 23 | 6 | 5 | 12 | 22 | 36 | 6 | 49 | 2,537 |
| 9 | Hartlepool United | 46 | 14 | 3 | 6 | 42 | 22 | 6 | 6 | 11 | 22 | 39 | 3 | 49 | 3,115 |
| 10 | Northampton Town | 46 | 11 | 7 | 5 | 42 | 26 | 7 | 6 | 10 | 23 | 41 | -2 | 49 | 2,305 |
| 11 | Wigan Athletic | 46 | 13 | 4 | 6 | 29 | 16 | 5 | 7 | 11 | 22 | 39 | -4 | 47 | 4,434 |
| 12 | Bury | 46 | 10 | 8 | 5 | 38 | 21 | 7 | 3 | 13 | 32 | 41 | 8 | 45 | 2,748 |
| 13 | AFC Bournemouth | 46 | 9 | 8 | 6 | 30 | 21 | 7 | 5 | 11 | 17 | 27 | -1 | 45 | 3,380 |
| 14 | Bradford City | 46 | 9 | 9 | 5 | 30 | 24 | 5 | 7 | 11 | 23 | 36 | -7 | 44 | 2,858 |
| 15 | Rochdale | 46 | 11 | 6 | 6 | 33 | 25 | 3 | 9 | 11 | 27 | 45 | -10 | 42 | 2,460 |
| 16 | Scunthorpe United | 46 | 8 | 12 | 3 | 40 | 31 | 3 | 8 | 12 | 20 | 38 | -9 | 42 | 2,357 |
| 17 | Torquay United | 46 | 13 | 2 | 8 | 38 | 26 | 5 | 3 | 15 | 17 | 37 | -8 | 41 | 2,050 |
| 18 | Crewe Alexandra | 46 | 10 | 7 | 6 | 28 | 20 | 3 | 7 | 13 | 20 | 41 | -13 | 40 | 2,909 |
| 19 | Port Vale | 46 | 10 | 8 | 5 | 40 | 23 | 2 | 7 | 14 | 17 | 47 | -13 | 39 | 2,738 |
| 20 | Stockport County | 46 | 10 | 5 | 8 | 29 | 25 | 6 | 2 | 15 | 15 | 32 | -13 | 39 | 2,335 |
| 21 | Tranmere Rovers | 46 | 12 | 5 | 6 | 41 | 24 | 1 | 5 | 17 | 18 | 49 | -14 | 36 | 1,901 |
| 22 | Hereford United | 46 | 8 | 8 | 7 | 29 | 20 | 3 | 5 | 15 | 9 | 42 | -24 | 35 | 2,444 |
| 23 | Halifax Town | 46 | 9 | 3 | 11 | 28 | 32 | 2 | 9 | 12 | 16 | 39 | -27 | 34 | 1,924 |
| 24 | York City | 46 | 10 | 2 | 11 | 31 | 23 | 2 | 7 | 14 | 16 | 43 | -19 | 33 | 2,245 |

Tranmere Rovers, Hereford United, Halifax Town and York City re-elected to the Football League

# 1981/82

*Three points for a win introduced*

## First Division

| | | Pld | W | D | L | F | A | W | D | L | F | A | GD | Pts | Ave Gate |
|---|---|---|---|---|---|---|---|---|---|---|---|---|---|---|---|
| 1 | Liverpool | 42 | 14 | 3 | 4 | 39 | 14 | 12 | 6 | 3 | 41 | 18 | 48 | 87 | 35,060 |
| 2 | Ipswich Town | 42 | 17 | 1 | 3 | 47 | 25 | 9 | 4 | 8 | 28 | 28 | 22 | 83 | 21,925 |
| 3 | Manchester United | 42 | 12 | 6 | 3 | 27 | 9 | 10 | 6 | 5 | 32 | 20 | 30 | 78 | 44,570 |
| 4 | Tottenham Hotspur | 42 | 12 | 4 | 5 | 41 | 26 | 8 | 7 | 6 | 26 | 22 | 19 | 71 | 35,099 |
| 5 | Arsenal | 42 | 13 | 5 | 3 | 27 | 15 | 7 | 6 | 8 | 21 | 22 | 11 | 71 | 25,493 |
| 6 | Swansea City | 42 | 13 | 3 | 5 | 34 | 16 | 8 | 3 | 10 | 24 | 35 | 7 | 69 | 18,225 |
| 7 | Southampton | 42 | 15 | 2 | 4 | 49 | 30 | 4 | 7 | 10 | 23 | 37 | 5 | 66 | 21,835 |
| 8 | Everton | 42 | 11 | 7 | 3 | 33 | 21 | 6 | 6 | 9 | 23 | 29 | 6 | 64 | 24,673 |
| 9 | West Ham United | 42 | 9 | 10 | 2 | 42 | 29 | 5 | 6 | 10 | 24 | 28 | 9 | 58 | 26,584 |
| 10 | Manchester City | 42 | 9 | 7 | 5 | 32 | 23 | 6 | 9 | 6 | 17 | 27 | -1 | 58 | 34,063 |
| 11 | Aston Villa | 42 | 9 | 6 | 6 | 28 | 24 | 6 | 6 | 9 | 27 | 29 | 2 | 57 | 26,875 |
| 12 | Nottingham Forest | 42 | 7 | 7 | 7 | 19 | 20 | 8 | 5 | 8 | 23 | 28 | -6 | 57 | 19,937 |
| 13 | Brighton & Hove Albion | 42 | 8 | 7 | 6 | 30 | 24 | 5 | 6 | 10 | 13 | 28 | -9 | 52 | 18,244 |
| 14 | Coventry City | 42 | 9 | 4 | 8 | 31 | 24 | 4 | 7 | 10 | 25 | 38 | -6 | 50 | 13,099 |
| 15 | Notts County | 42 | 8 | 5 | 8 | 32 | 33 | 5 | 3 | 13 | 29 | 36 | -8 | 47 | 11,627 |
| 16 | Birmingham City | 42 | 8 | 6 | 7 | 29 | 25 | 2 | 8 | 11 | 24 | 36 | -8 | 44 | 17,116 |
| 17 | West Bromwich Albion | 42 | 6 | 6 | 9 | 24 | 25 | 5 | 5 | 11 | 22 | 32 | -11 | 44 | 16,785 |
| 18 | Stoke City | 42 | 9 | 2 | 10 | 27 | 28 | 3 | 6 | 12 | 17 | 35 | -19 | 44 | 14,635 |
| 19 | Sunderland | 42 | 6 | 5 | 10 | 19 | 26 | 5 | 6 | 10 | 19 | 32 | -20 | 44 | 19,607 |
| 20 | Leeds United | 42 | 6 | 11 | 4 | 23 | 20 | 4 | 1 | 16 | 16 | 41 | -22 | 42 | 22,109 |
| 21 | Wolverhampton Wanderers | 42 | 8 | 5 | 8 | 19 | 20 | 2 | 5 | 14 | 13 | 43 | -31 | 40 | 15,242 |
| 22 | Middlesbrough | 42 | 5 | 9 | 7 | 20 | 24 | 3 | 6 | 12 | 14 | 28 | -18 | 39 | 13,412 |

## Second Division

| | | Pld | W | D | L | F | A | W | D | L | F | A | GD | Pts | Ave Gate |
|---|---|---|---|---|---|---|---|---|---|---|---|---|---|---|---|
| 1 | Luton Town | 42 | 16 | 3 | 2 | 48 | 19 | 9 | 10 | 2 | 38 | 27 | 40 | 88 | 11,880 |
| 2 | Watford | 42 | 13 | 6 | 2 | 46 | 16 | 10 | 5 | 6 | 30 | 26 | 34 | 80 | 14,631 |
| 3 | Norwich City | 42 | 14 | 3 | 4 | 41 | 19 | 8 | 2 | 11 | 23 | 31 | 14 | 71 | 14,183 |
| 4 | Sheffield Wednesday | 42 | 10 | 8 | 3 | 31 | 23 | 10 | 2 | 9 | 24 | 28 | 4 | 70 | 19,170 |
| 5 | Queens Park Rangers | 42 | 15 | 4 | 2 | 40 | 9 | 6 | 2 | 13 | 25 | 34 | 22 | 69 | 12,574 |
| 6 | Barnsley | 42 | 13 | 4 | 4 | 33 | 14 | 6 | 9 | 6 | 26 | 27 | 18 | 67 | 15,097 |
| 7 | Rotherham United | 42 | 13 | 5 | 3 | 42 | 19 | 7 | 2 | 12 | 24 | 35 | 12 | 67 | 9,856 |
| 8 | Leicester City | 42 | 12 | 5 | 4 | 31 | 19 | 6 | 7 | 8 | 25 | 29 | 8 | 66 | 14,182 |
| 9 | Newcastle United | 42 | 14 | 4 | 3 | 30 | 14 | 4 | 4 | 13 | 22 | 36 | 2 | 62 | 17,276 |
| 10 | Blackburn Rovers | 42 | 11 | 4 | 6 | 26 | 15 | 5 | 7 | 9 | 21 | 28 | 4 | 59 | 8,404 |
| 11 | Oldham Athletic | 42 | 9 | 9 | 3 | 28 | 23 | 6 | 5 | 10 | 22 | 28 | -1 | 59 | 7,022 |
| 12 | Chelsea | 42 | 10 | 4 | 6 | 37 | 30 | 5 | 7 | 9 | 23 | 30 | 0 | 57 | 13,131 |
| 13 | Charlton Athletic | 42 | 11 | 5 | 5 | 33 | 22 | 2 | 7 | 12 | 17 | 43 | -15 | 48 | 6,648 |
| 14 | Cambridge United | 42 | 11 | 4 | 6 | 31 | 19 | 2 | 5 | 14 | 17 | 34 | -5 | 48 | 5,073 |
| 15 | Crystal Palace | 42 | 9 | 2 | 10 | 25 | 26 | 4 | 7 | 10 | 9 | 19 | -11 | 48 | 10,380 |
| 16 | Derby County | 42 | 9 | 8 | 4 | 32 | 23 | 3 | 4 | 14 | 21 | 45 | -15 | 48 | 11,827 |
| 17 | Grimsby Town | 42 | 5 | 8 | 8 | 29 | 30 | 6 | 5 | 10 | 24 | 35 | -12 | 46 | 8,406 |
| 18 | Shrewsbury Town | 42 | 10 | 6 | 5 | 26 | 19 | 1 | 7 | 13 | 11 | 38 | -20 | 46 | 4,570 |
| 19 | Bolton Wanderers | 42 | 10 | 4 | 7 | 28 | 24 | 3 | 3 | 15 | 11 | 37 | -22 | 46 | 7,597 |
| 20 | Cardiff City | 42 | 9 | 2 | 10 | 28 | 32 | 3 | 6 | 12 | 17 | 29 | -16 | 44 | 5,573 |
| 21 | Wrexham | 42 | 9 | 4 | 8 | 22 | 22 | 2 | 7 | 12 | 18 | 34 | -16 | 44 | 4,309 |
| 22 | Orient | 42 | 6 | 8 | 7 | 23 | 24 | 4 | 1 | 16 | 13 | 37 | -25 | 39 | 4,419 |

# APPENDICES

## Third Division

| | | Pld | W | D | L | F | A | W | D | L | F | A | GD | Pts | Ave Gate |
|---|---|---|---|---|---|---|---|---|---|---|---|---|---|---|---|
| 1 | Burnley | 46 | 13 | 7 | 3 | 37 | 20 | 8 | 10 | 5 | 29 | 25 | 21 | 80 | 6,936 |
| 2 | Carlisle United | 46 | 17 | 4 | 2 | 44 | 21 | 6 | 7 | 10 | 21 | 29 | 15 | 80 | 4,409 |
| 3 | Fulham | 46 | 12 | 9 | 2 | 44 | 22 | 9 | 6 | 8 | 33 | 29 | 26 | 78 | 6,937 |
| 4 | Lincoln City | 46 | 13 | 7 | 3 | 40 | 16 | 8 | 7 | 8 | 26 | 24 | 26 | 77 | 4,222 |
| 5 | Oxford United | 46 | 10 | 8 | 5 | 28 | 18 | 9 | 6 | 8 | 35 | 31 | 14 | 71 | 5,850 |
| 6 | Gillingham | 46 | 14 | 5 | 4 | 44 | 26 | 6 | 6 | 11 | 20 | 30 | 8 | 71 | 5,241 |
| 7 | Southend United | 46 | 11 | 7 | 5 | 35 | 23 | 7 | 8 | 8 | 28 | 28 | 12 | 69 | 5,082 |
| 8 | Brentford | 46 | 8 | 6 | 9 | 28 | 22 | 11 | 5 | 7 | 28 | 25 | 9 | 68 | 5,692 |
| 9 | Millwall | 46 | 12 | 4 | 7 | 36 | 28 | 6 | 9 | 8 | 26 | 34 | 0 | 67 | 4,625 |
| 10 | Plymouth Argyle | 46 | 12 | 5 | 6 | 37 | 24 | 6 | 6 | 11 | 27 | 32 | 8 | 65 | 4,792 |
| 11 | Chesterfield | 46 | 12 | 4 | 7 | 33 | 27 | 6 | 6 | 11 | 24 | 31 | -1 | 64 | 4,752 |
| 12 | Reading | 46 | 11 | 6 | 6 | 43 | 35 | 6 | 5 | 12 | 24 | 40 | -8 | 62 | 4,017 |
| 13 | Portsmouth | 46 | 11 | 10 | 2 | 33 | 14 | 3 | 9 | 11 | 23 | 37 | 5 | 61 | 8,543 |
| 14 | Preston North End | 46 | 10 | 7 | 6 | 25 | 22 | 6 | 6 | 11 | 25 | 34 | -6 | 61 | 5,496 |
| 15 | Bristol Rovers | 46 | 12 | 4 | 7 | 35 | 28 | 6 | 5 | 12 | 23 | 37 | -7 | 61* | 5,599 |
| 16 | Newport County | 46 | 9 | 10 | 4 | 28 | 21 | 5 | 6 | 12 | 26 | 33 | 0 | 58 | 4,458 |
| 17 | Huddersfield Town | 46 | 10 | 5 | 8 | 38 | 25 | 5 | 7 | 11 | 26 | 34 | 5 | 57 | 6,745 |
| 18 | Exeter City | 46 | 14 | 4 | 5 | 46 | 33 | 2 | 5 | 16 | 25 | 51 | -13 | 57 | 3,857 |
| 19 | Doncaster Rovers | 46 | 9 | 9 | 5 | 31 | 24 | 4 | 8 | 11 | 24 | 44 | -13 | 56 | 5,234 |
| 20 | Walsall | 46 | 10 | 7 | 6 | 32 | 23 | 3 | 7 | 13 | 19 | 32 | -4 | 53 | 3,744 |
| 21 | Wimbledon | 46 | 10 | 6 | 7 | 33 | 27 | 4 | 5 | 14 | 28 | 48 | -14 | 53 | 2,595 |
| 22 | Swindon Town | 46 | 9 | 5 | 9 | 37 | 36 | 4 | 8 | 11 | 18 | 35 | -16 | 52 | 5,824 |
| 23 | Bristol City | 46 | 7 | 6 | 10 | 24 | 29 | 4 | 7 | 12 | 16 | 36 | -25 | 46 | 6,511 |
| 24 | Chester | 46 | 2 | 10 | 11 | 16 | 30 | 5 | 1 | 17 | 20 | 48 | -42 | 32 | 2,170 |

*Bristol Rovers deducted 2 points for fielding an unregistered player

## Fourth Division

| | | Pld | W | D | L | F | A | W | D | L | F | A | GD | Pts | Ave Gate |
|---|---|---|---|---|---|---|---|---|---|---|---|---|---|---|---|
| 1 | Sheffield United | 46 | 15 | 8 | 0 | 53 | 15 | 12 | 7 | 4 | 41 | 26 | 53 | 96 | 14,891 |
| 2 | Bradford City | 46 | 14 | 7 | 2 | 52 | 23 | 12 | 6 | 5 | 36 | 22 | 43 | 91 | 5,391 |
| 3 | Wigan Athletic | 46 | 17 | 5 | 1 | 47 | 18 | 9 | 8 | 6 | 33 | 28 | 34 | 91 | 5,839 |
| 4 | AFC Bournemouth | 46 | 12 | 10 | 1 | 37 | 15 | 11 | 9 | 3 | 25 | 15 | 32 | 88 | 5,933 |
| 5 | Peterborough United | 46 | 16 | 3 | 4 | 46 | 22 | 8 | 7 | 8 | 25 | 35 | 14 | 82 | 4,698 |
| 6 | Colchester United | 46 | 12 | 6 | 5 | 47 | 23 | 8 | 6 | 9 | 35 | 34 | 25 | 72 | 2,859 |
| 7 | Port Vale | 46 | 9 | 12 | 2 | 26 | 17 | 9 | 4 | 10 | 30 | 32 | 7 | 70 | 3,638 |
| 8 | Hull City | 46 | 14 | 3 | 6 | 36 | 23 | 5 | 9 | 9 | 34 | 38 | 9 | 69 | 3,992 |
| 9 | Bury | 46 | 13 | 7 | 3 | 53 | 26 | 4 | 10 | 9 | 27 | 33 | 21 | 68 | 3,557 |
| 10 | Hereford United | 46 | 10 | 9 | 4 | 36 | 25 | 6 | 10 | 7 | 28 | 33 | 6 | 67 | 2,592 |
| 11 | Tranmere Rovers | 46 | 7 | 9 | 7 | 27 | 25 | 7 | 9 | 7 | 24 | 31 | -5 | 60 | 1,735 |
| 12 | Blackpool | 46 | 11 | 5 | 7 | 40 | 26 | 4 | 8 | 11 | 26 | 34 | 6 | 58 | 4,223 |
| 13 | Darlington | 46 | 10 | 5 | 8 | 36 | 28 | 5 | 8 | 10 | 25 | 34 | -1 | 58 | 2,509 |
| 14 | Hartlepool United | 46 | 9 | 8 | 6 | 39 | 34 | 4 | 8 | 11 | 34 | 50 | -11 | 55 | 2,054 |
| 15 | Torquay United | 46 | 9 | 8 | 6 | 30 | 25 | 5 | 13 | 17 | 34 | -12 | 55 | 2,247 |
| 16 | Aldershot | 46 | 8 | 7 | 8 | 34 | 29 | 5 | 8 | 10 | 23 | 39 | -11 | 54 | 2,167 |
| 17 | York City | 46 | 9 | 5 | 9 | 45 | 37 | 5 | 3 | 15 | 24 | 54 | -22 | 50 | 2,360 |
| 18 | Stockport County | 46 | 10 | 5 | 8 | 34 | 28 | 2 | 8 | 13 | 14 | 39 | -19 | 49 | 2,547 |
| 19 | Halifax Town | 46 | 6 | 11 | 6 | 28 | 30 | 3 | 11 | 9 | 23 | 42 | -21 | 49 | 2,407 |
| 20 | Mansfield Town | 46 | 8 | 6 | 9 | 39 | 39 | 5 | 4 | 14 | 24 | 42 | -18 | 47* | 2,684 |
| 21 | Rochdale | 46 | 7 | 9 | 7 | 26 | 22 | 3 | 7 | 13 | 24 | 40 | -12 | 46 | 1,837 |
| 22 | Northampton Town | 46 | 9 | 5 | 9 | 32 | 27 | 2 | 4 | 17 | 25 | 57 | -27 | 42 | 2,305 |
| 23 | Scunthorpe United | 46 | 7 | 9 | 7 | 26 | 35 | 2 | 6 | 15 | 17 | 44 | -36 | 42 | 2,231 |
| 24 | Crewe Alexandra | 46 | 3 | 6 | 14 | 19 | 32 | 3 | 3 | 17 | 10 | 52 | -55 | 27 | 2,196 |

Rochdale, Northampton Town, Scunthorpe United and Crewe Alexandra re-elected to the Football League
*Mansfield Town deducted 2 points for fielding an ineligible player

# 1982/83

## First Division

| | | Pld | W | D | L | F | A | W | D | L | F | A | GD | Pts | Ave Gate |
|---|---|---|---|---|---|---|---|---|---|---|---|---|---|---|---|
| 1 | Liverpool | 42 | 16 | 4 | 1 | 55 | 16 | 8 | 6 | 7 | 32 | 21 | 50 | 82 | 34,834 |
| 2 | Watford | 42 | 16 | 2 | 3 | 49 | 20 | 6 | 3 | 12 | 25 | 37 | 17 | 71 | 19,454 |
| 3 | Manchester United | 42 | 14 | 7 | 0 | 39 | 10 | 5 | 6 | 10 | 17 | 28 | 18 | 70 | 41,573 |
| 4 | Tottenham Hotspur | 42 | 15 | 4 | 2 | 50 | 15 | 5 | 5 | 11 | 15 | 35 | 15 | 69 | 30,654 |
| 5 | Nottingham Forest | 42 | 12 | 5 | 4 | 34 | 18 | 8 | 4 | 9 | 28 | 32 | 12 | 69 | 17,826 |
| 6 | Aston Villa | 42 | 17 | 2 | 2 | 47 | 15 | 4 | 3 | 14 | 15 | 35 | 12 | 68 | 23,752 |
| 7 | Everton | 42 | 13 | 6 | 2 | 43 | 19 | 5 | 4 | 12 | 23 | 29 | 18 | 64 | 20,310 |
| 8 | West Ham United | 42 | 13 | 3 | 5 | 41 | 23 | 7 | 1 | 13 | 27 | 39 | 6 | 64 | 22,744 |
| 9 | Ipswich Town | 42 | 11 | 3 | 7 | 39 | 23 | 4 | 10 | 7 | 25 | 27 | 14 | 58 | 19,676 |
| 10 | Arsenal | 42 | 11 | 6 | 4 | 36 | 19 | 5 | 4 | 12 | 22 | 37 | 2 | 58 | 24,152 |
| 11 | West Bromwich Albion | 42 | 11 | 5 | 5 | 35 | 20 | 4 | 7 | 10 | 16 | 29 | 2 | 57 | 15,255 |
| 12 | Southampton | 42 | 11 | 5 | 5 | 36 | 22 | 4 | 7 | 10 | 18 | 36 | -4 | 57 | 18,717 |
| 13 | Stoke City | 42 | 13 | 4 | 4 | 34 | 21 | 3 | 5 | 13 | 19 | 43 | -11 | 57 | 16,627 |
| 14 | Norwich City | 42 | 10 | 6 | 5 | 30 | 18 | 4 | 6 | 11 | 22 | 40 | -6 | 54 | 17,678 |
| 15 | Notts County | 42 | 12 | 4 | 5 | 37 | 25 | 3 | 3 | 15 | 18 | 46 | -16 | 52 | 10,264 |
| 16 | Sunderland | 42 | 7 | 10 | 4 | 30 | 22 | 5 | 4 | 12 | 18 | 39 | -13 | 50 | 17,353 |
| 17 | Birmingham City | 42 | 9 | 7 | 5 | 29 | 24 | 3 | 7 | 11 | 11 | 31 | -15 | 50 | 15,880 |
| 18 | Luton Town | 42 | 7 | 7 | 7 | 34 | 33 | 5 | 6 | 10 | 31 | 51 | -19 | 49 | 13,452 |
| 19 | Coventry City | 42 | 10 | 5 | 6 | 29 | 17 | 3 | 4 | 14 | 19 | 42 | -11 | 48 | 10,479 |
| 20 | Manchester City | 42 | 9 | 5 | 7 | 26 | 23 | 4 | 3 | 14 | 21 | 47 | -23 | 47 | 26,792 |
| 21 | Swansea City | 42 | 10 | 4 | 7 | 32 | 29 | 0 | 7 | 14 | 19 | 40 | -18 | 41 | 11,682 |
| 22 | Brighton & Hove Albion | 42 | 8 | 7 | 6 | 25 | 22 | 1 | 6 | 14 | 13 | 46 | -30 | 40 | 14,669 |

## Second Division

| | | Pld | W | D | L | F | A | W | D | L | F | A | GD | Pts | Ave Gate |
|---|---|---|---|---|---|---|---|---|---|---|---|---|---|---|---|
| 1 | Queens Park Rangers | 42 | 16 | 3 | 2 | 51 | 16 | 10 | 4 | 7 | 26 | 20 | 41 | 85 | 12,806 |
| 2 | Wolverhampton Wanderers | 42 | 14 | 5 | 2 | 42 | 16 | 6 | 10 | 5 | 26 | 28 | 24 | 75 | 15,683 |
| 3 | Leicester City | 42 | 11 | 4 | 6 | 36 | 15 | 9 | 6 | 6 | 36 | 29 | 28 | 70 | 12,819 |
| 4 | Fulham | 42 | 13 | 5 | 3 | 36 | 20 | 7 | 4 | 10 | 28 | 27 | 17 | 69 | 10,836 |
| 5 | Newcastle United | 42 | 13 | 6 | 2 | 43 | 21 | 5 | 7 | 9 | 32 | 32 | 22 | 67 | 24,179 |
| 6 | Sheffield Wednesday | 42 | 9 | 8 | 4 | 33 | 23 | 7 | 7 | 7 | 27 | 24 | 13 | 63 | 16,657 |
| 7 | Oldham Athletic | 42 | 8 | 10 | 3 | 38 | 24 | 6 | 9 | 6 | 26 | 23 | 17 | 61 | 6,981 |
| 8 | Leeds United | 42 | 7 | 11 | 3 | 28 | 22 | 6 | 10 | 5 | 23 | 24 | 5 | 60 | 16,008 |
| 9 | Shrewsbury Town | 42 | 8 | 9 | 4 | 20 | 15 | 7 | 5 | 9 | 28 | 33 | 0 | 59 | 5,275 |
| 10 | Barnsley | 42 | 9 | 8 | 4 | 37 | 28 | 5 | 7 | 9 | 20 | 27 | 2 | 57 | 12,320 |
| 11 | Blackburn Rovers | 42 | 11 | 7 | 3 | 38 | 21 | 4 | 5 | 12 | 20 | 37 | 0 | 57 | 7,116 |
| 12 | Cambridge United | 42 | 11 | 7 | 3 | 26 | 17 | 2 | 5 | 14 | 16 | 43 | -18 | 51 | 4,532 |
| 13 | Derby County | 42 | 7 | 10 | 4 | 27 | 24 | 3 | 9 | 9 | 22 | 34 | -9 | 49 | 13,599 |
| 14 | Carlisle United | 42 | 10 | 6 | 5 | 44 | 28 | 2 | 6 | 13 | 24 | 42 | -2 | 48 | 5,943 |
| 15 | Crystal Palace | 42 | 11 | 7 | 3 | 31 | 17 | 1 | 5 | 15 | 12 | 35 | -9 | 48 | 9,848 |
| 16 | Middlesbrough | 42 | 8 | 7 | 6 | 27 | 29 | 3 | 8 | 10 | 19 | 38 | -21 | 48 | 10,011 |
| 17 | Charlton Athletic | 42 | 11 | 3 | 7 | 40 | 31 | 2 | 6 | 13 | 23 | 55 | -23 | 48 | 7,193 |
| 18 | Chelsea | 42 | 8 | 8 | 5 | 31 | 22 | 3 | 4 | 12 | 20 | 39 | -10 | 47 | 12,728 |
| 19 | Grimsby Town | 42 | 9 | 7 | 5 | 32 | 26 | 3 | 4 | 14 | 13 | 44 | -25 | 47 | 7,745 |
| 20 | Rotherham United | 42 | 6 | 7 | 8 | 22 | 29 | 4 | 8 | 9 | 23 | 39 | -23 | 45 | 8,316 |
| 21 | Burnley | 42 | 10 | 4 | 7 | 38 | 24 | 2 | 4 | 15 | 18 | 42 | -10 | 44 | 9,004 |
| 22 | Bolton Wanderers | 42 | 10 | 2 | 9 | 30 | 26 | 1 | 9 | 11 | 12 | 35 | -19 | 44 | 7,512 |

## Third Division

| | | Pld | W | D | L | F | A | W | D | L | F | A | GD | Pts | Ave Gate |
|---|---|---|---|---|---|---|---|---|---|---|---|---|---|---|---|
| 1 | Portsmouth | 46 | 16 | 4 | 3 | 43 | 19 | 11 | 6 | 6 | 31 | 22 | 33 | 91 | 14,057 |
| 2 | Cardiff City | 46 | 17 | 5 | 1 | 45 | 14 | 8 | 6 | 9 | 31 | 36 | 26 | 86 | 7,023 |
| 3 | Huddersfield Town | 46 | 15 | 8 | 0 | 56 | 18 | 8 | 5 | 10 | 28 | 31 | 35 | 82 | 9,263 |
| 4 | Newport County | 46 | 13 | 7 | 3 | 40 | 20 | 10 | 2 | 11 | 36 | 34 | 22 | 78 | 4,710 |
| 5 | Oxford United | 46 | 12 | 9 | 2 | 41 | 23 | 10 | 3 | 10 | 30 | 30 | 18 | 78 | 5,476 |
| 6 | Lincoln City | 46 | 17 | 1 | 5 | 55 | 22 | 6 | 6 | 11 | 22 | 29 | 26 | 76 | 4,749 |
| 7 | Bristol Rovers | 46 | 16 | 4 | 3 | 55 | 21 | 6 | 5 | 12 | 29 | 37 | 26 | 75 | 6,191 |
| 8 | Plymouth Argyle | 46 | 15 | 2 | 6 | 37 | 23 | 4 | 6 | 13 | 24 | 43 | -5 | 65 | 4,532 |
| 9 | Brentford | 46 | 14 | 4 | 5 | 50 | 28 | 4 | 6 | 13 | 38 | 49 | 11 | 64 | 6,615 |
| 10 | Walsall | 46 | 14 | 5 | 4 | 38 | 19 | 3 | 8 | 12 | 26 | 44 | 1 | 64 | 3,242 |
| 11 | Sheffield United | 46 | 16 | 3 | 4 | 44 | 20 | 3 | 4 | 16 | 18 | 44 | -2 | 64 | 11,806 |
| 12 | Bradford City | 46 | 11 | 7 | 5 | 41 | 27 | 5 | 6 | 12 | 27 | 42 | -1 | 61 | 4,832 |
| 13 | Gillingham | 46 | 12 | 4 | 7 | 37 | 29 | 4 | 9 | 10 | 21 | 30 | -1 | 61 | 4,147 |
| 14 | AFC Bournemouth | 46 | 11 | 7 | 5 | 35 | 20 | 5 | 6 | 12 | 24 | 48 | -9 | 61 | 5,723 |
| 15 | Southend United | 46 | 10 | 8 | 5 | 41 | 28 | 5 | 6 | 12 | 25 | 37 | 1 | 59 | 3,279 |
| 16 | Preston North End | 46 | 11 | 10 | 2 | 35 | 17 | 4 | 3 | 16 | 25 | 52 | -9 | 58 | 4,938 |
| 17 | Millwall | 46 | 12 | 7 | 4 | 41 | 24 | 2 | 6 | 15 | 23 | 53 | -13 | 55 | 4,031 |
| 18 | Wigan Athletic | 46 | 10 | 4 | 9 | 35 | 33 | 5 | 5 | 13 | 25 | 39 | -12 | 54 | 4,439 |
| 19 | Exeter City | 46 | 12 | 4 | 7 | 49 | 43 | 2 | 8 | 13 | 32 | 61 | -23 | 54 | 3,369 |
| 20 | Orient | 46 | 10 | 6 | 7 | 44 | 38 | 5 | 3 | 15 | 20 | 50 | -24 | 54 | 2,726 |
| 21 | Reading | 46 | 10 | 8 | 5 | 37 | 28 | 2 | 9 | 12 | 27 | 51 | -15 | 53 | 3,267 |
| 22 | Wrexham | 46 | 11 | 6 | 6 | 40 | 26 | 1 | 9 | 13 | 16 | 50 | -20 | 51 | 2,710 |
| 23 | Doncaster Rovers | 46 | 6 | 8 | 9 | 38 | 44 | 3 | 3 | 17 | 19 | 53 | -40 | 38 | 3,516 |
| 24 | Chesterfield | 46 | 6 | 6 | 11 | 28 | 28 | 2 | 7 | 14 | 15 | 40 | -25 | 37 | 3,251 |

## Division Four

| | | Pld | W | D | L | F | A | W | D | L | F | A | GD | Pts | Ave Gate |
|---|---|---|---|---|---|---|---|---|---|---|---|---|---|---|---|
| 1 | Wimbledon | 46 | 17 | 4 | 2 | 57 | 23 | 12 | 7 | 4 | 39 | 2 | 51 | 98 | 2,354 |
| 2 | Hull City | 46 | 14 | 8 | 1 | 48 | 14 | 11 | 7 | 5 | 27 | 20 | 41 | 90 | 6,942 |
| 3 | Port Vale | 46 | 15 | 4 | 4 | 37 | 16 | 11 | 6 | 6 | 30 | 18 | 33 | 88 | 4,819 |
| 4 | Scunthorpe United | 46 | 13 | 7 | 3 | 41 | 17 | 10 | 7 | 6 | 30 | 25 | 29 | 83 | 3,574 |
| 5 | Bury | 46 | 15 | 4 | 4 | 43 | 20 | 8 | 8 | 7 | 31 | 26 | 28 | 81 | 3,092 |
| 6 | Colchester United | 46 | 17 | 5 | 1 | 51 | 19 | 7 | 4 | 12 | 24 | 36 | 20 | 81 | 2,552 |
| 7 | York City | 46 | 18 | 4 | 1 | 59 | 19 | 4 | 9 | 10 | 29 | 39 | 30 | 79 | 3,243 |
| 8 | Swindon Town | 46 | 14 | 3 | 6 | 45 | 27 | 5 | 8 | 10 | 16 | 27 | 7 | 68 | 3,994 |
| 9 | Peterborough United | 46 | 13 | 6 | 4 | 38 | 23 | 4 | 7 | 12 | 20 | 29 | 6 | 64 | 2,795 |
| 10 | Mansfield Town | 46 | 11 | 6 | 6 | 32 | 26 | 5 | 7 | 11 | 29 | 44 | -9 | 61 | 2,312 |
| 11 | Halifax Town | 46 | 9 | 8 | 6 | 31 | 23 | 7 | 4 | 12 | 28 | 43 | -7 | 60 | 1,925 |
| 12 | Torquay United | 46 | 12 | 3 | 8 | 38 | 30 | 5 | 4 | 14 | 18 | 35 | -9 | 58 | 2,312 |
| 13 | Chester | 46 | 8 | 6 | 9 | 28 | 24 | 7 | 5 | 11 | 27 | 36 | -5 | 56 | 1,903 |
| 14 | Bristol City | 46 | 10 | 8 | 5 | 32 | 25 | 3 | 9 | 11 | 27 | 45 | -11 | 56 | 4,695 |
| 15 | Northampton Town | 46 | 10 | 8 | 5 | 43 | 29 | 4 | 4 | 15 | 22 | 46 | -10 | 54 | 2,595 |
| 16 | Stockport County | 46 | 11 | 8 | 4 | 41 | 31 | 3 | 4 | 16 | 19 | 48 | -19 | 54 | 2,303 |
| 17 | Darlington | 46 | 8 | 5 | 10 | 27 | 30 | 5 | 8 | 10 | 34 | 41 | -10 | 52 | 1,454 |
| 18 | Aldershot | 46 | 11 | 5 | 7 | 40 | 35 | 1 | 10 | 12 | 21 | 47 | -21 | 51 | 1,928 |
| 19 | Tranmere Rovers | 46 | 8 | 8 | 7 | 30 | 29 | 5 | 3 | 15 | 19 | 42 | -22 | 50 | 1,929 |
| 20 | Rochdale | 46 | 11 | 8 | 4 | 38 | 25 | 0 | 8 | 15 | 17 | 48 | -18 | 49 | 1,689 |
| 21 | Blackpool | 46 | 10 | 8 | 5 | 32 | 23 | 3 | 4 | 16 | 23 | 51 | -19 | 49* | 3,002 |
| 22 | Hartlepool United | 46 | 11 | 5 | 7 | 30 | 24 | 2 | 4 | 17 | 16 | 52 | -30 | 48 | 1,369 |
| 23 | Crewe Alexandra | 46 | 9 | 5 | 9 | 35 | 32 | 2 | 3 | 18 | 18 | 39 | -18 | 41 | 2,244 |
| 24 | Hereford United | 46 | 8 | 6 | 9 | 19 | 23 | 3 | 2 | 18 | 23 | 56 | -37 | 41 | 2,234 |

Blackpool, Hartlepool United, Crewe Alexandra and Hereford United re-elected to the Football League
*Blackpool deducted two points for fielding an ineligible player

# 1983/84

## First Division

| | | Pld | W | D | L | F | A | W | D | L | F | A | GD | Pts | Ave Gate |
|---|---|---|---|---|---|---|---|---|---|---|---|---|---|---|---|
| 1 | Liverpool | 42 | 14 | 5 | 2 | 50 | 12 | 8 | 9 | 4 | 23 | 20 | 41 | 80 | 31,974 |
| 2 | Southampton | 42 | 15 | 4 | 2 | 44 | 17 | 7 | 7 | 7 | 22 | 21 | 28 | 77 | 18,088 |
| 3 | Nottingham Forest | 42 | 14 | 4 | 3 | 47 | 17 | 8 | 4 | 9 | 29 | 28 | 31 | 74 | 17,698 |
| 4 | Manchester United | 42 | 14 | 3 | 4 | 43 | 18 | 6 | 11 | 4 | 28 | 23 | 30 | 74 | 42,534 |
| 5 | Queens Park Rangers | 42 | 14 | 4 | 3 | 37 | 12 | 8 | 3 | 10 | 30 | 25 | 30 | 73 | 15,370 |
| 6 | Arsenal | 42 | 10 | 5 | 6 | 41 | 29 | 8 | 4 | 9 | 33 | 31 | 14 | 63 | 28,116 |
| 7 | Everton | 42 | 9 | 9 | 3 | 21 | 12 | 7 | 5 | 9 | 23 | 30 | 2 | 62 | 19,343 |
| 8 | Tottenham Hotspur | 42 | 11 | 4 | 6 | 31 | 24 | 6 | 6 | 9 | 33 | 41 | -1 | 61 | 28,701 |
| 9 | West Ham United | 42 | 10 | 4 | 7 | 39 | 24 | 7 | 5 | 9 | 21 | 31 | 5 | 60 | 21,386 |
| 10 | Aston Villa | 42 | 14 | 3 | 4 | 34 | 22 | 3 | 6 | 12 | 25 | 39 | -2 | 60 | 21,370 |
| 11 | Watford | 42 | 9 | 7 | 5 | 36 | 31 | 7 | 2 | 12 | 32 | 46 | -9 | 57 | 16,510 |
| 12 | Ipswich Town | 42 | 11 | 4 | 6 | 34 | 23 | 4 | 4 | 13 | 21 | 34 | -2 | 53 | 17,464 |
| 13 | Sunderland | 42 | 8 | 9 | 4 | 26 | 18 | 5 | 4 | 12 | 16 | 35 | -11 | 52 | 16,180 |
| 14 | Norwich City | 42 | 9 | 8 | 4 | 34 | 20 | 3 | 7 | 11 | 14 | 29 | -1 | 51 | 15,659 |
| 15 | Leicester City | 42 | 11 | 5 | 5 | 40 | 30 | 2 | 7 | 12 | 25 | 38 | -3 | 51 | 14,923 |
| 16 | Luton Town | 42 | 7 | 5 | 9 | 30 | 33 | 7 | 4 | 10 | 23 | 33 | -13 | 51 | 11,938 |
| 17 | West Bromwich Albion | 42 | 10 | 4 | 7 | 30 | 25 | 4 | 5 | 12 | 18 | 37 | -14 | 51 | 14,568 |
| 18 | Stoke City | 42 | 11 | 4 | 6 | 30 | 23 | 2 | 7 | 12 | 14 | 40 | -19 | 50 | 13,900 |
| 19 | Coventry City | 42 | 8 | 5 | 8 | 33 | 33 | 5 | 6 | 10 | 24 | 44 | -20 | 50 | 12,572 |
| 20 | Birmingham City | 42 | 7 | 7 | 7 | 19 | 18 | 5 | 5 | 11 | 20 | 32 | -11 | 48 | 14,106 |
| 21 | Notts County | 42 | 6 | 7 | 8 | 31 | 36 | 4 | 4 | 13 | 19 | 36 | -22 | 41 | 9,463 |
| 22 | Wolverhampton Wanderers | 42 | 4 | 8 | 9 | 15 | 28 | 2 | 3 | 16 | 12 | 52 | -53 | 29 | 12,478 |

## Second Division

| | | Pld | W | D | L | F | A | W | D | L | F | A | GD | Pts | Ave Gate |
|---|---|---|---|---|---|---|---|---|---|---|---|---|---|---|---|
| 1 | Chelsea | 42 | 15 | 4 | 2 | 55 | 17 | 10 | 9 | 2 | 35 | 23 | 50 | 88 | 21,119 |
| 2 | Sheffield Wednesday | 42 | 16 | 4 | 1 | 47 | 16 | 10 | 6 | 5 | 25 | 18 | 38 | 88 | 22,770 |
| 3 | Newcastle United | 42 | 16 | 2 | 3 | 51 | 18 | 8 | 6 | 7 | 34 | 35 | 32 | 80 | 29,810 |
| 4 | Manchester City | 42 | 13 | 3 | 5 | 43 | 21 | 7 | 7 | 7 | 23 | 27 | 18 | 70 | 25,604 |
| 5 | Grimsby Town | 42 | 13 | 6 | 2 | 36 | 15 | 6 | 7 | 8 | 24 | 32 | 13 | 70 | 7,643 |
| 6 | Blackburn Rovers | 42 | 9 | 11 | 1 | 35 | 19 | 8 | 5 | 8 | 22 | 27 | 11 | 67 | 7,622 |
| 7 | Carlisle United | 42 | 10 | 9 | 2 | 29 | 13 | 6 | 7 | 8 | 19 | 28 | 7 | 64 | 5,611 |
| 8 | Shrewsbury Town | 42 | 13 | 5 | 3 | 34 | 18 | 4 | 5 | 12 | 15 | 35 | -4 | 61 | 4,740 |
| 9 | Brighton & Hove Albion | 42 | 11 | 6 | 4 | 42 | 17 | 6 | 3 | 12 | 27 | 43 | 9 | 60 | 12,275 |
| 10 | Leeds United | 42 | 13 | 4 | 4 | 33 | 16 | 3 | 8 | 10 | 22 | 40 | -1 | 60 | 15,493 |
| 11 | Fulham | 42 | 9 | 6 | 6 | 35 | 24 | 6 | 6 | 9 | 25 | 29 | 7 | 57 | 8,143 |
| 12 | Huddersfield Town | 42 | 8 | 6 | 7 | 27 | 20 | 6 | 9 | 6 | 29 | 29 | 7 | 57 | 11,044 |
| 13 | Charlton Athletic | 42 | 13 | 4 | 4 | 40 | 26 | 3 | 5 | 13 | 13 | 38 | -11 | 57 | 6,732 |
| 14 | Barnsley | 42 | 9 | 6 | 6 | 33 | 23 | 6 | 1 | 14 | 24 | 30 | 4 | 52 | 9,738 |
| 15 | Cardiff City | 42 | 11 | 3 | 7 | 32 | 27 | 4 | 3 | 14 | 21 | 39 | -13 | 51 | 7,067 |
| 16 | Portsmouth | 42 | 8 | 3 | 10 | 46 | 32 | 6 | 4 | 11 | 27 | 32 | 9 | 49 | 13,196 |
| 17 | Middlesbrough | 42 | 9 | 8 | 4 | 26 | 18 | 3 | 5 | 13 | 15 | 29 | -6 | 49 | 8,474 |
| 18 | Crystal Palace | 42 | 8 | 5 | 8 | 18 | 18 | 4 | 6 | 11 | 24 | 34 | -10 | 47 | 8,199 |
| 19 | Oldham Athletic | 42 | 10 | 6 | 5 | 33 | 27 | 3 | 2 | 16 | 14 | 46 | -26 | 47 | 6,035 |
| 20 | Derby County | 42 | 9 | 5 | 7 | 26 | 26 | 2 | 4 | 15 | 10 | 46 | -36 | 42 | 12,858 |
| 21 | Swansea City | 42 | 7 | 4 | 10 | 20 | 28 | 0 | 4 | 17 | 16 | 57 | -49 | 29 | 6,980 |
| 22 | Cambridge United | 42 | 4 | 7 | 10 | 20 | 33 | 0 | 5 | 16 | 8 | 44 | -49 | 24 | 4,070 |

## Third Division

| | | Pld | W | D | L | F | A | W | D | L | F | A | GD | Pts | Ave Gate |
|---|---|---|---|---|---|---|---|---|---|---|---|---|---|---|---|
| 1 | Oxford United | 46 | 17 | 5 | 1 | 58 | 22 | 11 | 6 | 6 | 33 | 28 | 41 | 95 | 7,870 |
| 2 | Wimbledon | 46 | 15 | 5 | 3 | 58 | 35 | 11 | 4 | 8 | 39 | 41 | 21 | 87 | 3,459 |
| 3 | Sheffield United | 46 | 14 | 7 | 2 | 56 | 18 | 10 | 4 | 9 | 30 | 35 | 33 | 83 | 12,881 |
| 4 | Hull City | 46 | 16 | 5 | 2 | 42 | 11 | 7 | 9 | 7 | 29 | 27 | 33 | 83 | 8,135 |
| 5 | Bristol Rovers | 46 | 16 | 5 | 2 | 47 | 21 | 6 | 8 | 9 | 21 | 33 | 14 | 79 | 5,550 |
| 6 | Walsall | 46 | 14 | 4 | 5 | 44 | 22 | 8 | 5 | 10 | 24 | 39 | 7 | 75 | 5,017 |
| 7 | Bradford City | 46 | 11 | 9 | 3 | 46 | 30 | 9 | 2 | 12 | 27 | 35 | 8 | 71 | 4,203 |
| 8 | Gillingham | 46 | 13 | 4 | 6 | 50 | 29 | 7 | 6 | 10 | 24 | 40 | 5 | 70 | 3,916 |
| 9 | Millwall | 46 | 16 | 4 | 3 | 42 | 18 | 2 | 9 | 12 | 29 | 47 | 6 | 67 | 4,351 |
| 10 | Bolton Wanderers | 46 | 13 | 4 | 6 | 36 | 17 | 5 | 6 | 12 | 20 | 43 | -4 | 64 | 5,892 |
| 11 | Orient | 46 | 13 | 5 | 5 | 40 | 27 | 5 | 4 | 14 | 31 | 54 | -10 | 63 | 3,222 |
| 12 | Burnley | 46 | 12 | 5 | 6 | 52 | 25 | 4 | 9 | 10 | 24 | 36 | 15 | 62 | 6,625 |
| 13 | Newport County | 46 | 11 | 9 | 3 | 35 | 27 | 5 | 5 | 13 | 23 | 48 | -17 | 62 | 3,135 |
| 14 | Lincoln City | 46 | 11 | 4 | 8 | 42 | 29 | 6 | 6 | 11 | 17 | 33 | -3 | 61 | 3,148 |
| 15 | Wigan Athletic | 46 | 11 | 5 | 7 | 26 | 18 | 5 | 8 | 10 | 20 | 38 | -10 | 61 | 3,899 |
| 16 | Preston North End | 46 | 12 | 5 | 6 | 42 | 27 | 3 | 6 | 14 | 24 | 39 | 0 | 56 | 4,571 |
| 17 | AFC Bournemouth | 46 | 11 | 5 | 7 | 38 | 27 | 5 | 2 | 16 | 25 | 46 | -10 | 55 | 4,039 |
| 18 | Rotherham United | 46 | 10 | 5 | 8 | 29 | 17 | 5 | 4 | 14 | 28 | 47 | -7 | 54 | 4,645 |
| 19 | Plymouth Argyle | 46 | 11 | 8 | 4 | 38 | 17 | 2 | 4 | 17 | 18 | 45 | -6 | 51 | 5,336 |
| 20 | Brentford | 46 | 8 | 9 | 6 | 41 | 30 | 3 | 7 | 13 | 28 | 49 | -10 | 49 | 4,735 |
| 21 | Scunthorpe United | 46 | 9 | 9 | 5 | 40 | 31 | 0 | 10 | 13 | 14 | 42 | -19 | 46 | 3,349 |
| 22 | Southend United | 46 | 8 | 9 | 6 | 34 | 24 | 2 | 5 | 16 | 21 | 52 | -21 | 44 | 3,142 |
| 23 | Port Vale | 46 | 10 | 4 | 9 | 33 | 29 | 1 | 6 | 16 | 18 | 54 | -32 | 43 | 4,023 |
| 24 | Exeter City | 46 | 4 | 8 | 11 | 27 | 39 | 2 | 7 | 14 | 23 | 45 | -34 | 33 | 3,380 |

## Fourth Division

| | | Pld | W | D | L | F | A | W | D | L | F | A | GD | Pts | Ave Gate |
|---|---|---|---|---|---|---|---|---|---|---|---|---|---|---|---|
| 1 | York City | 46 | 18 | 4 | 1 | 58 | 16 | 13 | 4 | 6 | 38 | 23 | 57 | 101 | 5,008 |
| 2 | Doncaster Rovers | 46 | 15 | 6 | 2 | 46 | 22 | 9 | 7 | 7 | 36 | 32 | 28 | 85 | 3,778 |
| 3 | Reading | 46 | 17 | 6 | 0 | 51 | 14 | 5 | 10 | 8 | 33 | 42 | 28 | 82 | 4,471 |
| 4 | Bristol City | 46 | 18 | 3 | 2 | 51 | 14 | 6 | 7 | 10 | 19 | 27 | 26 | 82 | 7,287 |
| 5 | Aldershot | 46 | 14 | 6 | 3 | 49 | 29 | 8 | 3 | 12 | 27 | 40 | 7 | 75 | 2,483 |
| 6 | Blackpool | 46 | 15 | 4 | 4 | 47 | 19 | 6 | 5 | 12 | 23 | 33 | 18 | 72 | 3,936 |
| 7 | Peterborough United | 46 | 15 | 5 | 3 | 52 | 16 | 3 | 9 | 11 | 20 | 32 | 24 | 68 | 3,424 |
| 8 | Colchester United | 46 | 14 | 7 | 2 | 45 | 14 | 3 | 9 | 11 | 24 | 39 | 16 | 67 | 2,220 |
| 9 | Torquay United | 46 | 13 | 7 | 3 | 32 | 18 | 5 | 6 | 12 | 27 | 46 | -5 | 67 | 1,922 |
| 10 | Tranmere Rovers | 46 | 11 | 5 | 7 | 33 | 26 | 6 | 10 | 7 | 20 | 27 | 0 | 66 | 2,138 |
| 11 | Hereford United | 46 | 11 | 6 | 6 | 31 | 21 | 5 | 9 | 9 | 23 | 32 | 1 | 63 | 2,984 |
| 12 | Stockport County | 46 | 12 | 5 | 6 | 34 | 25 | 5 | 6 | 12 | 26 | 39 | -4 | 62 | 2,098 |
| 13 | Chesterfield | 46 | 10 | 11 | 2 | 34 | 24 | 5 | 4 | 14 | 25 | 37 | -2 | 60 | 3,414 |
| 14 | Darlington | 46 | 13 | 4 | 6 | 31 | 19 | 4 | 4 | 15 | 18 | 31 | -1 | 59 | 1,507 |
| 15 | Bury | 46 | 9 | 7 | 7 | 34 | 32 | 6 | 7 | 10 | 27 | 32 | -3 | 59 | 2,104 |
| 16 | Crewe Alexandra | 46 | 10 | 8 | 5 | 35 | 27 | 6 | 3 | 14 | 21 | 40 | -11 | 59 | 2,454 |
| 17 | Swindon Town | 46 | 11 | 7 | 5 | 34 | 23 | 4 | 6 | 13 | 24 | 33 | 2 | 58 | 3,344 |
| 18 | Northampton Town | 46 | 10 | 8 | 5 | 32 | 32 | 3 | 6 | 14 | 21 | 46 | -25 | 53 | 2,343 |
| 19 | Mansfield Town | 46 | 9 | 7 | 7 | 44 | 27 | 4 | 6 | 13 | 22 | 43 | -4 | 52 | 2,440 |
| 20 | Wrexham | 46 | 7 | 6 | 10 | 34 | 33 | 4 | 9 | 10 | 25 | 41 | -15 | 48 | 2,083 |
| 21 | Halifax Town | 46 | 11 | 6 | 6 | 36 | 25 | 1 | 6 | 16 | 19 | 64 | -34 | 48 | 1,412 |
| 22 | Rochdale | 46 | 8 | 9 | 6 | 35 | 31 | 3 | 4 | 16 | 17 | 49 | -28 | 46 | 1,491 |
| 23 | Hartlepool United | 46 | 7 | 8 | 8 | 31 | 28 | 3 | 2 | 18 | 16 | 57 | -38 | 40 | 1,505 |
| 24 | Chester City | 46 | 7 | 5 | 11 | 23 | 35 | 0 | 8 | 15 | 22 | 47 | -37 | 34 | 1,764 |

Halifax Town, Rochdale, Hartlepool United, and Chester City re-elected to the Football League

# 1984/85

## First Division

| | | Pld | W | D | L | F | A | W | D | L | F | A | GD | Pts | Ave Gate |
|---|---|---|---|---|---|---|---|---|---|---|---|---|---|---|---|
| 1 | Everton | 42 | 16 | 3 | 2 | 58 | 17 | 12 | 3 | 6 | 30 | 26 | 45 | 90 | 32,725 |
| 2 | Liverpool | 42 | 12 | 4 | 5 | 36 | 19 | 10 | 7 | 4 | 32 | 16 | 33 | 77 | 35,854 |
| 3 | Tottenham Hotspur | 42 | 11 | 3 | 7 | 46 | 31 | 12 | 5 | 4 | 32 | 20 | 27 | 77 | 28,932 |
| 4 | Manchester United | 42 | 13 | 6 | 2 | 47 | 13 | 9 | 4 | 8 | 30 | 34 | 30 | 76 | 45,074 |
| 5 | Southampton | 42 | 13 | 4 | 4 | 29 | 18 | 6 | 7 | 8 | 27 | 29 | 9 | 68 | 18,033 |
| 6 | Chelsea | 42 | 13 | 3 | 5 | 38 | 20 | 5 | 9 | 7 | 25 | 28 | 15 | 66 | 23,062 |
| 7 | Arsenal | 42 | 14 | 5 | 2 | 37 | 14 | 5 | 4 | 12 | 24 | 35 | 12 | 66 | 31,685 |
| 8 | Sheffield Wednesday | 42 | 12 | 7 | 2 | 39 | 21 | 5 | 7 | 9 | 19 | 24 | 13 | 65 | 27,762 |
| 9 | Nottingham Forest | 42 | 13 | 4 | 4 | 35 | 18 | 6 | 3 | 12 | 21 | 30 | 8 | 64 | 16,757 |
| 10 | Aston Villa | 42 | 10 | 7 | 4 | 34 | 20 | 5 | 4 | 12 | 26 | 40 | 0 | 56 | 18,289 |
| 11 | Watford | 42 | 10 | 5 | 6 | 48 | 30 | 4 | 8 | 9 | 33 | 41 | 10 | 55 | 18,375 |
| 12 | West Bromwich Albion | 42 | 11 | 4 | 6 | 36 | 23 | 5 | 3 | 13 | 22 | 39 | -4 | 55 | 14,121 |
| 13 | Luton Town | 42 | 12 | 5 | 4 | 40 | 22 | 3 | 4 | 14 | 17 | 39 | -4 | 54 | 10,816 |
| 14 | Newcastle United | 42 | 11 | 4 | 6 | 33 | 26 | 2 | 9 | 10 | 22 | 44 | -15 | 52 | 26,046 |
| 15 | Leicester City | 42 | 10 | 4 | 7 | 39 | 25 | 5 | 2 | 14 | 26 | 48 | -8 | 51 | 14,530 |
| 16 | West Ham United | 42 | 7 | 8 | 6 | 27 | 23 | 6 | 4 | 11 | 24 | 45 | -17 | 51 | 18,435 |
| 17 | Ipswich Town | 42 | 8 | 7 | 6 | 27 | 20 | 5 | 4 | 12 | 19 | 37 | -11 | 50 | 17,050 |
| 18 | Coventry City | 42 | 11 | 3 | 7 | 29 | 22 | 4 | 2 | 15 | 18 | 42 | -17 | 50 | 12,791 |
| 19 | Queens Park Rangers | 42 | 11 | 6 | 4 | 41 | 30 | 2 | 5 | 14 | 12 | 42 | -19 | 50 | 14,364 |
| 20 | Norwich City | 42 | 9 | 6 | 6 | 28 | 24 | 4 | 4 | 13 | 18 | 40 | -18 | 49 | 16,058 |
| 21 | Sunderland | 42 | 7 | 6 | 8 | 20 | 26 | 3 | 4 | 14 | 20 | 36 | -22 | 40 | 18,358 |
| 22 | Stoke City | 42 | 3 | 3 | 15 | 18 | 41 | 0 | 5 | 16 | 6 | 50 | -67 | 17 | 10,646 |

## Second Division

| | | Pld | W | D | L | F | A | W | D | L | F | A | GD | Pts | Ave Gate |
|---|---|---|---|---|---|---|---|---|---|---|---|---|---|---|---|
| 1 | Oxford United | 42 | 18 | 2 | 1 | 62 | 15 | 7 | 7 | 7 | 22 | 21 | 48 | 84 | 10,579 |
| 2 | Birmingham City | 42 | 12 | 6 | 3 | 30 | 15 | 13 | 1 | 7 | 29 | 18 | 26 | 82 | 12,522 |
| 3 | Manchester City | 42 | 14 | 4 | 3 | 42 | 16 | 7 | 7 | 7 | 24 | 24 | 26 | 74 | 24,206 |
| 4 | Portsmouth | 42 | 11 | 6 | 4 | 39 | 25 | 9 | 8 | 4 | 30 | 25 | 19 | 74 | 15,192 |
| 5 | Blackburn Rovers | 42 | 14 | 3 | 4 | 38 | 15 | 7 | 7 | 7 | 28 | 26 | 25 | 73 | 9,641 |
| 6 | Brighton & Hove Albion | 42 | 13 | 6 | 2 | 31 | 11 | 7 | 6 | 8 | 23 | 23 | 20 | 72 | 11,598 |
| 7 | Leeds United | 42 | 12 | 7 | 2 | 37 | 11 | 7 | 5 | 9 | 29 | 32 | 23 | 69 | 14,662 |
| 8 | Shrewsbury Town | 42 | 12 | 6 | 3 | 45 | 22 | 6 | 5 | 10 | 21 | 31 | 13 | 65 | 4,710 |
| 9 | Fulham | 42 | 13 | 3 | 5 | 35 | 26 | 6 | 5 | 10 | 33 | 38 | 4 | 65 | 6,178 |
| 10 | Grimsby Town | 42 | 13 | 1 | 7 | 47 | 32 | 5 | 7 | 9 | 25 | 32 | 8 | 62 | 6,640 |
| 11 | Barnsley | 42 | 11 | 7 | 3 | 27 | 12 | 3 | 9 | 9 | 15 | 30 | 0 | 58 | 7,225 |
| 12 | Wimbledon | 42 | 9 | 8 | 4 | 40 | 29 | 7 | 2 | 12 | 31 | 46 | -4 | 58 | 4,424 |
| 13 | Huddersfield Town | 42 | 9 | 5 | 7 | 28 | 29 | 6 | 5 | 10 | 24 | 35 | -12 | 55 | 7,238 |
| 14 | Oldham Athletic | 42 | 10 | 4 | 7 | 27 | 23 | 5 | 4 | 12 | 22 | 44 | -18 | 53 | 4,741 |
| 15 | Crystal Palace | 42 | 8 | 7 | 6 | 25 | 27 | 4 | 5 | 12 | 21 | 38 | -19 | 48 | 6,440 |
| 16 | Carlisle United | 42 | 8 | 5 | 8 | 27 | 23 | 5 | 3 | 13 | 23 | 44 | -17 | 47 | 4,081 |
| 17 | Charlton Athletic | 42 | 8 | 7 | 6 | 34 | 30 | 3 | 5 | 13 | 17 | 33 | -12 | 45 | 5,039 |
| 18 | Sheffield United | 42 | 7 | 6 | 8 | 31 | 28 | 3 | 8 | 10 | 23 | 38 | -12 | 44 | 12,415 |
| 19 | Middlesbrough | 42 | 6 | 8 | 7 | 22 | 26 | 4 | 2 | 15 | 19 | 31 | -16 | 40 | 5,127 |
| 20 | Notts County | 42 | 6 | 5 | 10 | 25 | 32 | 4 | 2 | 15 | 20 | 41 | -28 | 37 | 6,198 |
| 21 | Cardiff City | 42 | 5 | 3 | 13 | 24 | 42 | 4 | 5 | 12 | 23 | 37 | -32 | 35 | 4,369 |
| 22 | Wolverhampton Wanderers | 42 | 5 | 4 | 12 | 18 | 32 | 3 | 5 | 13 | 19 | 47 | -42 | 33 | 8,376 |

## Third Division

| | | Pld | W | D | L | F | A | W | D | L | F | A | GD | Pts | Ave Gate |
|---|---|---|---|---|---|---|---|---|---|---|---|---|---|---|---|
| 1 | Bradford City | 46 | 15 | 6 | 2 | 44 | 23 | 13 | 4 | 6 | 33 | 22 | 32 | 94 | 6,051 |
| 2 | Millwall | 46 | 18 | 5 | 0 | 44 | 12 | 8 | 7 | 8 | 29 | 30 | 31 | 90 | 6,442 |
| 3 | Hull City | 46 | 16 | 4 | 3 | 46 | 20 | 9 | 8 | 6 | 32 | 29 | 29 | 87 | 8,010 |
| 4 | Gillingham | 46 | 15 | 5 | 3 | 54 | 29 | 10 | 3 | 10 | 26 | 33 | 18 | 83 | 4,726 |
| 5 | Bristol City | 46 | 17 | 2 | 4 | 46 | 19 | 7 | 7 | 9 | 28 | 28 | 27 | 81 | 8,471 |
| 6 | Bristol Rovers | 46 | 15 | 6 | 2 | 37 | 13 | 6 | 6 | 11 | 29 | 35 | 18 | 75 | 4,963 |
| 7 | Derby County | 46 | 14 | 7 | 2 | 40 | 20 | 5 | 6 | 12 | 25 | 34 | 11 | 70 | 10,832 |
| 8 | York City | 46 | 13 | 5 | 5 | 42 | 22 | 7 | 4 | 12 | 28 | 35 | 13 | 69 | 5,526 |
| 9 | Reading | 46 | 8 | 7 | 8 | 31 | 29 | 11 | 5 | 7 | 37 | 33 | 6 | 69 | 3,465 |
| 10 | AFC Bournemouth | 46 | 16 | 3 | 4 | 42 | 16 | 3 | 8 | 12 | 15 | 30 | 11 | 68 | 3,766 |
| 11 | Walsall | 46 | 9 | 7 | 7 | 33 | 22 | 9 | 6 | 8 | 25 | 30 | 6 | 67 | 4,807 |
| 12 | Rotherham United | 46 | 11 | 6 | 6 | 36 | 24 | 7 | 5 | 11 | 19 | 31 | 0 | 65 | 4,441 |
| 13 | Brentford | 46 | 13 | 5 | 5 | 42 | 27 | 3 | 9 | 11 | 20 | 37 | -2 | 62 | 4,048 |
| 14 | Doncaster Rovers | 46 | 11 | 5 | 7 | 42 | 33 | 6 | 3 | 14 | 30 | 41 | -2 | 59 | 4,146 |
| 15 | Plymouth Argyle | 46 | 11 | 7 | 5 | 33 | 23 | 4 | 7 | 12 | 29 | 42 | -3 | 59 | 5,133 |
| 16 | Wigan Athletic | 46 | 12 | 6 | 5 | 36 | 22 | 3 | 8 | 12 | 24 | 42 | -4 | 59 | 3,264 |
| 17 | Bolton Wanderers | 46 | 12 | 5 | 6 | 38 | 22 | 4 | 1 | 18 | 31 | 53 | -6 | 54 | 4,951 |
| 18 | Newport County | 46 | 9 | 6 | 8 | 30 | 30 | 4 | 7 | 12 | 25 | 37 | -12 | 52 | 2,431 |
| 19 | Lincoln City | 46 | 8 | 11 | 4 | 32 | 20 | 3 | 7 | 13 | 18 | 31 | -1 | 51 | 2,550 |
| 20 | Swansea City | 46 | 7 | 5 | 11 | 31 | 39 | 5 | 6 | 12 | 22 | 41 | -27 | 47 | 4,397 |
| 21 | Burnley | 46 | 6 | 8 | 9 | 30 | 24 | 5 | 5 | 13 | 30 | 49 | -13 | 46 | 4,220 |
| 22 | Orient | 46 | 7 | 7 | 9 | 30 | 36 | 4 | 6 | 13 | 21 | 40 | -25 | 46 | 2,596 |
| 23 | Preston North End | 46 | 9 | 5 | 9 | 33 | 41 | 4 | 2 | 17 | 18 | 59 | -49 | 46 | 3,749 |
| 24 | Cambridge United | 46 | 2 | 3 | 18 | 17 | 48 | 2 | 6 | 15 | 20 | 47 | -58 | 21 | 2,102 |

## Fourth Division

| | | Pld | W | D | L | F | A | W | D | L | F | A | GD | Pts | Ave Gate |
|---|---|---|---|---|---|---|---|---|---|---|---|---|---|---|---|
| 1 | Chesterfield | 46 | 16 | 6 | 1 | 40 | 13 | 10 | 7 | 6 | 24 | 22 | 29 | 91 | 4,071 |
| 2 | Blackpool | 46 | 15 | 7 | 1 | 42 | 15 | 9 | 7 | 7 | 31 | 24 | 34 | 86 | 4,906 |
| 3 | Darlington | 46 | 16 | 4 | 3 | 41 | 22 | 8 | 9 | 6 | 25 | 27 | 17 | 85 | 3,772 |
| 4 | Bury | 46 | 15 | 6 | 2 | 46 | 20 | 9 | 6 | 8 | 30 | 30 | 26 | 84 | 3,461 |
| 5 | Hereford United | 46 | 16 | 2 | 5 | 38 | 21 | 6 | 9 | 8 | 27 | 26 | 18 | 77 | 3,881 |
| 6 | Tranmere Rovers | 46 | 17 | 1 | 5 | 50 | 21 | 7 | 2 | 14 | 33 | 45 | 17 | 75 | 1,688 |
| 7 | Colchester United | 46 | 13 | 7 | 3 | 49 | 29 | 7 | 7 | 9 | 38 | 36 | 22 | 74 | 2,076 |
| 8 | Swindon Town | 46 | 16 | 4 | 3 | 42 | 21 | 5 | 5 | 13 | 20 | 37 | 4 | 72 | 3,020 |
| 9 | Scunthorpe United | 46 | 14 | 6 | 3 | 61 | 33 | 5 | 8 | 10 | 22 | 29 | 21 | 71 | 2,065 |
| 10 | Crewe Alexandra | 46 | 10 | 7 | 6 | 32 | 28 | 8 | 5 | 10 | 33 | 41 | -4 | 66 | 2,275 |
| 11 | Peterborough United | 46 | 11 | 7 | 5 | 29 | 21 | 5 | 7 | 11 | 25 | 32 | 1 | 62 | 3,134 |
| 12 | Port Vale | 46 | 11 | 8 | 4 | 39 | 24 | 3 | 10 | 10 | 22 | 35 | 2 | 60 | 3,242 |
| 13 | Aldershot | 46 | 11 | 6 | 6 | 33 | 20 | 6 | 2 | 15 | 23 | 43 | -7 | 59 | 2,009 |
| 14 | Mansfield Town | 46 | 10 | 8 | 5 | 25 | 15 | 3 | 10 | 10 | 16 | 23 | 3 | 57 | 2,316 |
| 15 | Wrexham | 46 | 10 | 6 | 7 | 39 | 27 | 5 | 3 | 15 | 28 | 43 | -3 | 54 | 1,596 |
| 16 | Chester City | 46 | 11 | 3 | 9 | 35 | 30 | 4 | 6 | 13 | 25 | 42 | -12 | 54 | 1,879 |
| 17 | Rochdale | 46 | 8 | 7 | 8 | 33 | 30 | 5 | 7 | 11 | 22 | 39 | -14 | 53 | 1,454 |
| 18 | Exeter City | 46 | 9 | 7 | 7 | 30 | 27 | 4 | 7 | 12 | 27 | 52 | -22 | 53 | 2,348 |
| 19 | Hartlepool United | 46 | 10 | 6 | 7 | 34 | 29 | 4 | 4 | 15 | 20 | 38 | -13 | 52 | 2,340 |
| 20 | Southend United | 46 | 8 | 8 | 7 | 30 | 34 | 5 | 3 | 15 | 28 | 49 | -25 | 50 | 1,888 |
| 21 | Halifax Town | 46 | 9 | 3 | 11 | 26 | 32 | 6 | 2 | 15 | 16 | 37 | -27 | 50 | 1,381 |
| 22 | Stockport County | 46 | 11 | 5 | 7 | 40 | 26 | 2 | 3 | 18 | 18 | 53 | -21 | 47 | 1,895 |
| 23 | Northampton Town | 46 | 10 | 1 | 12 | 32 | 32 | 4 | 4 | 15 | 21 | 42 | -21 | 47 | 1,826 |
| 24 | Torquay United | 46 | 5 | 11 | 7 | 18 | 24 | 4 | 3 | 16 | 20 | 39 | -25 | 41 | 1,437 |

Halifax Town, Stockport County, Northampton Town and Torquay United re-elected to the Football League

# 1985/86

## First Division

| | | Pld | W | D | L | F | A | W | D | L | F | A | GD | Pts | Ave Gate |
|---|---|---|---|---|---|---|---|---|---|---|---|---|---|---|---|
| 1 | Liverpool | 42 | 16 | 4 | 1 | 58 | 14 | 10 | 6 | 5 | 31 | 23 | 52 | 88 | 35,271 |
| 2 | Everton | 42 | 16 | 3 | 2 | 54 | 18 | 10 | 5 | 6 | 33 | 23 | 46 | 86 | 32,226 |
| 3 | West Ham United | 42 | 17 | 2 | 2 | 48 | 16 | 9 | 4 | 8 | 26 | 24 | 34 | 84 | 21,179 |
| 4 | Manchester United | 42 | 12 | 5 | 4 | 35 | 12 | 10 | 5 | 6 | 35 | 24 | 34 | 76 | 46,321 |
| 5 | Sheffield Wednesday | 42 | 13 | 6 | 2 | 36 | 23 | 8 | 4 | 9 | 27 | 31 | 9 | 73 | 23,110 |
| 6 | Chelsea | 42 | 12 | 4 | 5 | 32 | 27 | 8 | 7 | 6 | 25 | 29 | 1 | 71 | 21,984 |
| 7 | Arsenal | 42 | 13 | 5 | 3 | 29 | 15 | 7 | 4 | 10 | 20 | 32 | 2 | 69 | 23,824 |
| 8 | Nottingham Forest | 42 | 11 | 5 | 5 | 38 | 25 | 8 | 6 | 7 | 31 | 28 | 16 | 68 | 16,808 |
| 9 | Luton Town | 42 | 12 | 6 | 3 | 37 | 15 | 6 | 6 | 9 | 24 | 29 | 17 | 66 | 11,062 |
| 10 | Tottenham Hotspur | 42 | 12 | 2 | 7 | 47 | 25 | 7 | 6 | 8 | 27 | 27 | 22 | 65 | 20,859 |
| 11 | Newcastle United | 42 | 12 | 5 | 4 | 46 | 31 | 5 | 7 | 9 | 21 | 41 | -5 | 63 | 23,433 |
| 12 | Watford | 42 | 11 | 6 | 4 | 40 | 22 | 5 | 5 | 11 | 29 | 40 | 7 | 59 | 15,359 |
| 13 | Queens Park Rangers | 42 | 12 | 3 | 6 | 33 | 20 | 3 | 4 | 14 | 20 | 44 | -11 | 52 | 12,664 |
| 14 | Southampton | 42 | 10 | 6 | 5 | 32 | 18 | 2 | 4 | 15 | 19 | 44 | -11 | 46 | 14,877 |
| 15 | Manchester City | 42 | 7 | 7 | 7 | 25 | 26 | 4 | 5 | 12 | 18 | 31 | -14 | 45 | 24,229 |
| 16 | Aston Villa | 42 | 7 | 6 | 8 | 27 | 28 | 3 | 8 | 10 | 24 | 39 | -16 | 44 | 15,237 |
| 17 | Coventry City | 42 | 6 | 5 | 10 | 31 | 35 | 5 | 5 | 11 | 17 | 36 | -23 | 43 | 11,589 |
| 18 | Oxford United | 42 | 7 | 7 | 7 | 34 | 27 | 3 | 5 | 13 | 28 | 53 | -18 | 42 | 11,009 |
| 19 | Leicester City | 42 | 7 | 8 | 6 | 35 | 35 | 3 | 4 | 14 | 19 | 41 | -22 | 42 | 11,792 |
| 20 | Ipswich Town | 42 | 8 | 5 | 8 | 20 | 24 | 3 | 3 | 15 | 12 | 31 | -23 | 41 | 14,468 |
| 21 | Birmingham City | 42 | 5 | 2 | 14 | 13 | 25 | 3 | 3 | 15 | 17 | 48 | -43 | 29 | 10,899 |
| 22 | West Bromwich Albion | 42 | 3 | 8 | 10 | 21 | 36 | 1 | 4 | 16 | 14 | 53 | -54 | 24 | 12,163 |

## Second Division

| | | Pld | W | D | L | F | A | W | D | L | F | A | GD | Pts | Ave Gate |
|---|---|---|---|---|---|---|---|---|---|---|---|---|---|---|---|
| 1 | Norwich City | 42 | 16 | 4 | 1 | 51 | 15 | 9 | 5 | 7 | 33 | 22 | 45 | 84 | 13,722 |
| 2 | Charlton Athletic | 42 | 14 | 5 | 2 | 44 | 15 | 8 | 6 | 7 | 34 | 30 | 33 | 77 | 6,028 |
| 3 | Wimbledon | 42 | 13 | 6 | 2 | 38 | 16 | 8 | 7 | 6 | 20 | 21 | 21 | 76 | 4,578 |
| 4 | Portsmouth | 42 | 13 | 4 | 4 | 43 | 17 | 9 | 3 | 9 | 26 | 24 | 28 | 73 | 13,614 |
| 5 | Crystal Palace | 42 | 12 | 3 | 6 | 29 | 22 | 7 | 6 | 8 | 28 | 30 | 5 | 66 | 6,787 |
| 6 | Hull City | 42 | 11 | 7 | 3 | 39 | 19 | 6 | 6 | 9 | 26 | 36 | 10 | 64 | 7,671 |
| 7 | Sheffield United | 42 | 10 | 7 | 4 | 36 | 24 | 7 | 4 | 10 | 28 | 39 | 1 | 62 | 10,798 |
| 8 | Oldham Athletic | 42 | 13 | 4 | 4 | 40 | 28 | 4 | 5 | 12 | 22 | 33 | 1 | 60 | 4,651 |
| 9 | Millwall | 42 | 12 | 3 | 6 | 39 | 24 | 5 | 5 | 11 | 25 | 41 | -1 | 59 | 5,459 |
| 10 | Stoke City | 42 | 8 | 11 | 2 | 29 | 16 | 6 | 4 | 11 | 19 | 34 | -2 | 57 | 8,288 |
| 11 | Brighton & Hove Albion | 42 | 10 | 5 | 6 | 42 | 30 | 6 | 3 | 12 | 22 | 34 | 2 | 56 | 9,725 |
| 12 | Barnsley | 42 | 9 | 6 | 6 | 29 | 26 | 5 | 8 | 8 | 18 | 24 | -3 | 56 | 6,067 |
| 13 | Bradford City | 42 | 14 | 1 | 6 | 36 | 24 | 2 | 5 | 14 | 15 | 39 | -12 | 54 | 5,815 |
| 14 | Leeds United | 42 | 9 | 7 | 5 | 30 | 22 | 6 | 1 | 14 | 26 | 50 | -16 | 53 | 13,258 |
| 15 | Grimsby Town | 42 | 11 | 4 | 6 | 35 | 24 | 3 | 6 | 12 | 23 | 38 | -4 | 52 | 5,157 |
| 16 | Huddersfield Town | 42 | 10 | 6 | 5 | 30 | 23 | 4 | 4 | 13 | 21 | 44 | -16 | 52 | 6,821 |
| 17 | Shrewsbury Town | 42 | 11 | 5 | 5 | 29 | 20 | 3 | 4 | 14 | 23 | 44 | -12 | 51 | 3,926 |
| 18 | Sunderland | 42 | 10 | 5 | 6 | 33 | 29 | 3 | 6 | 12 | 14 | 32 | -14 | 50 | 16,052 |
| 19 | Blackburn Rovers | 42 | 10 | 4 | 7 | 30 | 20 | 2 | 9 | 10 | 23 | 42 | -9 | 49 | 5,826 |
| 20 | Carlisle United | 42 | 10 | 2 | 9 | 30 | 28 | 3 | 5 | 13 | 17 | 43 | -24 | 46 | 4,010 |
| 21 | Middlesbrough | 42 | 8 | 6 | 7 | 26 | 23 | 4 | 3 | 14 | 18 | 30 | -9 | 45 | 6,257 |
| 22 | Fulham | 42 | 8 | 3 | 10 | 29 | 32 | 2 | 3 | 16 | 16 | 37 | -24 | 36 | 4,623 |

## Third Division

| | | Pld | W | D | L | F | A | W | D | L | F | A | GD | Pts | Ave Gate |
|---|---|---|---|---|---|---|---|---|---|---|---|---|---|---|---|
| 1 | Reading | 46 | 16 | 3 | 4 | 39 | 22 | 13 | 4 | 6 | 28 | 29 | 16 | 94 | 6,892 |
| 2 | Plymouth Argyle | 46 | 17 | 3 | 3 | 56 | 20 | 9 | 6 | 8 | 32 | 33 | 35 | 87 | 8,297 |
| 3 | Derby County | 46 | 13 | 7 | 3 | 45 | 20 | 10 | 8 | 5 | 35 | 21 | 39 | 84 | 12,386 |
| 4 | Wigan Athletic | 46 | 17 | 4 | 2 | 54 | 17 | 6 | 10 | 7 | 28 | 31 | 34 | 83 | 4,148 |
| 5 | Gillingham | 46 | 14 | 5 | 4 | 48 | 17 | 8 | 8 | 7 | 33 | 37 | 27 | 79 | 3,690 |
| 6 | Walsall | 46 | 15 | 7 | 1 | 59 | 23 | 7 | 2 | 14 | 31 | 41 | 26 | 75 | 4,890 |
| 7 | York City | 46 | 16 | 4 | 3 | 49 | 17 | 4 | 7 | 12 | 28 | 41 | 19 | 71 | 4,111 |
| 8 | Notts County | 46 | 12 | 6 | 5 | 42 | 26 | 7 | 8 | 8 | 29 | 34 | 11 | 71 | 4,403 |
| 9 | Bristol City | 46 | 14 | 5 | 4 | 43 | 19 | 4 | 9 | 10 | 26 | 41 | 9 | 68 | 6,599 |
| 10 | Brentford | 46 | 8 | 8 | 7 | 29 | 29 | 10 | 4 | 9 | 29 | 32 | -3 | 66 | 3,956 |
| 11 | Doncaster Rovers | 46 | 7 | 10 | 6 | 20 | 21 | 9 | 6 | 8 | 25 | 31 | -7 | 64 | 2,803 |
| 12 | Blackpool | 46 | 11 | 6 | 6 | 38 | 19 | 6 | 6 | 11 | 28 | 36 | 11 | 63 | 4,535 |
| 13 | Darlington | 46 | 10 | 7 | 6 | 39 | 33 | 5 | 6 | 12 | 22 | 45 | -17 | 58 | 3,026 |
| 14 | Rotherham United | 46 | 13 | 5 | 5 | 44 | 18 | 2 | 7 | 14 | 17 | 41 | 2 | 57 | 3,474 |
| 15 | AFC Bournemouth | 46 | 9 | 6 | 8 | 41 | 31 | 6 | 3 | 14 | 24 | 41 | -7 | 54 | 3,423 |
| 16 | Bristol Rovers | 46 | 9 | 8 | 6 | 27 | 21 | 5 | 4 | 14 | 24 | 54 | -24 | 54 | 4,195 |
| 17 | Chesterfield | 46 | 10 | 6 | 7 | 41 | 30 | 3 | 8 | 12 | 20 | 34 | -3 | 53 | 3,211 |
| 18 | Bolton Wanderers | 46 | 10 | 4 | 9 | 35 | 30 | 5 | 4 | 14 | 19 | 38 | -14 | 53 | 4,846 |
| 19 | Newport County | 46 | 7 | 8 | 8 | 35 | 33 | 4 | 10 | 9 | 17 | 32 | -13 | 51 | 2,493 |
| 20 | Bury | 46 | 11 | 7 | 5 | 46 | 26 | 1 | 6 | 16 | 17 | 41 | -4 | 49 | 2,888 |
| 21 | Lincoln City | 46 | 7 | 9 | 7 | 33 | 34 | 3 | 7 | 13 | 22 | 43 | -22 | 46 | 2,616 |
| 22 | Cardiff City | 46 | 7 | 5 | 11 | 22 | 29 | 5 | 4 | 14 | 31 | 54 | -30 | 45 | 3,061 |
| 23 | Wolverhampton Wanderers | 46 | 6 | 6 | 11 | 29 | 47 | 5 | 4 | 14 | 28 | 51 | -41 | 43 | 4,019 |
| 24 | Swansea City | 46 | 9 | 6 | 8 | 27 | 27 | 2 | 4 | 17 | 16 | 60 | -44 | 43 | 4,305 |

## Fourth Division

| | | Pld | W | D | L | F | A | W | D | L | F | A | GD | Pts | Ave Gate |
|---|---|---|---|---|---|---|---|---|---|---|---|---|---|---|---|
| 1 | Swindon Town | 46 | 20 | 2 | 1 | 52 | 19 | 12 | 4 | 7 | 30 | 24 | 39 | 102 | 6,531 |
| 2 | Chester City | 46 | 15 | 5 | 3 | 44 | 16 | 8 | 10 | 5 | 39 | 34 | 33 | 84 | 2,956 |
| 3 | Mansfield Town | 46 | 13 | 8 | 2 | 43 | 17 | 10 | 4 | 9 | 31 | 30 | 27 | 81 | 3,764 |
| 4 | Port Vale | 46 | 13 | 9 | 1 | 42 | 11 | 8 | 7 | 8 | 25 | 26 | 30 | 79 | 3,581 |
| 5 | Orient | 46 | 11 | 6 | 6 | 39 | 21 | 9 | 6 | 8 | 40 | 43 | 15 | 72 | 2,628 |
| 6 | Colchester United | 46 | 12 | 6 | 5 | 51 | 22 | 7 | 7 | 9 | 37 | 41 | 25 | 70 | 2,327 |
| 7 | Hartlepool United | 46 | 15 | 6 | 2 | 41 | 20 | 5 | 4 | 14 | 27 | 47 | 1 | 70 | 2,593 |
| 8 | Northampton Town | 46 | 9 | 7 | 7 | 44 | 29 | 9 | 3 | 11 | 35 | 29 | 21 | 64 | 2,384 |
| 9 | Southend United | 46 | 13 | 4 | 6 | 43 | 27 | 5 | 6 | 12 | 26 | 40 | 2 | 64 | 2,784 |
| 10 | Hereford United | 46 | 15 | 6 | 2 | 55 | 30 | 3 | 4 | 16 | 19 | 43 | 1 | 64 | 2,755 |
| 11 | Stockport County | 46 | 9 | 9 | 5 | 35 | 28 | 8 | 4 | 11 | 28 | 43 | -8 | 64 | 2,666 |
| 12 | Crewe Alexandra | 46 | 10 | 6 | 7 | 35 | 26 | 8 | 3 | 12 | 19 | 35 | -7 | 63 | 1,817 |
| 13 | Wrexham | 46 | 11 | 5 | 7 | 34 | 24 | 6 | 4 | 13 | 34 | 56 | -12 | 60 | 1,820 |
| 14 | Burnley | 46 | 11 | 3 | 9 | 35 | 30 | 5 | 8 | 10 | 25 | 35 | -5 | 59 | 3,203 |
| 15 | Scunthorpe United | 46 | 11 | 7 | 5 | 33 | 23 | 4 | 7 | 12 | 17 | 32 | -5 | 59 | 1,777 |
| 16 | Aldershot | 46 | 12 | 5 | 6 | 45 | 25 | 5 | 2 | 16 | 21 | 49 | -8 | 58 | 1,479 |
| 17 | Peterborough United | 46 | 9 | 11 | 3 | 31 | 19 | 4 | 6 | 13 | 21 | 45 | -12 | 56 | 2,590 |
| 18 | Rochdale | 46 | 12 | 7 | 4 | 41 | 29 | 2 | 6 | 15 | 16 | 48 | -20 | 55 | 1,789 |
| 19 | Tranmere Rovers | 46 | 9 | 1 | 13 | 46 | 41 | 6 | 8 | 9 | 28 | 32 | 1 | 54 | 1,566 |
| 20 | Halifax Town | 46 | 10 | 8 | 5 | 35 | 27 | 4 | 4 | 15 | 25 | 44 | -11 | 54 | 1,405 |
| 21 | Exeter City | 46 | 10 | 4 | 9 | 26 | 25 | 3 | 11 | 9 | 21 | 34 | -12 | 54 | 1,972 |
| 22 | Cambridge United | 46 | 12 | 2 | 9 | 45 | 38 | 3 | 7 | 13 | 20 | 42 | -15 | 54 | 2,089 |
| 23 | Preston North End | 46 | 7 | 4 | 12 | 32 | 41 | 4 | 6 | 13 | 22 | 48 | -35 | 43 | 3,502 |
| 24 | Torquay United | 46 | 8 | 5 | 10 | 29 | 32 | 1 | 5 | 17 | 14 | 56 | -45 | 37 | 1,239 |

Exeter City, Cambridge United, Preston North End and Torquay United re-elected to the Football League

# 1986/87
## First Division

| | Club | Pld | W | D | L | F | A | W | D | L | F | A | GD | Pts | Ave Gate |
|---|---|---|---|---|---|---|---|---|---|---|---|---|---|---|---|
| 1 | Everton | 42 | 16 | 4 | 1 | 49 | 11 | 10 | 4 | 7 | 27 | 20 | 45 | 86 | 32,935 |
| 2 | Liverpool | 42 | 15 | 3 | 3 | 43 | 16 | 8 | 5 | 8 | 29 | 26 | 30 | 77 | 36,285 |
| 3 | Tottenham Hotspur | 42 | 14 | 3 | 4 | 40 | 14 | 7 | 5 | 9 | 28 | 29 | 25 | 71 | 25,881 |
| 4 | Arsenal | 42 | 12 | 5 | 4 | 31 | 12 | 8 | 5 | 8 | 27 | 23 | 23 | 70 | 29,022 |
| 5 | Norwich City | 42 | 9 | 10 | 2 | 27 | 20 | 8 | 7 | 6 | 26 | 31 | 2 | 68 | 17,564 |
| 6 | Wimbledon | 42 | 11 | 5 | 5 | 32 | 22 | 8 | 4 | 9 | 25 | 28 | 7 | 66 | 7,810 |
| 7 | Luton Town | 42 | 14 | 5 | 2 | 29 | 13 | 4 | 7 | 10 | 18 | 32 | 2 | 66 | 10,256 |
| 8 | Nottingham Forest | 42 | 12 | 8 | 1 | 36 | 14 | 6 | 3 | 12 | 28 | 37 | 13 | 65 | 19,086 |
| 9 | Watford | 42 | 12 | 5 | 4 | 38 | 20 | 6 | 4 | 11 | 29 | 34 | 13 | 63 | 15,799 |
| 10 | Coventry City | 42 | 14 | 4 | 3 | 35 | 17 | 3 | 8 | 10 | 15 | 28 | 5 | 63 | 16,119 |
| 11 | Manchester United | 42 | 13 | 3 | 5 | 38 | 18 | 1 | 11 | 9 | 14 | 27 | 7 | 56 | 40,594 |
| 12 | Southampton | 42 | 11 | 5 | 5 | 44 | 24 | 3 | 5 | 13 | 25 | 44 | 1 | 52 | 14,949 |
| 13 | Sheffield Wednesday | 42 | 9 | 7 | 5 | 39 | 24 | 4 | 6 | 11 | 19 | 35 | -1 | 52 | 23,147 |
| 14 | Chelsea | 42 | 8 | 6 | 7 | 30 | 30 | 5 | 7 | 9 | 23 | 34 | -11 | 52 | 17,694 |
| 15 | West Ham United | 42 | 10 | 4 | 7 | 33 | 28 | 4 | 6 | 11 | 19 | 39 | -15 | 52 | 20,607 |
| 16 | Queens Park Rangers | 42 | 9 | 7 | 5 | 31 | 27 | 4 | 4 | 13 | 17 | 37 | -16 | 50 | 11,753 |
| 17 | Newcastle United | 42 | 10 | 4 | 7 | 33 | 29 | 2 | 7 | 12 | 14 | 36 | -18 | 47 | 24,791 |
| 18 | Oxford United | 42 | 8 | 8 | 5 | 30 | 25 | 3 | 5 | 13 | 14 | 44 | -25 | 46 | 10,357 |
| 19 | Charlton Athletic | 42 | 7 | 7 | 7 | 26 | 22 | 4 | 4 | 13 | 19 | 33 | -10 | 44 | 9,012 |
| 20 | Leicester City | 42 | 9 | 7 | 5 | 39 | 24 | 2 | 2 | 17 | 15 | 52 | -22 | 42 | 11,697 |
| 21 | Manchester City | 42 | 8 | 6 | 7 | 28 | 24 | 0 | 9 | 12 | 8 | 33 | -21 | 39 | 21,922 |
| 22 | Aston Villa | 42 | 7 | 7 | 7 | 25 | 25 | 1 | 5 | 15 | 20 | 54 | -34 | 36 | 18,171 |

Play-offs introduced at the end of the 1986/87 season. Fourth-bottom club in Division One in the play-offs with the three teams who finished 3rd, 4th and 5th in Division Two – Charlton Athletic, Oldham Athletic, Leeds United and Ipswich Town. Two-legged semi-finals and a two-legged final. The final, Charlton Athletic v Leeds United, ended 1-1 on aggregate after two legs. Charlton Athletic won the replay 2-1 and retained their place in Division One.

## Second Division

| | Club | Pld | W | D | L | F | A | W | D | L | F | A | GD | Pts | Ave Gate |
|---|---|---|---|---|---|---|---|---|---|---|---|---|---|---|---|
| 1 | Derby County | 42 | 14 | 6 | 1 | 42 | 18 | 11 | 3 | 7 | 22 | 20 | 26 | 84 | 15,539 |
| 2 | Portsmouth | 42 | 17 | 2 | 2 | 37 | 11 | 6 | 7 | 8 | 16 | 17 | 25 | 78 | 13,404 |
| 3 | Oldham Athletic | 42 | 13 | 6 | 2 | 36 | 16 | 9 | 3 | 9 | 29 | 28 | 21 | 75 | 6,883 |
| 4 | Leeds United | 42 | 15 | 4 | 2 | 43 | 16 | 4 | 7 | 10 | 15 | 28 | 14 | 68 | 17,612 |
| 5 | Ipswich Town | 42 | 12 | 6 | 3 | 29 | 10 | 5 | 7 | 9 | 30 | 33 | 16 | 64 | 12,123 |
| 6 | Crystal Palace | 42 | 12 | 4 | 5 | 35 | 20 | 7 | 1 | 13 | 16 | 33 | -2 | 62 | 7,583 |
| 7 | Plymouth Argyle | 42 | 12 | 6 | 3 | 40 | 23 | 4 | 7 | 10 | 22 | 34 | 5 | 61 | 12,387 |
| 8 | Stoke City | 42 | 11 | 5 | 5 | 40 | 21 | 5 | 5 | 11 | 23 | 32 | 10 | 58 | 9,987 |
| 9 | Sheffield United | 42 | 10 | 8 | 3 | 31 | 19 | 5 | 5 | 11 | 19 | 30 | 1 | 58 | 9,991 |
| 10 | Bradford City | 42 | 10 | 5 | 6 | 36 | 27 | 5 | 5 | 11 | 26 | 35 | 0 | 55 | 8,246 |
| 11 | Barnsley | 42 | 8 | 7 | 6 | 26 | 23 | 6 | 6 | 9 | 23 | 29 | -3 | 55 | 5,870 |
| 12 | Blackburn Rovers | 42 | 11 | 4 | 6 | 30 | 22 | 4 | 6 | 11 | 15 | 33 | -10 | 55 | 6,772 |
| 13 | Reading | 42 | 11 | 4 | 6 | 33 | 23 | 3 | 7 | 11 | 19 | 36 | -7 | 53 | 6,883 |
| 14 | Hull City | 42 | 10 | 4 | 6 | 25 | 22 | 3 | 8 | 10 | 16 | 33 | -14 | 53 | 6,674 |
| 15 | West Bromwich Albion | 42 | 8 | 6 | 7 | 29 | 22 | 5 | 6 | 10 | 22 | 27 | 2 | 51 | 9,133 |
| 16 | Millwall | 42 | 10 | 5 | 6 | 27 | 16 | 4 | 4 | 13 | 12 | 29 | -6 | 51 | 4,304 |
| 17 | Huddersfield Town | 42 | 9 | 6 | 6 | 38 | 30 | 4 | 6 | 11 | 16 | 31 | -7 | 51 | 6,617 |
| 18 | Shrewsbury Town | 42 | 11 | 3 | 7 | 24 | 14 | 4 | 3 | 14 | 17 | 39 | -12 | 51 | 4,097 |
| 19 | Birmingham City | 42 | 8 | 9 | 4 | 27 | 21 | 3 | 8 | 10 | 20 | 38 | -12 | 50 | 7,426 |
| 20 | Sunderland | 42 | 8 | 6 | 7 | 25 | 23 | 4 | 6 | 11 | 24 | 36 | -10 | 48 | 13,600 |
| 21 | Grimsby Town | 42 | 5 | 8 | 8 | 18 | 21 | 5 | 6 | 10 | 21 | 38 | -20 | 44 | 5,050 |
| 22 | Brighton & Hove Albion | 42 | 7 | 6 | 8 | 22 | 20 | 2 | 6 | 13 | 15 | 34 | -17 | 39 | 8,293 |

Third-bottom club in Division Two in the play-offs with 3rd, 4th and 5th in Division Three – Sunderland, Swindon Town, Wigan Athletic and Gillingham. Two-legged semi-finals and a two-legged final. The final, Swindon Town v Gillingham, ended 2-2 on aggregate after two legs. Swindon Town won the replay 2-0 and were promoted to Division Two. Sunderland were relegated to Division Three.

## Third Division

| | | Pld | W | D | L | F | A | W | D | L | F | A | GD | Pts | Ave Gate |
|---|---|---|---|---|---|---|---|---|---|---|---|---|---|---|---|
| 1 | AFC Bournemouth | 46 | 19 | 3 | 1 | 44 | 14 | 10 | 7 | 6 | 32 | 26 | 36 | 97 | 6,610 |
| 2 | Middlesbrough | 46 | 16 | 5 | 2 | 38 | 11 | 12 | 5 | 6 | 29 | 19 | 37 | 94 | 10,174 |
| 3 | Swindon Town | 46 | 14 | 5 | 4 | 37 | 19 | 11 | 7 | 5 | 40 | 28 | 30 | 87 | 7,708 |
| 4 | Wigan Athletic | 46 | 15 | 5 | 3 | 47 | 26 | 10 | 5 | 8 | 36 | 34 | 23 | 85 | 3,397 |
| 5 | Gillingham | 46 | 16 | 5 | 2 | 42 | 14 | 7 | 4 | 12 | 23 | 34 | 17 | 78 | 4,971 |
| 6 | Bristol City | 46 | 14 | 6 | 3 | 42 | 15 | 7 | 8 | 8 | 21 | 21 | 27 | 77 | 9,441 |
| 7 | Notts County | 46 | 14 | 6 | 3 | 52 | 24 | 7 | 9 | 7 | 25 | 32 | 21 | 76 | 4,728 |
| 8 | Walsall | 46 | 16 | 4 | 3 | 50 | 27 | 6 | 5 | 12 | 30 | 40 | 13 | 75 | 5,312 |
| 9 | Blackpool | 46 | 11 | 7 | 5 | 35 | 20 | 5 | 9 | 9 | 39 | 39 | 15 | 64 | 3,866 |
| 10 | Mansfield Town | 46 | 9 | 9 | 5 | 30 | 23 | 6 | 7 | 10 | 22 | 32 | -3 | 61 | 3,215 |
| 11 | Brentford | 46 | 9 | 7 | 7 | 39 | 32 | 6 | 8 | 9 | 25 | 34 | -2 | 60 | 3,918 |
| 12 | Port Vale | 46 | 8 | 6 | 9 | 43 | 36 | 7 | 6 | 10 | 33 | 34 | 6 | 57 | 3,312 |
| 13 | Doncaster Rovers | 46 | 11 | 8 | 4 | 32 | 19 | 3 | 7 | 13 | 24 | 43 | -6 | 57 | 2,408 |
| 14 | Rotherham United | 46 | 10 | 6 | 7 | 29 | 23 | 5 | 6 | 12 | 19 | 34 | -9 | 57 | 2,983 |
| 15 | Chester City | 46 | 7 | 9 | 7 | 32 | 28 | 6 | 8 | 9 | 29 | 31 | 2 | 56 | 2,731 |
| 16 | Bury | 46 | 9 | 7 | 7 | 30 | 26 | 5 | 6 | 12 | 24 | 34 | -6 | 55 | 2,501 |
| 17 | Chesterfield | 46 | 11 | 5 | 7 | 36 | 33 | 2 | 10 | 11 | 20 | 36 | -13 | 54 | 2,575 |
| 18 | Fulham | 46 | 8 | 8 | 7 | 35 | 41 | 4 | 9 | 10 | 24 | 36 | -18 | 53 | 4,085 |
| 19 | Bristol Rovers | 46 | 7 | 8 | 8 | 26 | 29 | 6 | 4 | 13 | 23 | 46 | -26 | 51 | 3,245 |
| 20 | York City | 46 | 11 | 8 | 4 | 34 | 29 | 1 | 5 | 17 | 21 | 50 | -24 | 49 | 3,432 |
| 21 | Bolton Wanderers | 46 | 8 | 5 | 10 | 29 | 26 | 2 | 10 | 11 | 17 | 32 | -12 | 45 | 4,851 |
| 22 | Carlisle United | 46 | 7 | 5 | 11 | 26 | 35 | 3 | 3 | 17 | 13 | 43 | -39 | 38 | 2,644 |
| 23 | Darlington | 46 | 6 | 10 | 7 | 25 | 28 | 1 | 6 | 16 | 20 | 49 | -32 | 37 | 2,036 |
| 24 | Newport County | 46 | 4 | 9 | 10 | 26 | 34 | 4 | 4 | 15 | 23 | 52 | -37 | 37 | 2,063 |

Fourth-bottom club in Division Three in the play-offs with 4th, 5th and 6th in Division Four – Bolton Wanderers, Wolverhampton Wanderers, Colchester United and Aldershot. Two-legged semi-finals and a two-legged final. The final, Aldershot v Wolverhampton Wanderers, ended 3-0 to Aldershot on aggregate after two legs. Aldershot promoted to Division Three. Bolton Wanderers relegated to Division Four.

## Fourth Division

| | | Pld | W | D | L | F | A | W | D | L | F | A | GD | Pts | Ave Gate |
|---|---|---|---|---|---|---|---|---|---|---|---|---|---|---|---|
| 1 | Northampton Town | 46 | 20 | 2 | 1 | 56 | 20 | 10 | 7 | 6 | 47 | 33 | 50 | 99 | 6,316 |
| 2 | Preston North End | 46 | 16 | 4 | 3 | 36 | 18 | 10 | 8 | 5 | 36 | 29 | 25 | 90 | 8,079 |
| 3 | Southend United | 46 | 14 | 4 | 5 | 43 | 27 | 11 | 1 | 11 | 25 | 28 | 13 | 80 | 3,686 |
| 4 | Wolverhampton Wanderers | 46 | 12 | 3 | 8 | 36 | 24 | 12 | 4 | 7 | 33 | 26 | 19 | 79 | 5,754 |
| 5 | Colchester United | 46 | 15 | 3 | 5 | 41 | 20 | 6 | 4 | 13 | 23 | 36 | 8 | 70 | 2,740 |
| 6 | Aldershot | 46 | 13 | 5 | 5 | 40 | 22 | 7 | 5 | 11 | 24 | 35 | 7 | 70 | 2,358 |
| 7 | Orient | 46 | 15 | 2 | 6 | 40 | 25 | 5 | 7 | 11 | 24 | 36 | 3 | 69 | 2,857 |
| 8 | Scunthorpe United | 46 | 15 | 3 | 5 | 52 | 27 | 3 | 9 | 11 | 21 | 30 | 16 | 66 | 2,126 |
| 9 | Wrexham | 46 | 8 | 13 | 2 | 38 | 24 | 7 | 7 | 9 | 32 | 27 | 19 | 65 | 2,521 |
| 10 | Peterborough United | 46 | 10 | 7 | 6 | 29 | 21 | 7 | 7 | 9 | 28 | 29 | 7 | 65 | 3,714 |
| 11 | Cambridge United | 46 | 12 | 6 | 5 | 37 | 23 | 5 | 5 | 13 | 23 | 39 | -2 | 62 | 2,779 |
| 12 | Swansea City | 46 | 13 | 3 | 7 | 31 | 21 | 4 | 8 | 11 | 25 | 40 | -5 | 62 | 5,169 |
| 13 | Cardiff City | 46 | 6 | 12 | 5 | 24 | 18 | 9 | 4 | 10 | 24 | 32 | -2 | 61 | 2,826 |
| 14 | Exeter City | 46 | 11 | 10 | 2 | 37 | 17 | 0 | 13 | 10 | 16 | 32 | 4 | 56 | 2,627 |
| 15 | Halifax Town | 46 | 10 | 5 | 8 | 32 | 32 | 5 | 5 | 13 | 27 | 42 | -15 | 55 | 1,327 |
| 16 | Hereford United | 46 | 10 | 5 | 8 | 33 | 23 | 4 | 5 | 14 | 27 | 38 | -1 | 53 | 2,583 |
| 17 | Crewe Alexandra | 46 | 8 | 9 | 6 | 38 | 35 | 5 | 5 | 13 | 32 | 37 | -2 | 53 | 1,931 |
| 18 | Hartlepool United | 46 | 6 | 11 | 6 | 24 | 30 | 5 | 7 | 11 | 20 | 35 | -21 | 51 | 1,650 |
| 19 | Stockport County | 46 | 9 | 6 | 8 | 25 | 27 | 4 | 5 | 14 | 15 | 42 | -29 | 51 | 2,113 |
| 20 | Tranmere Rovers | 46 | 6 | 10 | 7 | 32 | 37 | 5 | 7 | 11 | 22 | 35 | -18 | 50 | 2,126 |
| 21 | Rochdale | 46 | 8 | 8 | 7 | 31 | 30 | 3 | 9 | 11 | 23 | 43 | -19 | 50 | 2,151 |
| 22 | Burnley | 46 | 9 | 7 | 7 | 31 | 35 | 3 | 6 | 14 | 22 | 39 | -21 | 49 | 3,342 |
| 23 | Torquay United | 46 | 8 | 8 | 7 | 28 | 29 | 2 | 10 | 11 | 28 | 43 | -16 | 48 | 1,777 |
| 24 | Lincoln City | 46 | 8 | 7 | 8 | 30 | 27 | 4 | 5 | 14 | 15 | 38 | -20 | 48 | 2,022 |

Automatic relegation/promotion introduced
Lincoln City relegated from the Football League; Scarborough promoted to the Football League

# 1987/88

## First Division

| | | Pld | W | D | L | F | A | W | D | L | F | A | GD | Pts | Ave Gate |
|---|---|---|---|---|---|---|---|---|---|---|---|---|---|---|---|
| 1 | Liverpool | 40 | 15 | 5 | 0 | 49 | 9 | 11 | 7 | 2 | 38 | 15 | 63 | 90 | 39,582 |
| 2 | Manchester United | 40 | 14 | 5 | 1 | 41 | 17 | 9 | 7 | 4 | 30 | 21 | 33 | 81 | 39,151 |
| 3 | Nottingham Forest | 40 | 11 | 7 | 2 | 40 | 17 | 9 | 6 | 5 | 27 | 22 | 28 | 73 | 19,670 |
| 4 | Everton | 40 | 14 | 4 | 2 | 34 | 11 | 5 | 9 | 6 | 19 | 16 | 26 | 70 | 27,770 |
| 5 | Queens Park Rangers | 40 | 12 | 4 | 4 | 30 | 14 | 7 | 6 | 7 | 18 | 24 | 10 | 67 | 13,267 |
| 6 | Arsenal | 40 | 11 | 4 | 5 | 35 | 16 | 7 | 8 | 5 | 23 | 23 | 19 | 66 | 29,910 |
| 7 | Wimbledon | 40 | 8 | 9 | 3 | 32 | 20 | 6 | 8 | 6 | 26 | 27 | 11 | 57 | 7,994 |
| 8 | Newcastle United | 40 | 9 | 6 | 5 | 32 | 23 | 5 | 8 | 7 | 23 | 30 | 2 | 56 | 21,058 |
| 9 | Luton Town | 40 | 11 | 6 | 3 | 40 | 21 | 3 | 5 | 12 | 17 | 37 | -1 | 53 | 8,038 |
| 10 | Coventry City | 40 | 6 | 8 | 6 | 23 | 25 | 7 | 6 | 7 | 23 | 28 | -7 | 53 | 17,509 |
| 11 | Sheffield Wednesday | 40 | 10 | 2 | 8 | 27 | 30 | 5 | 6 | 9 | 25 | 36 | -14 | 53 | 19,796 |
| 12 | Southampton | 40 | 6 | 8 | 6 | 27 | 26 | 6 | 6 | 8 | 22 | 27 | -4 | 50 | 14,543 |
| 13 | Tottenham Hotspur | 40 | 9 | 5 | 6 | 26 | 23 | 3 | 6 | 11 | 12 | 25 | -10 | 47 | 25,921 |
| 14 | Norwich City | 40 | 7 | 5 | 8 | 26 | 26 | 5 | 4 | 11 | 14 | 26 | -12 | 45 | 15,942 |
| 15 | Derby County | 40 | 6 | 7 | 7 | 18 | 17 | 4 | 6 | 10 | 17 | 28 | -10 | 43 | 17,153 |
| 16 | West Ham United | 40 | 6 | 9 | 5 | 23 | 21 | 3 | 6 | 11 | 17 | 31 | -12 | 42 | 19,802 |
| 17 | Charlton Athletic | 40 | 7 | 7 | 6 | 23 | 21 | 2 | 8 | 10 | 15 | 31 | -14 | 42 | 8,684 |
| 18 | Chelsea | 40 | 7 | 11 | 2 | 24 | 17 | 2 | 4 | 14 | 26 | 51 | -18 | 42 | 20,117 |
| 19 | Portsmouth | 40 | 4 | 8 | 8 | 21 | 27 | 3 | 6 | 11 | 15 | 39 | -30 | 35 | 15,923 |
| 20 | Watford | 40 | 4 | 5 | 11 | 15 | 24 | 3 | 6 | 11 | 12 | 27 | -24 | 32 | 14,529 |
| 21 | Oxford United | 40 | 5 | 7 | 8 | 24 | 34 | 1 | 6 | 13 | 20 | 46 | -36 | 31 | 8,355 |

First Division reduced to 21 clubs following three clubs relegated and two clubs promoted at the end of 1986/87. Fourth-bottom club in Division One in the play-offs with the three teams who finished 3rd, 4th and 5th in Division Two – Chelsea, Middlesbrough, Bradford City and Blackburn Rovers. Two-legged semi-finals and a two-legged final. The final, Middlesbrough v Chelsea, won by Middlesbrough 2-1 on aggregate after two legs. Middlesbrough promoted to Division One. Chelsea relegated to Division Two.

## Second Division

| | | Pld | W | D | L | F | A | W | D | L | F | A | GD | Pts | Ave Gate |
|---|---|---|---|---|---|---|---|---|---|---|---|---|---|---|---|
| 1 | Millwall | 44 | 15 | 3 | 4 | 45 | 23 | 10 | 4 | 8 | 27 | 29 | 20 | 82 | 8,416 |
| 2 | Aston Villa | 44 | 9 | 7 | 6 | 31 | 21 | 13 | 5 | 4 | 37 | 20 | 27 | 78 | 18,341 |
| 3 | Middlesbrough | 44 | 15 | 4 | 3 | 44 | 16 | 7 | 8 | 7 | 19 | 20 | 27 | 78 | 14,509 |
| 4 | Bradford City | 44 | 14 | 3 | 5 | 49 | 26 | 8 | 6 | 8 | 25 | 28 | 20 | 77 | 12,905 |
| 5 | Blackburn Rovers | 44 | 12 | 8 | 2 | 38 | 22 | 9 | 6 | 7 | 30 | 30 | 16 | 77 | 9,502 |
| 6 | Crystal Palace | 44 | 16 | 3 | 3 | 50 | 21 | 6 | 6 | 10 | 36 | 38 | 27 | 75 | 9,745 |
| 7 | Leeds United | 44 | 14 | 4 | 4 | 37 | 18 | 5 | 8 | 9 | 24 | 33 | 10 | 69 | 20,272 |
| 8 | Ipswich Town | 44 | 14 | 3 | 5 | 38 | 17 | 5 | 6 | 11 | 23 | 35 | 9 | 66 | 11,807 |
| 9 | Manchester City | 44 | 11 | 4 | 7 | 50 | 28 | 8 | 4 | 10 | 30 | 32 | 20 | 65 | 19,471 |
| 10 | Oldham Athletic | 44 | 13 | 4 | 5 | 43 | 27 | 5 | 7 | 10 | 29 | 37 | 8 | 65 | 6,906 |
| 11 | Stoke City | 44 | 12 | 6 | 4 | 34 | 22 | 5 | 5 | 12 | 16 | 35 | -7 | 62 | 9,606 |
| 12 | Swindon Town | 44 | 10 | 7 | 5 | 43 | 25 | 6 | 4 | 12 | 30 | 35 | 13 | 59 | 9,541 |
| 13 | Leicester City | 44 | 12 | 5 | 5 | 35 | 20 | 4 | 6 | 12 | 27 | 41 | 1 | 59 | 10,157 |
| 14 | Barnsley | 44 | 11 | 4 | 7 | 42 | 32 | 4 | 8 | 10 | 19 | 30 | -1 | 57 | 7,682 |
| 15 | Hull City | 44 | 10 | 8 | 4 | 32 | 22 | 4 | 7 | 11 | 22 | 38 | -6 | 57 | 8,134 |
| 16 | Plymouth Argyle | 44 | 12 | 4 | 6 | 44 | 26 | 4 | 4 | 14 | 21 | 41 | -2 | 56 | 10,280 |
| 17 | AFC Bournemouth | 44 | 7 | 7 | 8 | 36 | 30 | 6 | 3 | 13 | 20 | 38 | -12 | 49 | 7,873 |
| 18 | Shrewsbury Town | 44 | 8 | 7 | 7 | 23 | 22 | 4 | 8 | 10 | 19 | 32 | -12 | 49 | 4,944 |
| 19 | Birmingham City | 44 | 7 | 9 | 6 | 20 | 24 | 4 | 6 | 12 | 21 | 42 | -25 | 48 | 8,578 |
| 20 | West Bromwich Albion | 44 | 8 | 7 | 7 | 29 | 26 | 4 | 4 | 14 | 21 | 43 | -19 | 47 | 10,126 |
| 21 | Sheffield United | 44 | 8 | 6 | 8 | 27 | 28 | 5 | 1 | 16 | 18 | 46 | -29 | 46 | 10,206 |
| 22 | Reading | 44 | 5 | 7 | 10 | 20 | 25 | 5 | 5 | 12 | 24 | 45 | -26 | 42 | 6,945 |
| 23 | Huddersfield Town | 44 | 4 | 6 | 12 | 20 | 38 | 2 | 4 | 16 | 21 | 62 | -59 | 28 | 6,841 |

Second Division increased to 23 clubs as a result of three clubs relegated to Division Two and two clubs promoted from it at the end of 1986/87.
Third-bottom club in Division Two in the play-offs with the three teams who finished 3rd, 4th and 5th in Division Three – Sheffield United, Walsall, Notts County and Bristol City. Two-legged semi-finals and a two-legged final. The final, Walsall v Bristol City, ended 3-3 on aggregate after two legs. Walsall won the replay 4-0 and were promoted to Division Two. Sheffield United relegated to Division Three.

270

## Third Division

| | | Pld | W | D | L | F | A | W | D | L | F | A | GD | Pts | Ave Gate |
|---|---|---|---|---|---|---|---|---|---|---|---|---|---|---|---|
| 1 | Sunderland | 46 | 14 | 7 | 2 | 51 | 22 | 13 | 5 | 5 | 41 | 26 | 44 | 93 | 17,424 |
| 2 | Brighton & Hove Albion | 46 | 15 | 7 | 1 | 37 | 16 | 8 | 8 | 7 | 32 | 31 | 22 | 84 | 8,964 |
| 3 | Walsall | 46 | 15 | 6 | 2 | 39 | 22 | 8 | 7 | 8 | 29 | 28 | 18 | 82 | 5,597 |
| 4 | Notts County | 46 | 14 | 4 | 5 | 53 | 24 | 9 | 8 | 6 | 29 | 25 | 33 | 81 | 6,336 |
| 5 | Bristol City | 46 | 14 | 6 | 3 | 51 | 30 | 7 | 6 | 10 | 26 | 32 | 15 | 75 | 9,817 |
| 6 | Northampton Town | 46 | 12 | 8 | 3 | 36 | 18 | 6 | 11 | 6 | 34 | 33 | 19 | 73 | 5,514 |
| 7 | Wigan Athletic | 46 | 11 | 8 | 4 | 36 | 23 | 9 | 4 | 10 | 34 | 38 | 9 | 72 | 3,758 |
| 8 | Bristol Rovers | 46 | 14 | 5 | 4 | 43 | 19 | 4 | 7 | 12 | 25 | 37 | 12 | 66 | 3,652 |
| 9 | Fulham | 46 | 10 | 5 | 8 | 36 | 24 | 9 | 4 | 10 | 33 | 36 | 9 | 66 | 4,921 |
| 10 | Blackpool | 46 | 13 | 4 | 6 | 45 | 27 | 4 | 10 | 9 | 26 | 35 | 9 | 65 | 4,077 |
| 11 | Port Vale | 46 | 12 | 8 | 3 | 36 | 19 | 6 | 3 | 14 | 22 | 37 | 2 | 65 | 3,847 |
| 12 | Brentford | 46 | 9 | 8 | 6 | 27 | 23 | 7 | 6 | 10 | 26 | 36 | -6 | 62 | 4,581 |
| 13 | Gillingham | 46 | 8 | 9 | 6 | 45 | 21 | 6 | 8 | 9 | 32 | 40 | 16 | 59 | 4,595 |
| 14 | Bury | 46 | 9 | 7 | 7 | 33 | 26 | 6 | 7 | 10 | 25 | 31 | 1 | 59 | 2,565 |
| 15 | Chester City | 46 | 9 | 8 | 6 | 29 | 30 | 5 | 8 | 10 | 22 | 32 | -11 | 58 | 2,663 |
| 16 | Preston North End | 46 | 10 | 6 | 7 | 30 | 23 | 5 | 7 | 11 | 18 | 36 | -11 | 58 | 6,194 |
| 17 | Southend United | 46 | 10 | 6 | 7 | 42 | 33 | 4 | 7 | 12 | 23 | 50 | -18 | 55 | 3,621 |
| 18 | Chesterfield | 46 | 10 | 5 | 8 | 25 | 28 | 5 | 5 | 13 | 16 | 42 | -29 | 55 | 2,661 |
| 19 | Mansfield Town | 46 | 10 | 6 | 7 | 25 | 21 | 4 | 6 | 13 | 23 | 38 | -11 | 54 | 3,810 |
| 20 | Aldershot | 46 | 12 | 3 | 8 | 45 | 32 | 3 | 5 | 15 | 19 | 42 | -10 | 53 | 3,259 |
| 21 | Rotherham United | 46 | 8 | 8 | 7 | 28 | 25 | 4 | 8 | 11 | 22 | 41 | -16 | 52 | 3,665 |
| 22 | Grimsby Town | 46 | 6 | 7 | 10 | 25 | 29 | 6 | 7 | 10 | 23 | 29 | -10 | 50 | 3,416 |
| 23 | York City | 46 | 4 | 7 | 12 | 27 | 45 | 4 | 2 | 17 | 21 | 46 | -43 | 33 | 2,760 |
| 24 | Doncaster Rovers | 46 | 6 | 5 | 12 | 25 | 36 | 2 | 4 | 17 | 15 | 48 | -44 | 33 | 1,912 |

Fourth-bottom club in Division Three in the play-offs with the three teams who finished 4th, 5th and 6th in Division Four – Rotherham United, Scunthorpe United, Torquay United and Swansea City. Two-legged semi-finals and a two-legged final. The final, Swansea City v Torquay United, won by Swansea City 5-4 on aggregate. Swansea City promoted to Division Three. Rotherham United relegated to Division Four.

## Fourth Division

| | | Pld | W | D | L | F | A | W | D | L | F | A | GD | Pts | Ave Gate |
|---|---|---|---|---|---|---|---|---|---|---|---|---|---|---|---|
| 1 | Wolverhampton Wanderers | 46 | 15 | 3 | 5 | 47 | 19 | 12 | 6 | 5 | 35 | 24 | 39 | 90 | 9,854 |
| 2 | Cardiff City | 46 | 15 | 6 | 2 | 39 | 14 | 9 | 7 | 7 | 27 | 27 | 25 | 85 | 4,389 |
| 3 | Bolton Wanderers | 46 | 15 | 6 | 2 | 42 | 12 | 7 | 6 | 10 | 24 | 30 | 24 | 78 | 5,017 |
| 4 | Scunthorpe United | 46 | 14 | 5 | 4 | 42 | 20 | 6 | 12 | 5 | 34 | 31 | 25 | 77 | 3,233 |
| 5 | Torquay United | 46 | 10 | 7 | 6 | 34 | 16 | 11 | 7 | 5 | 32 | 25 | 25 | 77 | 3,005 |
| 6 | Swansea City | 46 | 9 | 7 | 7 | 35 | 28 | 11 | 3 | 9 | 27 | 28 | 6 | 70 | 4,471 |
| 7 | Peterborough United | 46 | 10 | 5 | 8 | 28 | 26 | 10 | 5 | 8 | 28 | 24 | -1 | 70 | 3,204 |
| 8 | Leyton Orient | 46 | 13 | 4 | 6 | 55 | 27 | 6 | 8 | 9 | 30 | 36 | 22 | 69 | 3,932 |
| 9 | Colchester United | 46 | 10 | 5 | 8 | 23 | 22 | 9 | 5 | 9 | 24 | 29 | -4 | 67 | 1,754 |
| 10 | Burnley | 46 | 12 | 5 | 6 | 31 | 22 | 8 | 2 | 13 | 26 | 40 | -5 | 67 | 6,281 |
| 11 | Wrexham | 46 | 13 | 3 | 7 | 46 | 26 | 7 | 3 | 13 | 23 | 32 | 11 | 66 | 2,195 |
| 12 | Scarborough | 46 | 12 | 8 | 3 | 38 | 19 | 5 | 6 | 12 | 18 | 29 | 8 | 65 | 3,003 |
| 13 | Darlington | 46 | 13 | 6 | 4 | 39 | 25 | 5 | 5 | 13 | 32 | 44 | 2 | 65 | 2,190 |
| 14 | Tranmere Rovers | 46 | 14 | 2 | 7 | 43 | 20 | 5 | 7 | 11 | 18 | 33 | 8 | 64* | 3,321 |
| 15 | Cambridge United | 46 | 10 | 6 | 7 | 32 | 24 | 6 | 7 | 10 | 18 | 28 | -2 | 61 | 2,264 |
| 16 | Hartlepool United | 46 | 9 | 7 | 7 | 25 | 25 | 6 | 7 | 10 | 25 | 32 | -7 | 59 | 2,128 |
| 17 | Crewe Alexandra | 46 | 7 | 11 | 5 | 25 | 19 | 6 | 8 | 9 | 32 | 34 | 4 | 58 | 2,280 |
| 18 | Halifax Town | 46 | 11 | 7 | 5 | 37 | 25 | 3 | 7 | 13 | 17 | 34 | -5 | 55* | 1,595 |
| 19 | Hereford United | 46 | 8 | 7 | 8 | 25 | 27 | 6 | 5 | 12 | 16 | 32 | -18 | 54 | 2,257 |
| 20 | Stockport County | 46 | 7 | 7 | 9 | 26 | 26 | 5 | 8 | 10 | 18 | 32 | -14 | 51 | 2,271 |
| 21 | Rochdale | 46 | 5 | 9 | 9 | 28 | 34 | 6 | 6 | 11 | 19 | 42 | -29 | 48 | 1,939 |
| 22 | Exeter City | 46 | 8 | 6 | 9 | 33 | 29 | 3 | 7 | 13 | 20 | 39 | -15 | 46 | 2,463 |
| 23 | Carlisle United | 46 | 9 | 5 | 9 | 38 | 33 | 3 | 3 | 17 | 19 | 53 | -29 | 44 | 2,235 |
| 24 | Newport County | 46 | 4 | 5 | 14 | 19 | 36 | 2 | 2 | 19 | 16 | 69 | -70 | 25 | 1,762 |

Newport County relegated from the Football League; Lincoln City promoted to the Football League
*Tranmere Rovers deducted two points for failing to fulfil a fixture, Halifax Town deducted one point for playing an unregistered player

# 1988/89

## First Division

| | | Pld | W | D | L | F | A | W | D | L | F | A | GD | Pts | Ave Gate |
|---|---|---|---|---|---|---|---|---|---|---|---|---|---|---|---|
| 1 | Arsenal | 38 | 10 | 6 | 3 | 35 | 19 | 12 | 4 | 3 | 38 | 17 | 37 | 76 | 35,595 |
| 2 | Liverpool | 38 | 11 | 5 | 3 | 33 | 11 | 11 | 5 | 3 | 32 | 17 | 37 | 76 | 38,574 |
| 3 | Nottingham Forest | 38 | 8 | 7 | 4 | 31 | 16 | 9 | 6 | 4 | 33 | 27 | 21 | 64 | 20,785 |
| 4 | Norwich City | 38 | 8 | 7 | 4 | 23 | 20 | 9 | 4 | 6 | 25 | 25 | 3 | 62 | 16,785 |
| 5 | Derby County | 38 | 9 | 3 | 7 | 23 | 18 | 8 | 4 | 7 | 17 | 20 | 2 | 58 | 17,536 |
| 6 | Tottenham Hotspur | 38 | 8 | 6 | 5 | 31 | 24 | 7 | 6 | 6 | 29 | 22 | 14 | 57 | 24,467 |
| 7 | Coventry City | 38 | 9 | 4 | 6 | 28 | 23 | 5 | 9 | 5 | 19 | 19 | 5 | 55 | 16,040 |
| 8 | Everton | 38 | 10 | 7 | 2 | 33 | 18 | 4 | 5 | 10 | 17 | 27 | 5 | 54 | 27,765 |
| 9 | Queens Park Rangers | 38 | 9 | 5 | 5 | 23 | 16 | 5 | 6 | 8 | 20 | 21 | 6 | 53 | 12,281 |
| 10 | Millwall | 38 | 10 | 3 | 6 | 27 | 21 | 4 | 8 | 7 | 20 | 31 | -5 | 53 | 15,416 |
| 11 | Manchester United | 38 | 10 | 5 | 4 | 27 | 13 | 3 | 7 | 9 | 18 | 22 | 10 | 51 | 36,488 |
| 12 | Wimbledon | 38 | 10 | 3 | 6 | 30 | 19 | 4 | 6 | 9 | 20 | 27 | 4 | 51 | 7,824 |
| 13 | Southampton | 38 | 6 | 7 | 6 | 25 | 26 | 4 | 8 | 7 | 27 | 40 | -14 | 45 | 15,590 |
| 14 | Charlton Athletic | 38 | 6 | 7 | 6 | 25 | 24 | 4 | 5 | 10 | 19 | 34 | -14 | 42 | 9,398 |
| 15 | Sheffield Wednesday | 38 | 6 | 6 | 7 | 21 | 25 | 4 | 6 | 9 | 13 | 26 | -17 | 42 | 20,037 |
| 16 | Luton Town | 38 | 8 | 6 | 5 | 32 | 21 | 2 | 5 | 12 | 10 | 31 | -10 | 41 | 9,504 |
| 17 | Aston Villa | 38 | 7 | 6 | 6 | 25 | 22 | 2 | 7 | 10 | 20 | 34 | -11 | 40 | 23,310 |
| 18 | Middlesbrough | 38 | 6 | 7 | 6 | 28 | 30 | 3 | 5 | 11 | 16 | 31 | -17 | 39 | 19,999 |
| 19 | West Ham United | 38 | 3 | 6 | 10 | 19 | 30 | 7 | 2 | 10 | 18 | 32 | -25 | 38 | 20,738 |
| 20 | Newcastle United | 38 | 3 | 6 | 10 | 19 | 28 | 4 | 4 | 11 | 13 | 35 | -31 | 31 | 22,921 |

A change to the play-offs for 1988/89 – relegation-threatened clubs were excluded from the play-offs. The four clubs finishing immediately outside the automatic promotion places qualified for the play-offs – two-legged semi-finals and a two-legged final.

## Second Division

| | | Pld | W | D | L | F | A | W | D | L | F | A | GD | Pts | Ave Gate |
|---|---|---|---|---|---|---|---|---|---|---|---|---|---|---|---|
| 1 | Chelsea | 46 | 15 | 6 | 2 | 50 | 25 | 14 | 6 | 3 | 46 | 25 | 46 | 99 | 15,731 |
| 2 | Manchester City | 46 | 12 | 8 | 3 | 48 | 28 | 11 | 5 | 7 | 29 | 25 | 24 | 82 | 23,500 |
| 3 | Crystal Palace | 46 | 15 | 6 | 2 | 42 | 17 | 8 | 6 | 9 | 29 | 32 | 22 | 81 | 10,655 |
| 4 | Watford | 46 | 14 | 5 | 4 | 41 | 18 | 8 | 7 | 8 | 33 | 30 | 26 | 78 | 12,292 |
| 5 | Blackburn Rovers | 46 | 16 | 4 | 3 | 50 | 22 | 6 | 7 | 10 | 24 | 37 | 15 | 77 | 8,891 |
| 6 | Swindon Town | 46 | 13 | 8 | 2 | 35 | 15 | 7 | 8 | 8 | 33 | 38 | 15 | 76 | 8,687 |
| 7 | Barnsley | 46 | 12 | 8 | 3 | 37 | 21 | 8 | 6 | 9 | 29 | 37 | 8 | 74 | 7,215 |
| 8 | Ipswich Town | 46 | 13 | 3 | 7 | 42 | 23 | 9 | 4 | 10 | 29 | 38 | 10 | 73 | 12,650 |
| 9 | West Bromwich Albion | 46 | 13 | 7 | 3 | 43 | 18 | 5 | 11 | 7 | 22 | 23 | 24 | 72 | 12,757 |
| 10 | Leeds United | 46 | 12 | 6 | 5 | 34 | 20 | 5 | 10 | 8 | 25 | 30 | 9 | 67 | 21,811 |
| 11 | Sunderland | 46 | 12 | 8 | 3 | 40 | 23 | 4 | 7 | 12 | 20 | 37 | 0 | 63 | 14,878 |
| 12 | AFC Bournemouth | 46 | 13 | 3 | 7 | 32 | 20 | 5 | 5 | 13 | 21 | 42 | -9 | 62 | 8,087 |
| 13 | Stoke City | 46 | 10 | 9 | 4 | 33 | 25 | 5 | 5 | 13 | 24 | 47 | -15 | 59 | 9,817 |
| 14 | Bradford City | 46 | 8 | 11 | 4 | 29 | 22 | 5 | 6 | 12 | 23 | 37 | -7 | 56 | 10,524 |
| 15 | Leicester City | 46 | 11 | 6 | 6 | 31 | 20 | 2 | 10 | 11 | 25 | 43 | -7 | 55 | 10,694 |
| 16 | Oldham Athletic | 46 | 9 | 10 | 4 | 49 | 32 | 2 | 11 | 10 | 26 | 40 | 3 | 54 | 7,204 |
| 17 | Oxford United | 46 | 11 | 6 | 6 | 40 | 34 | 3 | 6 | 14 | 22 | 36 | -8 | 54 | 6,352 |
| 18 | Plymouth Argyle | 46 | 11 | 4 | 8 | 35 | 22 | 3 | 8 | 12 | 20 | 44 | -11 | 54 | 8,628 |
| 19 | Brighton & Hove Albion | 46 | 11 | 5 | 7 | 36 | 24 | 3 | 4 | 16 | 21 | 42 | -9 | 51 | 9,048 |
| 20 | Portsmouth | 46 | 10 | 6 | 7 | 33 | 21 | 3 | 6 | 14 | 20 | 41 | -9 | 51 | 10,201 |
| 21 | Hull City | 46 | 7 | 9 | 7 | 31 | 25 | 4 | 5 | 14 | 21 | 43 | -16 | 47 | 6,666 |
| 22 | Shrewsbury Town | 46 | 4 | 11 | 8 | 25 | 31 | 4 | 7 | 12 | 15 | 36 | -27 | 42 | 4,706 |
| 23 | Birmingham City | 46 | 6 | 4 | 13 | 21 | 33 | 2 | 7 | 14 | 10 | 43 | -45 | 35 | 6,265 |
| 24 | Walsall | 46 | 3 | 10 | 10 | 27 | 42 | 2 | 6 | 15 | 14 | 38 | -39 | 31 | 6,108 |

Crystal Palace, Watford, Blackburn Rovers and Swindon Town qualified for the two-legged semi-finals. Crystal Palace defeated Blackburn Rovers 4-3 on aggregate in the two-legged final and were promoted to Division One.

## Third Division

| | | Pld | W | D | L | F | A | W | D | L | F | A | GD | Pts | Ave Gate |
|---|---|---|---|---|---|---|---|---|---|---|---|---|---|---|---|
| 1 | Wolverhampton Wanderers | 46 | 18 | 4 | 1 | 61 | 19 | 8 | 10 | 5 | 35 | 30 | 47 | 92 | 14,392 |
| 2 | Sheffield United | 46 | 16 | 3 | 4 | 57 | 21 | 9 | 6 | 8 | 36 | 33 | 39 | 84 | 12,222 |
| 3 | Port Vale | 46 | 15 | 3 | 5 | 46 | 21 | 9 | 9 | 5 | 32 | 27 | 30 | 84 | 6,731 |
| 4 | Fulham | 46 | 12 | 7 | 4 | 42 | 28 | 10 | 2 | 11 | 27 | 39 | 2 | 75 | 4,938 |
| 5 | Bristol Rovers | 46 | 9 | 11 | 3 | 34 | 21 | 10 | 6 | 7 | 33 | 30 | 16 | 74 | 5,259 |
| 6 | Preston North End | 46 | 14 | 7 | 2 | 56 | 31 | 5 | 8 | 10 | 23 | 29 | 19 | 72 | 7,737 |
| 7 | Brentford | 46 | 14 | 5 | 4 | 36 | 21 | 4 | 9 | 10 | 30 | 40 | 5 | 68 | 5,681 |
| 8 | Chester City | 46 | 12 | 6 | 5 | 38 | 18 | 7 | 5 | 11 | 26 | 43 | 3 | 68 | 3,055 |
| 9 | Notts County | 46 | 11 | 7 | 5 | 37 | 22 | 7 | 6 | 10 | 27 | 32 | 10 | 67 | 5,675 |
| 10 | Bolton Wanderers | 46 | 12 | 8 | 3 | 42 | 23 | 4 | 8 | 11 | 16 | 31 | 4 | 64 | 5,528 |
| 11 | Bristol City | 46 | 10 | 3 | 10 | 32 | 25 | 8 | 6 | 9 | 21 | 30 | -2 | 63 | 8,120 |
| 12 | Swansea City | 46 | 11 | 8 | 4 | 33 | 22 | 4 | 8 | 11 | 18 | 31 | -2 | 61 | 4,896 |
| 13 | Bury | 46 | 11 | 7 | 5 | 27 | 22 | 5 | 6 | 12 | 28 | 45 | -12 | 61 | 3,367 |
| 14 | Huddersfield Town | 46 | 10 | 8 | 5 | 35 | 25 | 7 | 1 | 15 | 28 | 48 | -10 | 60 | 5,821 |
| 15 | Mansfield Town | 46 | 10 | 8 | 5 | 32 | 22 | 4 | 9 | 10 | 16 | 30 | -4 | 59 | 4,005 |
| 16 | Cardiff City | 46 | 10 | 9 | 4 | 30 | 16 | 4 | 6 | 13 | 14 | 40 | -12 | 57 | 4,384 |
| 17 | Wigan Athletic | 46 | 9 | 5 | 9 | 28 | 22 | 5 | 9 | 9 | 27 | 31 | 2 | 56 | 3,151 |
| 18 | Reading | 46 | 10 | 6 | 7 | 37 | 29 | 5 | 5 | 13 | 31 | 43 | -4 | 56 | 5,105 |
| 19 | Blackpool | 46 | 10 | 6 | 7 | 36 | 29 | 4 | 7 | 12 | 20 | 30 | -3 | 55 | 4,276 |
| 20 | Northampton Town | 46 | 11 | 2 | 10 | 41 | 34 | 5 | 4 | 14 | 25 | 42 | -10 | 54 | 3,918 |
| 21 | Southend United | 46 | 10 | 9 | 4 | 33 | 26 | 3 | 6 | 14 | 23 | 49 | -19 | 54 | 3,699 |
| 22 | Chesterfield | 46 | 9 | 5 | 9 | 35 | 35 | 5 | 2 | 16 | 16 | 51 | -35 | 49 | 3,717 |
| 23 | Gillingham | 46 | 7 | 3 | 13 | 25 | 32 | 5 | 1 | 17 | 22 | 49 | -34 | 40 | 3,675 |
| 24 | Aldershot | 46 | 7 | 6 | 10 | 29 | 29 | 1 | 7 | 15 | 19 | 49 | -30 | 37 | 2,609 |

Port Vale, Fulham, Bristol Rovers and Preston North End qualified for the two-legged semi-finals. Port Vale defeated Bristol Rovers 2-1 on aggregate in the two-legged final and were promoted to Division Two.

## Fourth Division

| | | Pld | W | D | L | F | A | W | D | L | F | A | GD | Pts | Ave Gate |
|---|---|---|---|---|---|---|---|---|---|---|---|---|---|---|---|
| 1 | Rotherham United | 46 | 13 | 6 | 4 | 44 | 18 | 9 | 10 | 4 | 32 | 17 | 41 | 82 | 5,063 |
| 2 | Tranmere Rovers | 46 | 15 | 6 | 2 | 34 | 13 | 6 | 11 | 6 | 28 | 30 | 19 | 80 | 5,331 |
| 3 | Crewe Alexandra | 46 | 13 | 7 | 3 | 42 | 24 | 8 | 8 | 7 | 25 | 24 | 19 | 78 | 3,296 |
| 4 | Scunthorpe United | 46 | 11 | 9 | 3 | 40 | 22 | 10 | 5 | 8 | 37 | 35 | 20 | 77 | 4,547 |
| 5 | Scarborough | 46 | 12 | 7 | 4 | 33 | 23 | 9 | 7 | 7 | 34 | 29 | 15 | 77 | 2,961 |
| 6 | Leyton Orient | 46 | 16 | 2 | 5 | 61 | 19 | 5 | 10 | 8 | 25 | 31 | 36 | 75 | 3,793 |
| 7 | Wrexham | 46 | 12 | 7 | 4 | 44 | 28 | 7 | 7 | 9 | 33 | 35 | 14 | 71 | 2,636 |
| 8 | Cambridge United | 46 | 13 | 7 | 3 | 45 | 25 | 5 | 7 | 11 | 26 | 37 | 9 | 68 | 2,653 |
| 9 | Grimsby Town | 46 | 11 | 9 | 3 | 33 | 18 | 6 | 6 | 11 | 32 | 41 | 6 | 66 | 4,302 |
| 10 | Lincoln City | 46 | 12 | 6 | 5 | 39 | 26 | 6 | 4 | 13 | 25 | 34 | 4 | 64 | 3,887 |
| 11 | York City | 46 | 10 | 8 | 5 | 43 | 27 | 7 | 5 | 11 | 19 | 36 | -1 | 64 | 2,613 |
| 12 | Carlisle United | 46 | 9 | 6 | 8 | 26 | 25 | 6 | 9 | 8 | 27 | 27 | 1 | 60 | 3,176 |
| 13 | Exeter City | 46 | 14 | 4 | 5 | 46 | 23 | 4 | 2 | 17 | 19 | 45 | -3 | 60 | 2,679 |
| 14 | Torquay United | 46 | 15 | 2 | 6 | 32 | 23 | 2 | 6 | 15 | 13 | 37 | -15 | 59 | 2,349 |
| 15 | Hereford United | 46 | 11 | 8 | 4 | 40 | 27 | 3 | 8 | 12 | 26 | 45 | -6 | 58 | 2,132 |
| 16 | Burnley | 46 | 12 | 6 | 5 | 35 | 20 | 2 | 7 | 14 | 17 | 41 | -9 | 55 | 7,062 |
| 17 | Peterborough United | 46 | 10 | 3 | 10 | 29 | 32 | 4 | 9 | 10 | 23 | 42 | -22 | 54 | 3,264 |
| 18 | Rochdale | 46 | 10 | 10 | 3 | 32 | 26 | 3 | 4 | 16 | 24 | 56 | -26 | 53 | 1,968 |
| 19 | Hartlepool United | 46 | 10 | 6 | 7 | 33 | 33 | 4 | 4 | 15 | 17 | 45 | -28 | 52 | 2,048 |
| 20 | Stockport County | 46 | 8 | 10 | 5 | 31 | 20 | 2 | 11 | 10 | 23 | 32 | 2 | 51 | 2,792 |
| 21 | Halifax Town | 46 | 10 | 7 | 6 | 42 | 27 | 3 | 4 | 16 | 27 | 48 | -6 | 50 | 1,946 |
| 22 | Colchester United | 46 | 8 | 7 | 8 | 35 | 30 | 4 | 7 | 12 | 25 | 48 | -18 | 50 | 2,893 |
| 23 | Doncaster Rovers | 46 | 9 | 6 | 8 | 32 | 32 | 4 | 4 | 15 | 17 | 46 | -29 | 49 | 2,158 |
| 24 | Darlington | 46 | 3 | 12 | 8 | 28 | 38 | 5 | 6 | 12 | 25 | 38 | -23 | 42 | 2,316 |

Scunthorpe United, Scarborough, Leyton Orient and Wrexham qualified for the play-offs' two-legged semi-finals. Leyton Orient defeated Wrexham 2-1 in the two-legged final and were promoted to Division Three. Darlington relegated from the Football League; Maidstone United promoted to the Football League.

# 1989/90

## First Division

| | | Pld | W | D | L | F | A | W | D | L | F | A | GD | Pts | Ave Gate |
|---|---|---|---|---|---|---|---|---|---|---|---|---|---|---|---|
| 1 | Liverpool | 38 | 13 | 5 | 1 | 38 | 15 | 10 | 5 | 4 | 40 | 22 | 41 | 79 | 36,589 |
| 2 | Aston Villa | 38 | 13 | 3 | 3 | 36 | 20 | 8 | 4 | 7 | 21 | 18 | 19 | 70 | 25,544 |
| 3 | Tottenham Hotspur | 38 | 12 | 1 | 6 | 35 | 24 | 7 | 5 | 7 | 24 | 23 | 12 | 63 | 26,588 |
| 4 | Arsenal | 38 | 14 | 3 | 2 | 38 | 11 | 4 | 5 | 10 | 16 | 27 | 16 | 62 | 33,713 |
| 5 | Chelsea | 38 | 8 | 7 | 4 | 31 | 24 | 8 | 5 | 6 | 27 | 26 | 8 | 60 | 21,531 |
| 6 | Everton | 38 | 14 | 3 | 2 | 40 | 16 | 3 | 5 | 11 | 17 | 30 | 11 | 59 | 26,280 |
| 7 | Southampton | 38 | 10 | 5 | 4 | 40 | 27 | 5 | 5 | 9 | 31 | 36 | 8 | 55 | 16,463 |
| 8 | Wimbledon | 38 | 5 | 8 | 6 | 22 | 23 | 8 | 8 | 3 | 25 | 17 | 7 | 55 | 7,756 |
| 9 | Nottingham Forest | 38 | 9 | 4 | 6 | 31 | 21 | 6 | 5 | 8 | 24 | 26 | 8 | 54 | 20,606 |
| 10 | Norwich City | 38 | 7 | 10 | 2 | 24 | 14 | 6 | 4 | 9 | 20 | 28 | 2 | 53 | 16,737 |
| 11 | Queens Park Rangers | 38 | 9 | 4 | 6 | 27 | 22 | 4 | 7 | 8 | 18 | 22 | 1 | 50 | 13,218 |
| 12 | Coventry City | 38 | 11 | 2 | 6 | 24 | 25 | 3 | 5 | 11 | 15 | 34 | -20 | 49 | 14,312 |
| 13 | Manchester United | 38 | 8 | 6 | 5 | 26 | 14 | 5 | 3 | 11 | 20 | 33 | -1 | 48 | 39,077 |
| 14 | Manchester City | 38 | 9 | 4 | 6 | 26 | 21 | 3 | 8 | 8 | 17 | 31 | -9 | 48 | 27,975 |
| 15 | Crystal Palace | 38 | 8 | 7 | 4 | 27 | 23 | 5 | 2 | 12 | 15 | 43 | -24 | 48 | 17,105 |
| 16 | Derby County | 38 | 9 | 1 | 9 | 29 | 21 | 4 | 6 | 9 | 14 | 19 | 3 | 46 | 17,426 |
| 17 | Luton Town | 38 | 8 | 8 | 3 | 24 | 18 | 2 | 5 | 12 | 19 | 39 | -14 | 43 | 9,886 |
| 18 | Sheffield Wednesday | 38 | 8 | 6 | 5 | 21 | 17 | 3 | 4 | 12 | 14 | 34 | -16 | 43 | 20,930 |
| 19 | Charlton Athletic | 38 | 4 | 6 | 9 | 18 | 25 | 3 | 3 | 13 | 13 | 32 | -26 | 30 | 10,748 |
| 20 | Millwall | 38 | 4 | 6 | 9 | 23 | 25 | 1 | 5 | 13 | 16 | 40 | -26 | 26 | 12,413 |

## Second Division

| | | Pld | W | D | L | F | A | W | D | L | F | A | GD | Pts | Ave Gate |
|---|---|---|---|---|---|---|---|---|---|---|---|---|---|---|---|
| 1 | Leeds United | 46 | 16 | 6 | 1 | 46 | 18 | 8 | 7 | 8 | 33 | 34 | 27 | 85 | 28,210 |
| 2 | Sheffield United | 46 | 14 | 5 | 4 | 43 | 27 | 10 | 8 | 5 | 35 | 31 | 20 | 85 | 16,989 |
| 3 | Newcastle United | 46 | 17 | 4 | 2 | 51 | 26 | 5 | 10 | 8 | 29 | 29 | 25 | 80 | 21,590 |
| 4 | Swindon Town* | 46 | 12 | 6 | 5 | 49 | 29 | 8 | 8 | 7 | 30 | 30 | 20 | 74 | 9,394 |
| 5 | Blackburn Rovers | 46 | 10 | 9 | 4 | 43 | 30 | 9 | 8 | 6 | 31 | 29 | 15 | 74 | 9,624 |
| 6 | Sunderland | 46 | 10 | 8 | 5 | 41 | 32 | 10 | 6 | 7 | 29 | 32 | 6 | 74 | 17,728 |
| 7 | West Ham United | 46 | 14 | 5 | 4 | 50 | 22 | 6 | 7 | 10 | 30 | 35 | 23 | 72 | 20,311 |
| 8 | Oldham Athletic | 46 | 15 | 7 | 1 | 50 | 23 | 4 | 7 | 12 | 20 | 34 | 13 | 71 | 9,727 |
| 9 | Ipswich Town | 46 | 13 | 7 | 3 | 38 | 22 | 6 | 5 | 12 | 29 | 44 | 1 | 69 | 12,913 |
| 10 | Wolverhampton Wanderers | 46 | 12 | 5 | 6 | 37 | 20 | 6 | 8 | 9 | 30 | 40 | 7 | 67 | 17,045 |
| 11 | Port Vale | 46 | 11 | 9 | 3 | 37 | 20 | 4 | 7 | 12 | 25 | 37 | 5 | 61 | 8,978 |
| 12 | Portsmouth | 46 | 9 | 8 | 6 | 40 | 34 | 6 | 8 | 9 | 22 | 31 | -3 | 61 | 8,959 |
| 13 | Leicester City | 46 | 10 | 8 | 5 | 34 | 29 | 5 | 6 | 12 | 33 | 50 | -12 | 59 | 11,716 |
| 14 | Hull City | 46 | 7 | 8 | 8 | 27 | 31 | 7 | 8 | 8 | 31 | 34 | -7 | 58 | 6,518 |
| 15 | Watford | 46 | 11 | 6 | 6 | 41 | 28 | 3 | 9 | 11 | 17 | 32 | -2 | 57 | 10,353 |
| 16 | Plymouth Argyle | 46 | 9 | 8 | 6 | 30 | 23 | 5 | 5 | 13 | 28 | 40 | -5 | 55 | 8,749 |
| 17 | Oxford United | 46 | 8 | 7 | 8 | 35 | 31 | 7 | 2 | 14 | 22 | 35 | -9 | 54 | 5,820 |
| 18 | Brighton & Hove Albion | 46 | 10 | 6 | 7 | 28 | 27 | 5 | 3 | 15 | 28 | 45 | -16 | 54 | 8,679 |
| 19 | Barnsley | 46 | 7 | 9 | 7 | 22 | 23 | 6 | 6 | 11 | 27 | 48 | -22 | 54 | 9,033 |
| 20 | West Bromwich Albion | 46 | 6 | 8 | 9 | 35 | 37 | 6 | 7 | 10 | 32 | 34 | -4 | 51 | 11,308 |
| 21 | Middlesbrough | 46 | 10 | 3 | 10 | 33 | 29 | 3 | 8 | 12 | 19 | 34 | -11 | 50 | 16,269 |
| 22 | AFC Bournemouth | 46 | 8 | 6 | 9 | 30 | 31 | 4 | 6 | 13 | 27 | 45 | -19 | 48 | 7,454 |
| 23 | Bradford City | 46 | 9 | 6 | 8 | 26 | 24 | 0 | 8 | 15 | 18 | 44 | -24 | 41 | 8,777 |
| 24 | Stoke City | 46 | 4 | 11 | 8 | 20 | 24 | 2 | 8 | 13 | 15 | 39 | -28 | 37 | 12,449 |

From 1989/90 the play-off finals were played at Wembley and were a one-off game.
Newcastle United, Blackburn Rovers, Swindon Town and Sunderland qualified for the play-offs – two-legged semi-finals. Swindon Town defeated Sunderland 1-0 in the final.
*Swindon Town were not promoted, Sunderland were promoted in their place. Swindon Town's board of directors admitted financial irregularities and penalised with no promotion.

## Third Division

| | | Pld | W | D | L | F | A | W | D | L | F | A | GD | Pts | Ave Gate |
|---|---|---|---|---|---|---|---|---|---|---|---|---|---|---|---|
| 1 | Bristol Rovers | 46 | 15 | 8 | 0 | 43 | 14 | 11 | 7 | 5 | 28 | 21 | 36 | 93 | 6,202 |
| 2 | Bristol City | 46 | 15 | 5 | 3 | 40 | 16 | 12 | 5 | 6 | 36 | 24 | 36 | 91 | 11,544 |
| 3 | Notts County | 46 | 17 | 4 | 2 | 40 | 18 | 8 | 8 | 7 | 33 | 35 | 20 | 87 | 6,151 |
| 4 | Tranmere Rovers | 46 | 15 | 3 | 5 | 54 | 22 | 8 | 6 | 9 | 32 | 27 | 37 | 80 | 7,449 |
| 5 | Bury | 46 | 11 | 7 | 5 | 35 | 19 | 10 | 4 | 9 | 35 | 30 | 21 | 74 | 3,450 |
| 6 | Bolton Wanderers | 46 | 12 | 7 | 4 | 32 | 19 | 6 | 8 | 9 | 27 | 29 | 11 | 69 | 7,286 |
| 7 | Birmingham City | 46 | 10 | 7 | 6 | 33 | 19 | 8 | 5 | 10 | 27 | 40 | 1 | 66 | 8,558 |
| 8 | Huddersfield Town | 46 | 11 | 5 | 7 | 30 | 23 | 6 | 9 | 8 | 31 | 39 | -1 | 65 | 5,630 |
| 9 | Rotherham United | 46 | 12 | 6 | 5 | 48 | 28 | 5 | 7 | 11 | 23 | 34 | 9 | 64 | 5,612 |
| 10 | Reading | 46 | 10 | 9 | 4 | 33 | 21 | 5 | 10 | 8 | 24 | 32 | 4 | 64 | 4,060 |
| 11 | Shrewsbury Town | 46 | 10 | 9 | 4 | 38 | 24 | 6 | 6 | 11 | 21 | 30 | 5 | 63 | 3,521 |
| 12 | Crewe Alexandra | 46 | 10 | 8 | 5 | 32 | 24 | 5 | 9 | 9 | 24 | 29 | 3 | 62 | 4,008 |
| 13 | Brentford | 46 | 11 | 4 | 8 | 41 | 31 | 7 | 3 | 13 | 25 | 35 | 0 | 61 | 5,662 |
| 14 | Leyton Orient | 46 | 9 | 6 | 8 | 28 | 24 | 7 | 4 | 12 | 24 | 32 | -4 | 58 | 4,365 |
| 15 | Mansfield Town | 46 | 13 | 2 | 8 | 34 | 25 | 3 | 5 | 15 | 16 | 40 | -15 | 55 | 3,129 |
| 16 | Chester City | 46 | 11 | 7 | 5 | 30 | 23 | 2 | 8 | 13 | 13 | 32 | -12 | 54 | 2,506 |
| 17 | Swansea City | 46 | 10 | 6 | 7 | 25 | 27 | 4 | 6 | 13 | 20 | 36 | -18 | 54 | 4,223 |
| 18 | Wigan Athletic | 46 | 10 | 6 | 7 | 29 | 22 | 3 | 8 | 12 | 19 | 42 | -16 | 53 | 2,758 |
| 19 | Preston North End | 46 | 10 | 7 | 6 | 42 | 30 | 4 | 3 | 16 | 23 | 49 | -14 | 52 | 6,313 |
| 20 | Fulham | 46 | 8 | 8 | 7 | 33 | 27 | 4 | 7 | 12 | 22 | 39 | -11 | 51 | 4,484 |
| 21 | Cardiff City | 46 | 6 | 9 | 8 | 30 | 35 | 6 | 5 | 12 | 21 | 35 | -19 | 50 | 3,642 |
| 22 | Northampton Town | 46 | 7 | 7 | 9 | 27 | 31 | 4 | 7 | 12 | 24 | 37 | -17 | 47 | 3,187 |
| 23 | Blackpool | 46 | 8 | 6 | 9 | 29 | 33 | 2 | 10 | 11 | 20 | 40 | -24 | 46 | 4,075 |
| 24 | Walsall | 46 | 6 | 8 | 9 | 23 | 30 | 3 | 6 | 14 | 17 | 42 | -32 | 41 | 4,077 |

Notts County, Tranmere Rovers, Bury and Bolton Wanderers qualified for the two-legged semi-finals play-offs. Notts County defeated Tranmere Rovers 2-0 in the final and were promoted to Division Two.

## Fourth Division

| | | Pld | W | D | L | F | A | W | D | L | F | A | GD | Pts | Ave Gate |
|---|---|---|---|---|---|---|---|---|---|---|---|---|---|---|---|
| 1 | Exeter City | 46 | 20 | 3 | 0 | 50 | 14 | 8 | 2 | 13 | 33 | 34 | 35 | 89 | 4,859 |
| 2 | Grimsby Town | 46 | 14 | 4 | 5 | 41 | 20 | 8 | 9 | 6 | 29 | 27 | 23 | 79 | 5,984 |
| 3 | Southend United | 46 | 15 | 3 | 5 | 35 | 14 | 7 | 6 | 10 | 26 | 34 | 13 | 75 | 3,836 |
| 4 | Stockport County | 46 | 13 | 6 | 4 | 45 | 27 | 8 | 5 | 10 | 23 | 35 | 6 | 74 | 3,899 |
| 5 | Maidstone United | 46 | 14 | 4 | 5 | 49 | 21 | 8 | 3 | 12 | 28 | 40 | 16 | 73 | 2,427 |
| 6 | Cambridge United | 46 | 14 | 3 | 6 | 45 | 30 | 7 | 7 | 9 | 31 | 36 | 10 | 73 | 3,359 |
| 7 | Chesterfield | 46 | 12 | 9 | 2 | 41 | 19 | 7 | 5 | 11 | 22 | 31 | 13 | 71 | 4,181 |
| 8 | Carlisle United | 46 | 15 | 4 | 4 | 38 | 20 | 6 | 4 | 13 | 23 | 40 | 1 | 71 | 4,740 |
| 9 | Peterborough United | 46 | 10 | 8 | 5 | 35 | 23 | 7 | 9 | 7 | 24 | 23 | 13 | 68 | 4,804 |
| 10 | Lincoln City | 46 | 11 | 6 | 6 | 30 | 27 | 7 | 8 | 8 | 18 | 21 | 0 | 68 | 4,071 |
| 11 | Scunthorpe United | 46 | 9 | 9 | 5 | 42 | 25 | 8 | 6 | 9 | 27 | 29 | 15 | 66 | 3,524 |
| 12 | Rochdale | 46 | 11 | 4 | 8 | 28 | 23 | 9 | 2 | 12 | 24 | 32 | -3 | 66 | 2,027 |
| 13 | York City | 46 | 10 | 5 | 8 | 29 | 24 | 6 | 11 | 6 | 26 | 29 | 2 | 64 | 2,615 |
| 14 | Gillingham | 46 | 9 | 8 | 6 | 28 | 21 | 8 | 3 | 12 | 18 | 27 | -2 | 62 | 3,887 |
| 15 | Torquay United | 46 | 12 | 2 | 9 | 33 | 29 | 3 | 10 | 10 | 20 | 37 | -13 | 57 | 2,147 |
| 16 | Burnley | 46 | 6 | 10 | 7 | 19 | 18 | 8 | 4 | 11 | 26 | 37 | -10 | 56 | 6,222 |
| 17 | Hereford United | 46 | 7 | 4 | 12 | 31 | 32 | 8 | 6 | 9 | 25 | 30 | -6 | 55 | 2,676 |
| 18 | Scarborough | 46 | 10 | 5 | 8 | 35 | 28 | 5 | 5 | 13 | 25 | 45 | -13 | 55 | 2,325 |
| 19 | Hartlepool United | 46 | 12 | 4 | 7 | 45 | 33 | 3 | 6 | 14 | 21 | 55 | -22 | 55 | 2,503 |
| 20 | Doncaster Rovers | 46 | 7 | 7 | 9 | 29 | 29 | 7 | 2 | 14 | 24 | 31 | -7 | 51 | 2,706 |
| 21 | Wrexham | 46 | 8 | 8 | 7 | 28 | 28 | 5 | 4 | 14 | 23 | 39 | -16 | 51 | 2,368 |
| 22 | Aldershot | 46 | 8 | 7 | 8 | 28 | 26 | 4 | 7 | 12 | 21 | 43 | -20 | 50 | 2,022 |
| 23 | Halifax Town | 46 | 5 | 9 | 9 | 31 | 29 | 7 | 4 | 12 | 26 | 36 | -8 | 49 | 1,895 |
| 24 | Colchester United | 46 | 9 | 3 | 11 | 26 | 25 | 2 | 7 | 14 | 22 | 50 | -27 | 43 | 3,150 |

Stockport County, Maidstone United, Cambridge United and Chesterfield qualified for the play-offs' two-legged semi-finals. Cambridge United defeated Chesterfield 1-0 in the final and were promoted to the Third Division. Colchester United relegated from the Football League; Darlington promoted to the Football League

# Appendix 2

## Football Association Challenge Cup Finals

**10 May 1980; Wembley; Attendance 100,000**
West Ham United 1 (Brooking) Arsenal 0

**9 May 1981; Wembley; Attendance 100,000**
Tottenham Hotspur 1 (Hutchinson og) Manchester City 1
(Hutchinson) after extra time

**Replay**
**14 May 1981; Wembley; Attendance 92,000**
Tottenham Hotspur 3 (Villa 2, Crooks) Manchester City 2
(Mackenzie, Reeves, pen)

**22 May 1982; Wembley; Attendance 100,000**
Tottenham Hotspur 1 (Hoddle) Queens Park Rangers 1
(Fenwick) after extra time

**Replay**
**27 May 1982; Wembley; Attendance 90,000**
Tottenham Hotspur 1 (Hoddle, pen) Queens Park
Rangers 0

**21 May 1983; Wembley; Attendance 100,000**
Manchester United 2 (Stapleton, Wilkins) Brighton &
Hove Albion 2 (Smith, Stevens)
after extra time

**Replay**
**26 May 1983; Wembley; Attendance 92,000**
Manchester United 4 (Robson 2, Whiteside, Muhren, pen)
Brighton & Hove Albion 0

**19 May 1984; Wembley; Attendance 100,000**
Everton 2 (Sharp, Gray) Watford 0

**18 May 1985; Wembley; Attendance 100,000**
Manchester United 1 (Whiteside) Everton 0 after extra time

**10 May 1986; Wembley; Attendance 98,000**
Liverpool 3 (Rush 2, Johnston) Everton 1 (Lineker)

**16 May 1987; Wembley; Attendance 98,000**
Coventry City 3 (Bennett, Houchen, Mabbutt og) Tottenham Hotspur 2 (Allen, Mabbutt) after extra time

**14 May 1988; Wembley; Attendance 98,203**
Wimbledon 1 (Sanchez) Liverpool 0

**20 May 1989; Wembley; Attendance 82,500**
Liverpool 3 (Aldridge, Rush 2) Everton 2 (McCall 2) after extra time

# Appendix 3

## Football League Cup Finals

**15 March 1980; Wembley; Attendance 100,000**
Wolverhampton Wanderers 1 (Gray) Nottingham Forest 0

**14 March 1981; Wembley; Attendance 100,000**
Liverpool 1 (A Kennedy) West Ham United 1 (Stewart)
after extra time

**Replay**
**1 April 1981; Villa Park; Attendance 36,693**
Liverpool 2 (Dalglish, Hansen) West Ham United 1
(Goddard)

**13 March 1982; Wembley; Attendance 100,000**
**Milk Cup**
Liverpool 3 (Whelan 2, Rush) Tottenham Hotspur 1
(Archibald) after extra time

**26 March 1983; Wembley; Attendance 100,000**
**Milk Cup**
Liverpool 2 (A Kennedy, Whelan) Manchester United 1
(Whiteside) after extra time

**25 March 1984; Wembley; Attendance 100,000**
**Milk Cup**
Liverpool 0 Everton 0 after extra time

**Replay**
**28 March 1984; Maine Road; Attendance 52,084**
Liverpool 1 (Souness) Everton 0

**24 March 1985; Wembley; Attendance 100,000**
**Milk Cup**
Norwich City 1 (Chisholm og) Sunderland 0

**20 April 1986; Wembley; Attendance 90,396**
**Milk Cup**
Oxford United 3 (Hebberd, Houghton, Charles) Queens
Park Rangers 0

**1 April 1987; Wembley; Attendance 96,000**
**Littlewoods Challenge Cup**
Arsenal 2 (Nicholas 2) Liverpool 1 (Rush)

**24 April 1988; Wembley; Attendance 95,732**
**Littlewoods Challenge Cup**
Luton Town 3 (Stein 2, Wilson) Arsenal 2 (Hayes, Smith)

**9 April 1989; Wembley; Attendance 76,130**
**Littlewoods Challenge Cup**
Nottingham Forest 3 (Clough 2, 1 pen, Webb) Luton Town
1 (Harford)

Sponsorship of the Football League Cup commenced
in 1982. The competition was known as the Milk Cup
1982–1986 inclusive, and as the Littlewoods Challenge Cup
1987–1990 inclusive.

# Appendix 4

## Football League Attendances

| Season | Total | Div 1 | Div 2 | Div 3 | Div 4 |
|---|---|---|---|---|---|
| 1979/80 | 24,623,975 | 12,163,002 | 6,112,025 | 3,999,328 | 2,349,620 |
| 1980/81 | 21,907,569 | 11,392,894 | 5,175,442 | 3,637,854 | 1,701,379 |
| 1981/82 | 20,006,961 | 10,420,793 | 4,750,463 | 2,836,915 | 1,998,790 |
| 1982/83 | 18,766,158 | 9,295,613 | 4,974,937 | 2,943,568 | 1,552,040 |
| 1983/84 | 18,358,631 | 8,711,448 | 5,359,757 | 2,729,942 | 1,557,484 |
| 1984/85 | 17,849,835 | 9,761,404 | 4,030,823 | 2,667,008 | 1,390,600 |
| 1985/86 | 16,488,577 | 9,037,854 | 3,551,968 | 2,490,481 | 1,408,274 |
| 1986/87 | 17,379,218 | 9,144,676 | 4,168,131 | 2,350,970 | 1,715,441 |
| 1987/88 | 17,959,732 | 8,094,571 | 5,341,599 | 2,751,275 | 1,772,287 |
| 1988/89 | 18,524,192 | 7,809,993 | 5,887,805 | 3,035,327 | 1,791,067 |
| 1989/90 | 19,445,442 | 7,883,039 | 6,867,674 | 2,803,551 | 1,891,178 |

# Appendix 5

## Footballer of the Year

| Season | Player | Club |
|--------|--------|------|
| 1979/80 | Terry McDermott | Liverpool |
| 1980/81 | Frans Thijssen | Ipswich Town |
| 1981/82 | Steve Perryman | Tottenham Hotspur |
| 1982/83 | Kenny Dalglish | Liverpool |
| 1983/84 | Ian Rush | Liverpool |
| 1984/85 | Neville Southall | Everton |
| 1985/86 | Gary Lineker | Everton |
| 1986/87 | Clive Allen | Tottenham Hotspur |
| 1987/88 | John Barnes | Liverpool |
| 1988/89 | Steve Nicol | Liverpool |
| 1989/90 | John Barnes | Liverpool |

## PFA Player of the Year

| | | |
|--------|--------|------|
| 1979/80 | Terry McDermott | Liverpool |
| 1980/81 | John Wark | Ipswich Town |
| 1981/82 | Kevin Keegan | Southampton |
| 1982/83 | Kenny Dalglish | Liverpool |
| 1983/84 | Ian Rush | Liverpool |
| 1984/85 | Peter Reid | Everton |
| 1985/86 | Gary Lineker | Everton |
| 1986/87 | Clive Allen | Tottenham Hotspur |
| 1987/88 | John Barnes | Liverpool |
| 1988/89 | Mark Hughes | Manchester United |
| 1989/90 | David Platt | Aston Villa |

The Footballer of the Year award is voted on and presented by the Football Writers' Association.

The PFA Player of the Year is voted on by the players and presented by the Professional Footballers' Association.

# Appendix 6

## Ballon d'Or – European Footballer of the Year

| Season | Player | Club |
|--------|--------|------|
| 1979/80 | Karl-Heinz Rummenigge | Bayern Munich |
| 1980/81 | Karl-Heinz Rummenigge | Bayern Munich |
| 1981/82 | Paolo Rossi | Juventus |
| 1982/83 | Michel Platini | Juventus |
| 1983/84 | Michel Platini | Juventus |
| 1984/85 | Michel Platini | Juventus |
| 1985/86 | Igor Belanov | Dynamo Kiev |
| 1986/87 | Ruud Gullit | AC Milan |
| 1987/88 | Marco van Basten | AC Milan |
| 1988/89 | Marco van Basten | AC Milan |
| 1989/90 | Lothar Matthaus | Inter Milan |

The Ballon d'Or is voted on by European-based journalists. It was presented annually from 1956–2009, then revived in 2016.

Michel Platini became the first player to win three awards in succession and joined Johan Cruyff in winning three awards.

# Bibliography

**Including source material used for this book**
Programmes from all First Division clubs and many in the lower divisions in the 1980s

Football magazines including *Shoot, World Soccer, When Saturday Comes, Backpass*
*The Star Green 'Un, The Star, Morning Telegraph* newspapers
Various National Newspapers
*Rothmans Football Yearbooks*
*The Football Grounds of England and Wales*, Simon Inglis,
    Collins Willow, 1983
*Football Grounds of Britain*, Simon Inglis,
    Collins Willow, 1996
*Dalglish: My Autobiography*, Kenny Dalglish, Hodder & Stoughton, 1996
*Joe Fagan, Reluctant Champion: The Authorised Biography*,
    Andrew Fagan and Mark Platt, Aurum, 2011
*From Where I was Standing: A Liverpool Supporter's View of the Heysel Stadium Tragedy*, Chris Rowland, GPRF Publishing, 2009
*Four Minutes to Hell: The Story of the Bradford City Fire*, Paul Firth, Parrs Wood Press, 2005
*56: The Story of the Bradford Fire*, Martin Fletcher, Bloomsbury, 2015
*Hillsborough: The Truth*, Phil Scraton, Mainstream Publishing, 2016

*The Hillsborough Stadium Disaster, 15 April 1989: Inquiry by Rt Hon Lord Justice Taylor, Interim report*, HMSO, August 1989

*The Day of the Hillsborough Disaster*, Rogan Taylor, Andrew Ward and Tim Newburn, Liverpool University Press, 1995

*And the Sun Shines Now*, Adrian Tempany, Faber and Faber, 2016

*Hillsborough Untold*, Norman Bettison, Biteback Publishing, 2016

*The Soccer Tribe*, Desmond Morris, Jonathan Cape, 1981

*Football and its Fans*, Rogan Taylor, Leicester University Press, 1992

*The Daily Telegraph Football Chronicle*, Norman Barrett, Stanley Paul Carlton, 1993

*The Official Illustrated History of the FA Cup*, Bryon Butler, Headline, 1996

*League Football and the men who made it*, Simon Inglis, Collins Willow, 1988

*The Rough Guide to English Football: A Fans' Handbook 2000–2001*, Dan Goldstein, Rough Guides, 2000

*Football Nation*, Andrew Ward and John Williams, Bloomsbury, 2009

*Kicking and Screaming*, Rogan Taylor & Andrew Ward, Robson Books, 1995

*The Book of Football Obituaries*, Ivan Ponting, Pitch Publishing, 2012

*Are You Watching the Match Tonight?*, Brian Barwick, Andre Deutsch, 2013

*From the Back Page to the Front Room*, Roger Domeneghetti, Ockley Books, 2017

*Blowing the Whistle*, Toni Schumacher, Star Books, 1988

*Sweet FA*, Graham Kelly, Collins Willow, 1999

# BIBLIOGRAPHY

*Kicking with Both Feet*, Frank Clark, Headline, 2000

*Cloughie: Walking on Water*, Brian Clough with John Sadler, Headline, 2002

*Settling the Score*, Dave Bassett, John Blake, 2002

*Playing Extra Time*, Alan Ball, Sidgwick & Jackson, 2004

*The Man in the Middle*, David Elleray, Time Warner Books, 2004

*Seeing Red*, Graham Poll, Harper Sport, 2007

*Motty*, John Motson, Virgin Books, 2009

*Big Hands Big Heart*, Eric Nixon, Trinity Mirror Sport Media, 2012

*Budgie: The Autobiography of a Goalkeeping Legend*, John Burridge, John Blake, 2013

*Added Time*, Mark Halsey with Ian Ridley, Floodlit Dreams, 2013

*Headlines Deadlines All My Life*, Norman Giller, NGB, 2015

*Three Sides of the Mersey*, Rogan Taylor and Andrew Ward with John Williams, Robson Books, 1994

*A Quarter of Wednesday: A New History of Sheffield Wednesday 1970–1995*, Daniel Gordon, Wednesday Publishing, 1995

*Regrets of a Football Maverick: The Terry Curran Autobiography*, Terry Curran with John Brindley, Vertical Editions, 2012

*Don Megson: A Life in Football*, Don Megson with Chris Olewicz, Vertical Editions, 2014

*It is What it is: The Carlton Palmer Story*, Carlton Palmer with Steven Jacobi, Vertical Editions, 2017

*Theo Give Us a Ball*, Theo Foley with Paul Foley, Apex Publishing Ltd, 2018

*Tommy: A Life at the Soccer Factory*, Tommy Tynan with Richard Cowdery, Bud Books, 1990

*Manchester United: The Betrayal of a Legend*, Michael Crick and David Smith, Pan Books, 1990

*Red Glory*, Martin Edwards, Michael O'Mara Books, 2017

*Hard Man Hard Knocks*, Terry Yorath with Grahame Lloyd, Celluloid, 2004

*Sheffield United: Match of My Life*, Nick Johnson, Pitch Publishing, 2012

*Blade Heart: The Tony Kenworthy Autobiography*, Tony Kenworthy with John Brindley, Vertical Editions, 2013

*The Matador: The Life and Career of Tony Currie*, E J Huntley, Pitch Publishing, 2015

*Black and Blue*, Paul Canoville, Headline, 2008

*61 Minutes in Munich: The Story of Liverpool FC's First Black Footballer*, Howard Gayle, de Coubertin Books, 2016

*It's Only Banter*, Leroy Rosenior, Pitch Publishing, 2018

*Henrik, Hairdryers and the Hand of God: Extraordinary Tales from the Press Box*, Edited by Brian Marjoribanks, BackPage Press, 2012

*Hackett's Law*, Keith Hackett, Collins Willow, 1986

*One in a Million: The Autobiography*, Trevor Francis with Keith Dixon, Pitch Publishing, 2019

*An Everton Diary*, Peter Reid with Peter Ball, Queen Anne Press, 1988

*Stan the Man: A Hard Life in Football*, Stan Ternent with Tony Livesey, John Blake Publishing, 2004

*Red Card Roy*: Roy McDonough with Bernie Friend, VSP, 2012

*The Binman Chronicles*, Neville Southall, de Coubertin Books, 2015

*Big Norm: Looking After No. 1*, Mark Crossley, 2011

*Life in a Jungle: My Autobiography*, Bruce Grobbelaar with Ragnhild Lund Ansnes, de Coubertin Books, 2018

*King of Clubs*, Anton Johnson, Grosvenor House Publishing Limited, 2012

*Monster!* Eric Hall, Boxtree, 1998

# BIBLIOGRAPHY

*Ticket to the Moon: Aston Villa: The Rise and Fall of a European Champion*, Richard Sydenham, de Coubertin Books, 2018

*Life's a Pitch: The Groundsman's Tale*, Ian Darler, G2 Entertainment, 2019

*No Such Thing as Society: A History of Britain in the 1980s*, Andy McSmith, Constable, 2011